From Pacification to Peacebuildir

'[This] timely and important book ... explains the need for global transformation [in conflict resolution] and identifies many ways to advance it.'
Louis Kriesberg, Maxwell Professor Emeritus of
Social Conflict Studies, Syracuse University, USA

'Diana Francis reminds us of the values and energy that prompt the best in us, which get lost in settling for expectations like pacification rather than peace.'
Sue Williams, Director, Summer Peacebuilding Institute,
Eastern Mennonite University, Virginia

'Diana Francis has done it again – another practical book mapping the road from peaceful aspirations to peaceful reality.'
Bruce Kent, Founding Chair and Vice President of
the Movement for the Abolition of War

'Diana Francis's profound reflections on the conflict transformation field will be an inspiration to aspiring peace workers everywhere.'
Hugh Miall, Professor of International Relations, University of Kent

'This book is a must both for scholars studying international relations and practitioners who engage in the fields of peace work, human rights and development.'
Dr. Martina Fischer, Deputy Director of the Berghof Research Center
for Constructive Conflict Management, Berlin, and Deputy Chair
of the German Foundation for Peace Research, Osnabrück

'Diana Francis ensures that questions of values (and morality) are never allowed to sink beneath the weight of policy and programme imperatives.'
Professor Andrew Rigby, Centre for Peace and
Reconciliation Studies, University of Coventry

'Diana Francis is a giant in this field. ... Each of the chapters in this book touches on key dilemmas and current debates. ... The book offers practitioners and academics alike a guide to exploring where we could go next.'
Catherine Sexton, Chief Executive, Responding To Conflict (RTC)

'The so-called "peace operations" that are proliferating around the world look increasingly like wars. Diana Francis challenges collusion with this military imposition of "order" and makes a radical re-statement of grass-roots peacebuilding and conflict transformation as an emancipatory praxis.'
Howard Clark, Chairperson, War Resisters' International

'A much-needed overview of recent work in the field of conflict transformation.'
Johan Galtung, Professor of Peace Studies Professor of Peace Studies at six universities
and founder of the International Peace Research Institute in Oslo

'Diana Francis asks tough questions about conflict transformation, peacebuilding and the use of force. She gives answers that provoke and inspire.'
Dan Smith, Director of International Alert

'Diana Francis has a voice of integrity and wisdom based on decades of experience as an academic and conflict transformation practitioner. Her writing helps to remind us that [peacebuilding] has its roots in the liberation struggles of both pacifism and feminism. But in moving from popular protests to professionalisation, we risk compromising the roots of our own radicalisation. ... Diana challenges us to rediscover our principles, values, and ideals.'
Andy Carl, Executive Director of Conciliation Resources, London

'We live in the most dangerous times since the collapse of Communism. New wars are being fought in new ways. We are all under threat. Diana Francis makes the case not just against war fighting but against war thinking.'
Martin Bell, OBE, former BBC war reporter and MP

FROM PACIFICATION TO PEACEBUILDING

A Call to Global Transformation

Diana Francis

First published 2010 by Pluto Press
345 Archway Road, London N6 5AA and
175 Fifth Avenue, New York, NY 10010

www.plutobooks.com

Distributed in the United States of America exclusively by
Palgrave Macmillan, a division of St. Martin's Press LLC,
175 Fifth Avenue, New York, NY 10010

British Library Cataloguing in Publication Data
A catalogue record for this book is available from the British Library

ISBN   978 0 7453 3027 3   Hardback
ISBN   978 0 7453 3026 6   Paperback

Library of Congress Cataloging in Publication Data applied for

This book is printed on paper suitable for recycling and made from fully managed and
sustained forest sources. Logging, pulping and manufacturing processes are expected to
conform to the environmental standards of the country of origin.

10   9   8   7   6   5   4   3   2   1

Designed and produced for Pluto Press by
Chase Publishing Services Ltd, 33 Livonia Road, Sidmouth, EX10 9JB, England
Typeset from disk by Stanford DTP Services, Northampton, England
Printed and bound in the European Union by
CPI Antony Rowe, Chippenham and Eastbourne

Contents

Acknowledgements   vii
Preface   viii

1. **Vision and Engagement**   1
   A Time of Ferment   2
   Training Requests   3
   Key Ideas and Terms   3
   From Solidarity to Partnership   8
   Fundamental Values   10

2. **Ongoing Development**   12
   Capacity Building   15
   Popular Education   21
   Media Work and Arts Projects   22
   Bridge Building   23
   Advocacy   26
   Peace Processes in Large-Scale Conflicts   29
   Recovery from Violence   31
   Ongoing Learning   34
   Influencing Policy   35

3. **Dilemmas and Limitations**   38
   Practical Matters   38
   Power in Mid-Conflict and Post-Conflict Transformation   45
   Making a Strategic Difference   53
   Conflict, States and Global Systems   66
   Facing the Global Challenge   68

4. **Peacebuilding and Pacification**   71
   Peace and Militarism   71
   Two Worldviews   73
   Addressing Violence: Dilemmas and Ethics   77
   Peacebuilding and International Relations   86
   States and the Limitations to their Sovereignty   89
   Fear, Control and Future Security   90
   Shifting the Culture and Bridging the Divide   91

5. Caught between Two Systems:
   Co-option or Transformation?   96
   Conflict Transformation and Realpolitik   96
   Violence and Nonviolence   99
   Nonviolent People-Power   100
   Resistance to Nonviolence   101
   Ethics and Culture   105
   Signs that the System Can Change   107
   Dialogue with Donors   109

6. Building the Praxis of Nonviolence   113
   People-Power in Conflict Transformation   113
   Forms of Violence   116
   Nonviolence   119
   Transformative Power: Building Capacities for
        Nonviolence   139

7. Challenging the System   146
   An Oppressive System that Has Had its Day   146
   Global Transformation: An Agenda for our Field   150
   Mobilisation: Building Alliances for Global
        Transformation   158

8. Agenda for Humanity   168
   Peace   169
   Economic Justice and Well-being   170
   Democracy   174
   Grounds for Hope   178
   Global Solidarity and the Power of Humanity   179

Appendix: Stages and Processes in Conflict Transformation 182
Bibliography   186
Index   189

Acknowledgements

In writing this book I have been greatly helped by the following people, whom I wish to thank: all my CCTS colleagues for the chance to learn with them over the years; Andy Carl and Dan Smith for sharing their perceptions with me in extended conversations; Martina Fischer, for initial encouragement in thinking that I had something to say; Veronique Dudouet, for reading early chapters and reassuring me that this was so, and for specific feedback; Bill Stern, for the gift of his time in copy-editing; Anne Rogers, for much-needed, skilled and time-consuming technical assistance; my husband Nick, for unfailing moral support; and Celia McKeon, for reading the whole draft and giving me the most uplifting, constructive, insightful and informed commentary that anyone could hope for.

Preface

I have been a peace campaigner all my life. When I wrote my first book, *People, Peace and Power*,[1] I did so as a professional consultant in the field of conflict transformation. But my activist background and my knowledge of 'nonviolence' and 'people power' around the world have informed all my thinking and writing.

My professional work began in the wake of the crumbling of the Soviet empire and the eventual collapse of the Soviet Union itself. New and violent conflicts were erupting and it was these that prompted the formation, in1992, of the lengthily-named Co-ordinating Committee for Conflict Resolution Training in Europe (CCCRTE), which later became the Committee for Conflict Transformation Support (CCTS).[2] As Howard Clark recounts in his history of the committee,[3] its creation was a 'response to a growing demand for conflict resolution training in the "post-Communist" countries of Eastern and Central Europe', particularly those of the former Yugoslavia. Gradually the committee evolved into a forum for organisations (and individuals) that were mostly UK-based but were working in every continent, in support of local people confronted by violent conflict and seeking to address it. It has been, as Howard says, 'one of the few places where ... practitioners have taken the space to share their dilemmas, in some cases their excitement and in some cases their disappointment, as they reflect on their work and on developments in the field'.

I have been part of CCTS for its whole life,[4] and served as its Chair from 1995 until the end of 2009, participating in almost all its meetings and seminars. At the same time, I have worked as a consultant to CCTS member organisations, along with many others, learning with and from them.

1. D. Francis, *People, Peace and Power*, London: Pluto Press, 2002.
2. See its website: <www.c-r.org/ccts>.
3. H. Clark, *The Evolution of the Committee for Conflict Transformation Support, 1992–2006*, p. 2 – available at <www.c-r.org/ccts>.
4. As I write, the committee's future rests in the balance. By the time this book is published it may have entered a new phase of its life, or its work may have come to an end. Either way, its contribution in support of good practice and the growth of understanding will remain.

CCTS discussions, whether in regular meetings, seminars, or the CCTS Review, have been a testing place and a stimulus for my own thinking. Through them we all have access to the concerns and ideas of partners and networks across the globe – North, South, East and West – so that our perspectives are constantly being shifted and challenged. While I would not claim to have a reliable overview of all that is happening in our field, I consider myself lucky to have had, through these connections, exposure to a wide and varied sample of practice and to rich sources of insight. It is largely on these, and on my own direct experience in 'the field', that I have drawn in my writing. (Nonetheless, I cannot, in the last analysis, step out of my shoes as a 64-year-old woman who looks out on the world from the West.)

My purpose in writing this book was, in the first place, to look back to the hopes and the vision with which we, as a committee, began. (Though there are different tendencies within this field, as there are in others, I believe these hopes and this vision will not have differed greatly from those of other networks.) I wanted to review the successes that have encouraged us and to discuss the dilemmas, obstacles and frustrations that we have faced. But I also wanted to relate this world-within-a-world to wider pressures and events, examining the impact of these and their implications for our work as professionals and our responsibilities as citizens. In this I have picked up on themes explored in my second book, *Rethinking War and Peace*.[5]

I have set out to show that working for conflict transformation in any locality, in the way that we are currently doing, vital as it is, can take us only so far when the big world is going in quite another direction; that unless we address the wider questions our little boat of conflict transformation will constantly be swept out of the water by the big ships of geopolitics and militarism, in which the dominant agenda is to subdue or 'pacify' those who threaten instability or insubordination. In this book I am calling on my profession, and indeed on all readers who espouse the values of peace, to recognise that, unless we take up our own responsibility for changing the political, social and ideological contexts in which we live and work, we shall not see our dreams fulfilled. We must ensure that we are not co-opted into an agenda founded on values very different from our own, and do everything in our power to change those values and the systems that embody them. And we must recognise that movements

5. D. Francis, *Rethinking War and Peace*, London: Pluto Press, 2002.

have a power that complements the work of 'peace practitioners', and that professionals and movements need each other.

This book, written for fellow peacemakers and peace campaigners around the world, is therefore not only a study but also an argument: my small but necessary contribution to what I see as the daunting but all-too-urgent project of global transformation – the fundamental change so desperately needed by humanity and our planet. Unless we take a more radical approach, we shall not get beyond fire-fighting and the seemingly endless task of recon- struction. Unless we transform the way we think about conflict, human relationships, and what it is to be successful, our very life as a species is under threat.

Our field is going through a time of intensive self-scrutiny.[6] The phase that began with the Soviet collapse has ended. For too many years we were caught up in the calamitous policies and actions that followed the events of 11 September 2001 in the US, and there were signs that a new Cold War was beginning. Then the advent of a new US president brought new hope.

Our field can be credited with many important achievements, which should be recognised and set out. The value of its work will continue. At the same time, we have come to recognise our limitations.

I have long argued that the field of conflict transformation needs to be brought together with the older one of active nonviolence and to incorporate its wisdom, energy and knowledge. That now needs to be said more forcefully, and related to the deep contradiction between the dominant culture and dynamics of power, which rest ultimately on coercion and violence, and the values and assumptions of conflict transformation. The discussions and debates that have taken place within our field should now be crystallised and brought to a wider audience.

Those who work for peace in their own country – even when that work is funded – are likely to see what they do as the activism of concerned citizens, rather than as a profession. Those whose work is largely focused on other people's societies, although their concern for peace may spring from the same values, may be so caught up in this professional work that they are not actively challenging their own societies or the policies of their governments – governments

6. See for example S. Fisher and L. Zimina, 'Just Wasting Our Time? Provocative Thoughts for Peacebuilders', in B. Schmezle and M. Fischer (eds), *Peacebuilding at a Crossroads? Dilemmas and Paths for Another Generation* (Berghof Handbook Dialogue No. 7), Berlin: Berghof Research Center, 2009.

that may perpetuate the violence they wish to address. It is time for these practitioners, and academics, in the field of conflict transformation to 'get political'. And it is time for peacemakers everywhere to look beyond their own specific context to the wider system of global militarism and to join forces to challenge and change it. In doing so they should connect with the wider peace movement, which is vital to the transformation of the cultural and structural context in which specific violence takes place and which, in turn, needs the insights and skills that peace professionals can bring.

It is also time for us to acknowledge that peace – positive peace – is not separate from justice (economic and social), from human rights, or from environmental protection. We need to make the connections more strongly: intellectually, politically and practically. These 'goods' are all essential to humanity, and war is their common enemy.

1
Vision and Engagement

What do we see, as we look around the world? Civil wars and endemic violence; threats and invasions; slaughter by bomb and machete; military occupation and misery following wars launched by foreign powers; a continuing arms race and the proliferation of nuclear weapons; the widespread violation and subjugation of women; exclusion and division; forced migration; endemic poverty and excesses of wealth; economic instability and environmental destruction.

Of course that is not all. Across the world there are some people who are having a good day today, some situations that are improving, some countries enjoying prosperity, many good people caring for others and working for change. But it is hard not to contrast the widespread violence, suffering and destruction with any notion of peace.

I dream of a world where conflict is accepted as part of life, inextricably linked with variety, movement and change – not seen as a reason for killing; a world where we all share responsibility for ensuring that conflict is handled in constructive, nonviolent ways; a world where people work to change the things that harm them, harm others, or threaten the future of our planet. That was my vision when I became involved in what was later named the Committee for Conflict Transformation Support (CCTS), in the early 1990s. I think it was a vision shared, more or less, by my colleagues.

It can be argued that such a vision was not to be achieved in a decade or two. But where have we got to, and are we heading in the right direction? Are there positive differences that can be detected, despite the gloom of this broad-brush picture – patches of light that can be expanded? Are they sufficient to give us hope that the transformation we dreamed of has begun, or does something need to change in our analysis and in what we do?

In the first three chapters of this book I review the work of conflict transformation over the past 15 to 20 years – its goals, achievements and limitations – discussing some of the reasons for success and failure and the problems of evaluation. In the fourth chapter I change gear, presenting my analysis of the profound gulf between the worldview shaping much of global politics and that on which conflict transformation is based, arguing that, in order to build our way towards the kind of peace our world needs, we are going to have to re-examine and transform prevailing assumptions and approaches to power. The remaining chapters will translate that analysis into an agenda for action.

In this short opening chapter I will go back in time and outline the context in which a particular group of practitioners came together, the work they were asked to do, key elements of the theory on which they drew, and the values that they shared. I will also introduce the notion of partnership, which has become axiomatic in the conflict-transformation field.

A TIME OF FERMENT

The time of international ferment that followed the collapse of the former Soviet Union saw a coming together of the fields of international relations and conflict resolution that engendered much new thinking and activity.[1]

At this time also, many activists who, from the 1960s on, had been campaigning against global militarism (particularly as symbolised by the nuclear arms race) and in support of nonviolent struggles for justice around the world, were drawn into this burgeoning professional and academic field – myself included. We could see that 'struggle' was not necessarily being applied in ways or with aims that coincided with our values, and that the discourse of justice and liberation were often used in pursuit of exclusive nationalist and separatist agendas that went against the needs of ordinary people. Armed violence was once again the method of choice. Little seemed to have been learned from the astonishing impact of 'people power' in the Philippines, Eastern Europe, the Soviet Union and South Africa, and 'identity' was becoming the rallying cry of demagogues.

In such a situation the insights and ethos of 'conflict resolution', with its tolerant, non-judgemental reasonableness, seemed to offer an importantly different approach and energy, complementing the more impassioned character of 'active nonviolence',[2] with its moral

---

1. H. Miall, O. Ramsbotham and T. Woodhouse, *Contemporary Conflict Resolution*, Cambridge: Polity Press, 1999, p. 2.
2. J. and H. Goss-Mayr, *The Gospel and the Struggle for Peace*, Alkmaar, The Netherlands: International Fellowship of Reconciliation, 1990.

conviction and commitment. War was producing not justice and liberty, but suffering, tyranny and exclusion. At such a point the need for accommodation and coexistence took centre-stage.

TRAINING REQUESTS

The formation in 1992 of the then CCCRTE (Coordinating Committee for Conflict Resolution Training in Europe – CCTS's original name) was a response to requests from different parts of the former Soviet empire for training in the ideas and skills of conflict resolution.[3] These requests came from what would now be termed 'civil society organisations', though in newly separate small states the overlap between 'people' and 'government' was often considerable. (One could be employed in a quite menial capacity in the week and do government work at the weekend – or be part of a protest movement one month and of a government the next.)

The focus of the training requested was varied. It included conflict analysis and consequent options for action; action strategies and planning; conflict resolution theory and processes (including those related to dialogue, mediation and negotiation – particularly using a problem-solving approach); communication skills for all purposes; conflict dynamics and conflict escalators such as fear, anger and prejudice; and the meanings and implications of culture and identity.

In the case of the highly sophisticated groups that were coming together in the former Yugoslavia, there were also requests for assistance in matters related to group and organisational formation, such as group dynamics, group facilitation, clarification of aims and policy, participatory evaluation, and self- and peer-assessment. Sometimes we were asked for training (or facilitated preparation) directed towards a particular undertaking, such as a programme of human rights education or outreach to a particular sector of the local population. (Some requests, specifically those for trauma-counselling skills, drew in trainers from other professions, though there was a high level of awareness in our circle of the danger of 'pathologising' normal human responses and introducing inappropriately professionalised therapeutic models.)

KEY IDEAS AND TERMS

Usage of terms has shifted during the life of CCTS, so that no definitions hold constant over time. Moreover, terms are used

3. Clark, *Evolution.*

differently by different people. What follows necessarily represents my personal and provisional understanding. Inevitably, I write from a Western perspective, reflecting on a discourse dominated by Western concepts.

'Conflict resolution' refers, strictly speaking, to the process of finding a way out of destructive conflict through constructive dialogue and negotiation (though it was and sometimes still is used also to describe the wider collection of processes otherwise encapsulated by the term 'conflict transformation').[4] Arguably, the single most important idea in 'conflict resolution' is that of 'basic human needs', elucidated first in this field by John Burton[5] but developed by many others. The theory encapsulated in this phrase is that, in order for a conflict to be resolved in a lasting way, the basic human needs of the different protagonists – for security, identity and participation – must be met. These needs will underlie the more specific 'interests' of the conflicting parties, which should form the basis for negotiation or joint thinking aimed at 'problem-solving' – radically different in approach from 'positional bargaining' – to find a way forward that will meet the needs of all parties to the conflict.

Much taken-for-granted theory is embodied in the analytical questions and tools used in training and in conflict resolution processes. What is the conflict about, as seen from the perspectives of different players? What are its roots and its more immediate triggers or 'drivers'? Who are the different parties or 'stakeholders'? Who is involved? Who has influence? What are the relationships between them? What is their power, and how is it exercised? What are their current positions as regards the rights and wrongs of the conflict? What are their needs and their fears, their perceptions and their interests? And what factors in the wider context are influencing the conduct of the conflict?

One popular tool of analysis comes in two versions, both suggesting a triumvirate of mutually influential factors. One version identifies these as behaviour, attitude and context;[6] the other as direct, cultural and structural violence (where violence is defined as 'avoidable insults to basic human needs', and culture means worldview, norms and assumptions, or whatever makes violence 'seem normal').[7] These simple classifications have been found to be

4. Including by Miall et al., *Contemporary Conflict Resolution*.
5. J. Burton (ed.), *Conflict: Human Needs Theory*, London: Macmillan, 1990.
6. C. R. Mitchell, *The Structure of International Conflict*, London: Macmillan, 1981.
7. J. Galtung, 'Cultural Violence', *Journal of Peace Research* 27: 3 (1990), pp. 291–305.

extremely useful in helping people to look beyond the immediate manifestations of conflict and develop a stronger understanding of what would need to be changed for the achievement of any kind of lasting transformation.

Such thinking reveals that the negotiations between conflicting parties that are emblematic of 'conflict resolution' are a small part of what is needed to bring peace. This means that there are many different roles to be played in the transforming of a conflict, going far beyond those of mediators and negotiators. Internal and external players may need to be involved; partisan roles are vital, as well as the work of cross-party and impartial actors.[8] Theory about the dynamics of conflict, variously elaborated,[9] was also found to be useful, helping people to 'read' what was happening in their own situation, and so to identify the kind of action that was needed to address what was tending towards violence and polarisation, and ways in which they could contribute to improving the conflict dynamics.

Implicit in different aspects of training was theory about how influence can be exercised and change achieved – 'theories of change'. For instance, a theoretical diagram that is still much in use was Lederach's pyramid of the different 'levels' of social and political actors,[10] indicating the few powerful decision-makers at the top, the broad base of grassroots players, and the band of middle-level people who enjoy the freedom of manoeuvre denied to top politicians and have the opportunity to influence both those 'above' and 'below' them. (In the language of peace negotiation processes, these levels are often referred to as 'tracks'.) This middle band, seen as pivotal, was where most trainees were located.

There was also some very basic theory related to skills in communication (about 'active listening', for instance, and clear, non-accusatory speech), accompanied by exercises to develop the related skills, and a set of basic assumptions about what mediation was (a facilitated process, non-judgemental, and leading to voluntary agreement – thereby differing from arbitration, which is favoured in many societies), together with ideas for how mediation processes can be structured.

8. Francis, *People, Peace and Power*, pp. 18–19.
9. For example, F. Glasl, *Konfliktmanagement: Ein Handbuch fur Fuhrungsk-rafte, Beraterinnen und Berater*, Bern: Reies Geistleben, 1997; and J. P. Lederach, *Building Peace: Sustainable Reconciliation in Divided Societies*, Tokyo: United Nations University Press, 1994.
10. Lederach, *Building Peace*.

The methods of training on prejudice, identity and culture were mostly processes for self-awareness and mental deconstruction, and did not involve explicit theory, though clearly they had an implicit theoretical base. Gender was more often than not treated (if at all) as one identity issue among many, though some groups (such as Women in Black), and no doubt some trainers, took a more radical, feminist approach.

Although those of us who came from a 'nonviolence' background had come to see that the idea of nonviolent struggle did not fit every situation, that a greater focus on accommodation was sometimes needed, and that not all conflicts could be seen in terms of oppressors versus oppressed, it was also clear to some of us that it would not do to see all situations as lending themselves, in the present, to conflict resolution. Conflict resolution is a voluntary process that is more likely to take place where there is relative power parity, since both (or all) sides have to be motivated to work for a solution that is acceptable to all. If one side is substantially more powerful than the other it is far less likely that it will consider negotiation to be desirable or necessary (unless the concessions they need to make are likely to be small).

Increasingly, committee members became clear that it was necessary to recognise and address power asymmetries in a more concerted way, and to give greater attention to the kind of 'empowerment' that was central to the field of nonviolence and the idea of 'people power', in order to make conflict resolution possible. The profile of 'conflict transformation' that was emerging implied clear values and the recognition that it was not conflict that needed to be prevented but violence, and that sometimes conflict was needed in order to bring about change. This implied a more value-laden approach to the analysis of conflict, a stronger focus on its underlying causes, and greater attention to the specific challenges of 'asymmetric' conflict,[11] in which the power of conflicting groups is markedly unequal (though it should perhaps be noted that this realisation did not noticeably change the practice of most organisations).

In the former Yugoslav countries, the level of popular activism was high, and many of those who were now resisting inter-ethnic violence had also been involved in resistance to Slobodan Milošević (and would be again). However, they now wanted to focus on bridging the ever-growing divide between different 'ethnic groups'

---

11. See Miall et al., *Contemporary Conflict Resolution*, p. 21.

(a concept that was anathema to many of them),[12] and resisting the dynamics of hatred and violence that were growing by the day.

By contrast, I remember that, in the first training I did in the Caucasus, around this time, many doubts were expressed about the possibility of 'conflict resolution' when the power disparities between parties were apparently overwhelming. It was in response to participant's questions about the relevance of mediation and problem-solving to their conflict that in 1994, with the help of a colleague – Guus Meijer – I developed the first version of a diagram I had been working on, depicting stages and processes in conflict transformation.

This diagram was inspired by a much earlier one from Adam Curle.[13] First published by others in simplified form,[14] and fully in my first book,[15] it depicts the very different types of activity that may be needed at different times in a process of conflict transformation, in which conflict resolution is one stage among others. In particular, it represents the partisan action that will need to be taken by oppressed or marginalised groups if they are to be taken seriously and included in a conflict-resolution process. It also points to the long process of recovery that will be necessary after any bitter conflict, even when some kind of settlement has been reached. It appears as an Appendix to this book.

The nettle that seemed hard to grasp – the idea that was difficult to integrate with the theory of conflict resolution, as such – was the right and necessity for people to engage in political struggle against injustice and for inclusion in social and political agreements. This did not fit with the value of non-judgemental impartiality that is fundamental to conflict-resolution processes. The original idea of 'conflict prevention' – that it was important to address the 'latent conflict' of injustices that might give rise to violence (by those who suffered them) – might have been expected to include nonviolent struggle. However, I would suggest that the term itself, which equates conflict with violence, reflects an underlying feeling that not only violence but conflict itself is best avoided.

The ethos of struggle – even nonviolent – with its political and ideological overtones, did not mix with the broadly humane ethos of conflict resolution, nor yet with the notion of the 'objective' academic. Nonviolence, like feminism, challenges the establishment

12. See D. Ugresic, *The Culture of Lies*, London: Phoenix, 1998.
13. A. Curle, *Making Peace*, London: Tavistock, 1971.
14. Miall et al., *Contemporary Conflict Resolution*, p. 17.
15. Francis, *People, Peace and Power*, p. 49.

and has never really come in from the cold. 'Conflict prevention' is a phrase used mainly to suggest not popular mobilisation but action (or influence brought to bear) from outside, predominantly (though not exclusively) by governments or intergovernmental agencies.

The term 'peacebuilding' is generally used to refer to the work that needs to be done once a settlement has been reached, particularly after violent conflict. It was originally brought into vogue by UN Secretary General Boutros Boutros-Ghali, in his *Agenda for Peace*.[16] In that agenda, 'peacebuilding' followed on from 'peacemaking' and 'peacekeeping' (though logically it would be just as well applied to 'conflict prevention'). It is a term widely used in government circles, and hence has increasingly tended to displace 'conflict transformation' in NGO circles. ('Conflict resolution' is not so central to governmental discourse, perhaps because it is not such a major part of their practice.)

I still choose the term 'conflict transformation', partly because it is embedded in the title of CCTS, and partly because of the ideas it embodies. 'Peacebuilding' is in itself an excellent term, suggesting the many elements of constructive work that peace requires, and which are carried out by individuals and organisations that take this work very seriously. In many ways it is a more generally understandable and positive expression. But it has also become the specious term for hegemonic agendas and violence-based activities that are diametrically opposed to the methods of conflict transformation, as I shall discuss in Chapter 5.

My other reason for choosing 'conflict transformation' to describe non-governmental work is that, when 'peacebuilding' is used by governments to describe constructive activities, they are usually referring to the establishment of institutions and economies rather than to the building of relationships, which are the primary focus of conflict transformation. In this sense it is seen largely in terms of 'intervention': something carried out or instigated by outsiders. Conflict transformation is achieved, first and foremost, by local people, with 'outsiders' taking a supporting or facilitating role. It is focused on people: their skills, attitudes, actions and relationships.

FROM SOLIDARITY TO PARTNERSHIP

In the early days of the CCTS, we found that we were asked not only for training but also for ongoing solidarity and support. As

16. B. Boutros-Ghali, *An Agenda for Peace*, New York: United Nations, 1992.

I have indicated, new groups were very grateful to have people to think with them about their direction and strategy, and to facilitate their organisational formation processes and the kind of ongoing review and orientation that could help them hold together and steer the most effective course through stormy waters. Perhaps even more important, however, was the sense of solidarity. The kind of moral and psychological support and recognition that we offered was experienced as a lifeline by people who otherwise found themselves isolated in very violent situations.

The energy that came from the courage and determination of local activists was powerful and infectious. They were taking the initiative and we were responding, in solidarity. This shaped our conviction that our role in any country was to support local activists, who should set the agenda. (It was this conviction, together with our alignment with the broader political perspective of 'conflict transformation', which led us to the name we eventually chose: Committee for Conflict Transformation *Support*.) We wanted it to be clear that we did not think that anyone from outside could transform a conflict. It was our task to pool our resources to meet any requests that came to us, and to reflect and learn together about the kind of support that worked for people dealing with conflict.

However, ad hoc responses to requests gradually gave way to a more strategic, programmatic approach on the part of responding organisations – one that had in fact been developing in some member organisations even at the time of the Committee's formation. In this model, the kind of ongoing accompaniment outlined above became programmatic, rather than remaining a matter of personal contact and sporadic visits of one sort or another.

This in turn meant that the work done by the Western ('International') NGOs began to have its own rationale and agenda. Though this was not, to my knowledge, articulated at the time, I believe it was awareness of this shift away from simple responsiveness and towards the development of their own strategic agendas that lay behind organisations' growing emphasis on 'partnership'. The language of partnership, though routine in our field, signals that same belief that, however much expertise may be brought to a situation by outsiders, only the people who live in a place can build peace there, and that their primary role should be honoured.

So local actors remain central to the vision of conflict transformation. But the potential in the partnership model for contradictions and tensions is self-evident, particularly given the fact that funding is usually made available to local groups via 'international' partners. More often than not it is outsiders who formulate and present a funding proposal for joint work, though they may do so in consultation with local organisations. It is they who are accountable to the donors for the way the money is used. There is a danger, therefore, that local partners become, in this sense, client organisations, and may find themselves adjusting their agendas to fit with those of their outside partners in order to sustain their own organisations.

This is very different from the earlier model, in which funds were raised for a particular piece of support work that would be done in response to a local request. The programme approach enables the kind of ongoing support – funding, complementary expertise, a fresh perspective and contacts – that can give a substantial boost to local action and enable it to grow and develop. But it also constitutes a major shift in power and accountability, and I have seen the anxiety and resentment this can create at the local level.

I have also seen the agonising these relationships cause among Western counterparts. They, too, need to sustain their organisations or departments, and are caught between donors and local partners. They have their own analysis and strategy for a given region – informed by local partners, but also coming from their own knowledge of the country in question (which may in some ways be broader, if less intimate), and their external perspective. Their power brings with it its own unavoidable responsibility.

FUNDAMENTAL VALUES

What are the impulses and values implicit in all this? Compassion, though not often named, is clearly fundamental. We were responding in the first place, I think, at a very human level, to the suffering occasioned by war. That impulse of compassion finds expression in the value of respect for the identity, needs and rights of others.

Bringing an end to violence was the object of our remedial work – first and foremost the immediate violence of war, but also the violence of human rights violations and injustices stemming from tyranny, division and exclusion. Nonviolence can therefore be seen as a key value, both as a means and as a goal. It is related to the values of care and respect, and the consequent commitment to the prevention of suffering and the safeguarding of well-being. Nonviolence is traditionally associated very much with the discourse of rights, of justice, and of struggle.

Conflict resolution is in essence a process that seeks to build agreement and restore relationships between those caught up in a conflictual situation. It is often described as non-judgemental and inclusive. Care and respect are to be given to all equally ('parity of esteem' is a phrase sometimes used), in shared problem-solving processes aimed at outcomes where the needs of all are met, rather than one party getting the better of another. There are (in theory at least) no winners or losers. This implies the valuing of cooperation over domination.[17]

I would argue, therefore, that respect and care are the values underlying the discourses of both non-violence and conflict resolution. I am making these values explicit here not only because they are at the heart of conflict transformation, but also because they are in sharp contrast to the values expressed in much that goes on in the wider world in which we all operate, and at odds with some of the things done in the name of 'peacemaking' and 'peacebuilding', as I will argue in Chapter 4.

17. R. Eisler, *The Chalice and the Blade: Our History, Our Future*, London: Unwin Paperbacks, 1990.

2
Ongoing Development

Over recent years a great deal of conflict-transformation work has been carried out on every continent by local actors – 'ordinary people' – and by international organisations supporting their work. Much of this work is courageous, dedicated and impressive, and both local and international organisations have grown in number, and often in size.

There must be many movements across the world that have no international organisations supporting them with their expertise, and no access to funding from governments or big foundations: movements that are made up of many different organisations that rely on the passion and commitment of volunteers and on tiny offices maintained by the donations of their members. They are not 'professionalised' and are only notionally recognised by the peace 'field' as being part of it, although their existence and work are at least as important – arguably far more so – than the professional efforts of NGOs.

There is also a world of day-to-day peace work that goes on informally, between family members and neighbours, within and between clans and communities, without any assistance, payment or record, but vital to the well-being of all concerned. And at the other end of the scale there is the work of government programmes, inter-governmental bodies and the major international aid, development and human rights organisations (and others) that can also be related to 'positive peace', and is increasingly being given the label of 'peacebuilding', along with institution building.

My focus in this chapter, however, will be on the conflict-trans-formation work of non-governmental organisations, programmes or projects devoted specifically to addressing conflict through the transformation of people and relationships. The account I give of this work and my reflections on it are based on my own experience and that of my colleagues and their organisations. I make no claim to comprehensiveness, and perhaps not all my observations are well founded. However, I have done my best to check my perceptions with others and to listen carefully to what they have had to say.

As I have struggled to find simple categories for different types of work, I have noticed that, despite all my efforts to the contrary, I see things from an 'international' perspective, and that what I am putting under the spotlight is largely the work of international organisations.[1] Nonetheless, I will draw on my firsthand knowledge of many of their local counterparts, who do the greatest part of the work to transform conflict.

Different organisations operate on what can be seen as the different social and political levels (or 'tracks') referred to in Chapter 1. Many international NGOs have local partners at more than one level, but most community-based or grassroots work is done by local activists or by the local staff NGOs.

The assumption made by international NGOs working at more than one level of a conflict is that this produces mutual influence and synergy between the different levels of operation. But, while the theory is that 'middle-level' leadership is pivotal in reaching both top decision-makers and the wider populace – or grassroots – it is not clear that this assumption is always, or perhaps even often, translated into practice. In some circumstances there is a wide gulf between the ranks of the educated and those whose opportunities have been more limited. Paul Stubbs, in his excellent article on the concept and reality of civil society,[2] argues that in the former Yugoslav countries there was a sharp division between educated, anti-nationalist activists and grassroots nationalists. However, some local and regional organisations have found ways of ensuring that links are made and channels of communication created, typically so that the people 'below' have the opportunity to be heard and to exercise influence on those 'above'. And some international NGOs have helped local partners to make representations to external governments.

It is perhaps worth noting that it is implicit in the discourse on conflict transformation that it is not only proper, in democratic terms, that the drive for peace should come from below and that the bulk of the population, situated at the bottom of the pyramid, should be involved in the peace process, but that in fact the political

1. For a more inclusive formulation of roles in conflict transformation, covering the activities of 'insiders and outsiders', see Francis, *People, Peace and Power*, Table 1.1, pp. 18, 19.
2. P. Stubbs, 'Civil Society or Ubleha', in H. Rill, T. Smidling and A. Bitoljanu (eds), *20 Pieces of Encouragement for Awakening and Change: Peacebuilding in the Region of Former Yugoslavia*, Belgrade – Sarajevo: Centre for Nonviolent Action, 2007, pp. 215–28.

will is unlikely to exist at the top if this is not the case. Certainly, the international NGOs of which I have most experience work mostly with non-governmental organisations rather than with governments, though increasingly they are working to influence policymakers and donors, and are sometimes invited to provide training for them.

It is interesting and reassuring to see how practice is often the forerunner of key terms and ideas: that the implicit theory behind what people do is later recognised and made explicit. The phrases 'more people' and 'key people',[3] which are now used to encapsulate the pre-existing twin strategies of many organisations, are a case in point. The 'key people' are sought out because they have the capacity to influence others, whether to act as 'multipliers' and bring in 'more people', or because they have access to decision-makers and therefore the capacity to influence or change things directly.

As I have said elsewhere,[4] large-scale conflicts are extremely complex, and have all sorts of manifestations and sub-conflicts embedded in them, which may be very different from the main conflict and may take place within a different time-frame, so requiring different kinds of action. Moreover, in many regions violence is endemic and fluctuates in intensity, so that for a long time there is no clear, single direction to the conflict. So, while it is still useful to think about the 'stage' of a given conflict (as in the Appendix to this volume), I have decided to arrange this discussion under headings that in some cases suggest rather general types of activity, while others are related more to specific conflict stages or to issues that thread their way through different aspects of this work.

One thing that I have realised is that the essence of almost all peace activities consists in constructive communication – about ideas, feelings, perceptions, analysis, needs, requests, proposals, arguments and ways of doing things. Ideally, of course, sound thinking and knowledge will underlie communication for it to be useful, and it will need to be sincere and well-intentioned. But communication is the vehicle, and the skills of attentive listening and appropriate, hear-able speaking are vital.

This communication can potentially be carried out by many different kinds of people, and needs to involve those who have chosen, or found themselves in, partisan, semi-partisan and

3. CDA, *Reflecting on Peace Practice*, Cambridge, MA: CDA Collaborative Learning Project, 2004.
4. Francis, *People, Peace and Power*, p. 52.

non-partisan roles.[5] It also takes place in many different formats, venues and contexts, as suggested by the subheadings below. The fact that constructive communication constitutes the common thread in all this work is not surprising, since that is indeed what transforms conflict, enabling it to be dealt with through shifts in understanding and attitude, and consequent changes in behaviour and policy, rather than through violence: 'jaw jaw, not war war'.

In the following discussion of the conflict-transformation work that has been going on, I speak, inevitably, in generalities. Any examples I might cite would be random and invidious, and would either be so brief as to be meaningless or would render this chapter impossibly long. There are some excellent sources for stories and case studies.[6]

CAPACITY BUILDING

'Capacity building' is a staple on the conflict-transformation menu, and can be related to all the other activities that appear below, for which capacity is a prerequisite. It takes a variety of forms. Chief among these, however, is 'training', and specifically the 'training workshop'.

Training and other workshops

When I was first working in this field, it was almost exclusively as a trainer – that is, I facilitated workshops that gave their participants the chance to think together (sometimes in opposition), in a concerted and structured way: about particular issues or situations, their options for responding to them, and how to implement those responses. For many, this was a process of what Paolo Freire called 'conscientisation' – becoming conscious of, or awake to, their circumstances and possibilities, and becoming 'empowered' in the process.[7] These workshops provided an opportunity for them to bring into awareness their own and each other's experience-based knowledge, giving it shape and focus. At the same time, they were

5. D. Francis and N. Ropers, *Peace Work by Civil Actors in Post-Communist Societies* (Berghof Occasional Paper No. 10) Berlin: Berghof Research Centre for Constructive Conflict Management, 1997, p. 20.
6. D. Mathews, *War Prevention Works: 50 Stories of People Resolving Conflict*, Oxford: Oxford Research Group, 2001; P. Van Tongeren, M. Brenk, M. Hellema, and J. Verhoeven (eds), *People Building Peace II: Successful Stories of Civil Society*, Boulder and London: Lynne Rienner, 2005.
7. Paulo Freire, *Pedagogy of the Oppressed*, London: Penguin, 1972.

able to learn from the concepts and stories their facilitators brought into the process, and to work with a variety of tools to analyse conflict and devise strategies for addressing it. The workshops also gave participants a chance to develop (through 'experiential' exercises such as role-playing) various key skills, notably those for communicating effectively in conflict.[8]

Sometimes these training workshops had a wide focus, taking examples from a variety of situations, and were designed for participants to develop general concepts and skills; sometimes they were focused on a specific conflict that was affecting all their participants.

The workshops I first facilitated had been requested by those who took part in them. They wanted someone to help them think about the kind of action they had in mind or were already engaged in. They hoped to learn from ideas and experiences already 'out there' that were relevant to them. Gradually, however, workshops became a favourite 'tool' for outside organisations, typically international NGOs, in pursuing their own strategies for stimulating and supporting conflict transformation. The participants would be invited by the international NGOs, at the suggestion of local contacts.

Sometimes these international organisations were able to use workshops to bring together participants from both or all of the communities affected by a conflict, in a way that local organisations would not be trusted to do. In this way, workshops became vehicles for an oblique form of dialogue, as well as for education and inspiration.

Some organisations offered open courses of various lengths, to which would-be participants could apply and for which bursaries were often available. These were often longer and more thorough, and brought together participants from a wide variety of contexts and cultures. The richness of experiences and examples contributed by students on such courses, and the stimulus and insights associated with comparative learning, had their own particular advantages, challenging and enriching students' thinking in ways that were indeed transformative.

Some such courses continue to be provided. Yet I was not sure whether to write those paragraphs in the past or present tense, because I know that the picture has shifted to some degree. Firstly, international NGOs began to shift their attention from 'introductory

---

8. For a longer discussion of workshops, see Francis, *People, Peace and Power*, pp. 85–130.

training' (seldom followed up with anything under the title of 'intermediate' or 'advanced') to 'training for trainers'. The idea was to expand the 'capacity' for 'capacity building'. I imagine that the decline I have noticed in the demand for 'international' trainers is partly a consequence of an increase in 'local capacity', and that the workshops are continuing with local or regional trainers, training new groups who really want what they can offer. I hope that is so.

However, I also have the impression that the enthusiasm for training sometimes exceeded its utility, and that some people – particularly the young and educated – were invited to one workshop after another. While most were probably sincerely interested in their content, I think they were also attracted by the thought of a week (or whatever) in a relatively comfortable hotel or conference centre, in a place they would not otherwise have had the chance to visit, and in the company of an interesting group of people – and sometimes also by the 'per diems' that in some contexts accompanied such opportunities.

The workshops were often designed to bring participants to the point of sustained action of a kind that was quite new for them, or was at least different from what they had done before. In addition, there was sometimes an assumption that they would undertake work with fellow participants whom they had not met before. Given that only some of the participants had such a level of commitment as to make serious activism a priority in their lives, and that the circles within which these invitations were issued were limited and overlapping, I suspect that such workshops were subject to the law of diminishing returns.

Another weakness in the 'workshop-to-action' model was that, even when the participants knew in advance that action would be an expected outcome and participated in the workshop on that understanding, they did not really take their own 'action plans' seriously, but still regarded them as only an exercise. The only exceptions to this that I experienced were achieved when action plans were translated into project proposals and the international NGO concerned had raised the money to support their implementation. I do not know whether the new action generated in those cases was sustained when those funds came to an end, but hopefully those with their own rooted commitment may have found ways of continuing what they had begun. ('Sustainability' and funding will be discussed in Chapter 3.)

I believe that training workshops are most effective in supporting change when they are designed from scratch, in response to the needs of those who are themselves already determined to try to address a specific situation, and are looking for help in working out how to do so; or who already know what they want to do, and need assistance in preparing themselves; or who have an interest in talking to 'the other side' in an oblique way (not forced to talk about their own conflict, but able to if they so decide) and are being offered the chance to do this in a training workshop; or who have been looking for an opportunity to learn about conflict more generally, and nonviolent approaches to it, because they want to become politically engaged. In other words, workshops are worthwhile when they are already wanted or needed by those who are or want to be activists – that is, when they are designed for a particular purpose, creatively and responsively (and, I would add, when they are facilitated by people with knowledge, skill and humility, so that they encourage sober commitment rather than too-easy optimism).

Although some parts of the world might seem to have been saturated with training, there are still plenty of places where people are eager for more exposure to the ideas of conflict transformation, and are looking for new ways of approaching the problems that confront them. Some of those places are neglected by the 'international community', and are hard for people from outside to enter and work in. But there are now trainers from many different parts of the world who can provide this kind of support.

In the meantime a second wave of training seems to be underway, which is taking place in the light of experience and going deeper into areas and issues that have proved problematic or that need further exploration. This training is being organised for and by organisations, for themselves and others. It is also being taken increasingly to government departments, development organisations and military institutions whose personnel wish to understand conflict better and to design and carry out their work in 'conflict-sensitive' ways – or, in the case of organisations that deliver emergency aid, to understand how to negotiate, where necessary, with armed groups.

Capacity building sometimes takes place in the more prestigious guise of seminars, with keynote speakers and polished tables. At other times it goes on in the jungle or otherwise out of sight – for instance, with the leaders of 'unofficial' military groups who need to learn the skills of negotiation. This is one example of the kind of training that is concentrated on conflict parties who are at a disadvantage in terms of education and experience. It can help them to engage in processes with the potential to bring an end to violence or prevent its recurrence, enabling them to feel they have a chance of doing so as equals, and so to rely less heavily on violence to achieve their goals.

Training in how to avoid or deal with conflict is also being provided for people who undertake key roles in social institutions (for instance, in establishing the rule of law) that do not come directly under the 'peace' rubric, but whose role will be important in creating peaceable norms.

Although I am sure that not all training has been as relevant, empowering and inspiring as it might have been, and that not all participants have been the 'right' ones, I do believe that work carried out under this heading has enabled many hard-pressed and dedicated people to find new perspectives and a greater sense of possibility, as well as to play their roles more effectively.

Development of groups and organisations

As I suggested in Chapter 1, strengthening groups and organisations can be seen as an important aspect of capacity building. It often involves training. Know-how and facilitation are sometimes provided by larger, external organisations, which also foot the bill. Work that began informally often needs, as it grows, to become more structured, in terms of both personnel and procedures, and the lessons of early efforts need to be learned, so that future work can be effectively grounded and directed.

Evaluation processes that are planned by or with those whose work is being evaluated, and conducted in a participatory way, can be helpful in pointing up what has been achieved, as well as clarifying what can be improved, developed, or even abandoned. Making time for regular review is vital for any team. As a community worker once pointed out to me, regular evaluation plays a vital role in encouraging activists, because it makes them aware of how much they have done. It does not necessitate external facilitation and special venues; it can be carried out under a tree or in the meeting room, with group members taking turns in leading it. What matters is that it is collectively owned, and conducted in a way that gives energy rather than depleting it. A good outside facilitator, especially one who knows and understands the group, can help from time to time by providing the framework and focus, along with affirmation and fresh perspectives, questions and insights, enabling others to participate freely without being responsible for the process.

While support for organisational development can indeed help people to become more effective in the work they do for peace, the 'professionalisation' of peace work can take those involved in it away from their roots and make it harder for their fellow community members to be part of what they do, so increasing the gap between grassroots work and the 'middle level' world of NGOs. And this is related to the question of money.

Money

Access to funds can support developments in capacity and enable new abilities to be put to use. Training in fundraising and direct financial support can therefore be hugely enabling. But obtaining substantial amounts of money to fund an organisation's work must nowadays involve hiring accountants and learning to struggle with 'logframes' ('logical frameworks' or analytical grids) and other mechanisms that may be intended to support effectiveness and accountability, but that sometimes become an end in themselves – or, worse still, a contrivance that masks reality. They put pressure on organisations to predict the unpredictable and exaggerate the claims they make about outcomes. This is in many ways a debilitating world to enter. I have heard of genuine grassroots initiatives, run from village huts by community members, that were turned into slick, well-funded operations that no longer had any place for their initiators.

Monitoring and evaluation nowadays constitute a lucrative sphere of business. Consultants and others who were once employed to provide training and accompaniment for hands-on work are used instead (often by large contractors) to monitor and evaluate it in response to the demands of donors. Clearly it is important that funds are allocated judiciously and that their use is clearly accounted for, but there are problems associated with the way the goals of accountability are being pursued, which I will discuss later.

Know-how and sharing resources

I know of a wonderful women's organisation that makes all kinds of resources available to its network: knowledge of what others are doing; updates on particular legislation and the way it is being used; information and 'how-to' packs, available online, ready to be used as and when they are wanted.[9] I expect that others are doing similar things. (Having worked with all-women groups and organisations as well as others, I have noticed a particularly strong sense of equality, common purpose and solidarity among women

---

9. The Women Peacemakers Program of the International Fellowship of Reconciliation (<www.ifor.org/WPP>).

who work in the peace field.) There are also organisations whose sole purpose is to support groups of all kinds that are working for peace, helping them to develop their organisational skills.

Capacity-building activities are increasingly carried out by local people who have well-developed expertise and who are attuned to the specific needs of their own societies. Not only do they share their skills with others: it is they who, by and large, carry out the transformative activities discussed below.

POPULAR EDUCATION

While much of the capacity-building work outlined above can be seen as educational, it is focused on those who are seen as activists (at least potentially). Those activists in turn may eventually train others, but they may also do educational work that is designed to reach into their own communities and change the ways in which people think and behave, so that even if the people they train do not become active campaigners or bridge-builders, they are less likely to support war, aggravate inter-group relations, fight in the playground, or whatever, and will have some skills for dealing constructively with conflict.

Some peace-education work is done in schools, through visits from outside or through modules and materials designed for inclusion in the curriculum. Some schools have gone one step further and introduced peer-training and mediation schemes, which not only have an immediate impact in specific situations but help to shift the 'conflict culture' within the school, and even in the children's homes and communities.

Children are, as we are often told, 'the future'. However, it is not fair or reasonable to expect them to carry some of our more far-fetched hopes for them or to sort out what we have messed up! While they are young, they are subject to all the constraints and pressures of societies over which they currently have little influence. However, it may be empowering for them to have some alternative models for their own responses to the situations in which they find themselves; and they may, like any other people, be able to influence others.

Other educational programmes, some of them rolled out by international organisations or movements, are directed at adults who are thought of as being particularly at risk of involvement in violence (for instance, prisoners, ex-prisoners and former soldiers). I know of one in particular that has been popular in a great many different countries,[10] and whose clear, upbeat message and lively processes seem to have a strong impact on its participants. It must be hard for the impact of this work to withstand the pressures that come from life beyond the institutions in which many of these educational experiences take place – but the more such work is done, the better chance it has of influencing ways of life more widely and withstanding violent tendencies.

MEDIA WORK AND ARTS PROJECTS

Popular media, particularly radio and TV, can be a powerful vehicle for an even broader form of education, and many local NGOs (often with international backing) are involved in making feature films and running regular programmes that challenge stereotypes and dominant perspectives in conflictual situations. Sometimes films are made to introduce people from one side of a conflict divide to audiences on the other. They may be made by a third party and used as a channel of communication between different communities in conflict, or by members of those communities themselves. They can enable silenced voices to be heard and things to become known that have been kept hidden.

As with so much of this work, it is hard to prove the impact of these efforts at contributing to change in popular understanding, but their rationale is good, and it is hard to think that, if there were enough high-quality work of this kind, being done in such a way as to attract listeners and viewers, and being transmitted through popular channels, it would not have quite an influence. I have certainly seen some very powerful footage.

Many international NGOs have provided training for journalists in how to report in non-inflammatory ways, making them aware of their responsibility to do so, and enabling them to consider the ethical issues related to a reporter's job to inform, and to the potential effect of the way in which news is conveyed in shaping public opinion – and specifically in heightening or decreasing tension and hatred, or encouraging public support for violent or peaceful policies.

With all the work discussed so far, the question is not simply whether there is a good rationale for it, but whether it is done well enough to have the effect intended. The quality of trainers, trainees, advisers, journalists, camera crews, and so on, will make a huge

10. The Alternatives to Violence Project (<www.avpinternational.org>).

difference – their innate capabilities, their commitment to learning and following through on what they have learned, their personal influence and connections, the opportunities that present themselves, and what is going on when the programme is transmitted. Some of these elements can be legislated for, at least to some degree; others less so, or not at all. But mass communication is clearly influential where the newspaper or channel in question is to some degree liked and/or trusted.

The frequency of presentation and the way in which men and women are presented in the media (in most places still heavily male-dominated) have, I believe, a huge impact on social attitudes.[11] This is just one factor in the way articles are written or illustrated and programmes are made that will affect their immediate impact and longer-term influence.

Art has a way of presenting reality and expressing experiences and feelings that can touch people more deeply than at the purely rational level. It can also challenge familiar arguments and assumptions. Arts projects – plays, exhibitions, concerts, graffiti, and so on – have been used to raise the profile of particular aspects of a conflict, and to provide an opportunity for communication, both private and public, that can help 'reframe' familiar situations and encourage fresh thinking and new perspectives.

BRIDGE BUILDING

Bridges between 'enemies'

Building bridges between different sides in a conflict is archetypal peace work. These include bridges of communication and understanding as well as bridges to the discovery of shared agendas, and thence to cooperation. As I observed above, some 'training' workshops have a bridge-building function, but local activists and leaders across the world find all sorts of ways of forging connections with and between people who have become alienated – from making a personal approach to a neighbouring community to convening a vast and lengthy inter-clan meeting.

If they are successful, meetings can lead to new structures that have a mediatory or bridge-building function: an intercommunal peace committee, elders' group, youth organisation or women's

11. See, for example, D. Minic, 'Feminist Media Theory and Activism: Different Worlds of Possible Cooperation', in Rill et al., *20 Pieces of Encouragement*, pp. 282–308.

network; a religious or interreligious council that can transcend other loyalties; a system for 'trouble-shooting' and rebuilding trust, for instance through regular cross-border communications; or a live-in community that brings together members of groups that elsewhere are in conflict, providing a resource for peacemaking between those communities.

In specific situations, bridges have been built with adults or children recruited into armies (often through violent coercion) who now want to return to their communities. Initial contacts from those communities have been consolidated into ongoing systems for reception and reintegration. The reintegration of combatants is usually seen as a 'post-conflict' activity, but it sometimes goes on even while the violence continues, with the receiving groups also helping conscripts to escape.

Where practical cooperation is urgently needed, this can be an incentive to take the necessary risks. Sometimes economic activity acts as a bridge – whether by design or necessity. I remember hearing of a divided community in which one section had traditionally spun the wool for rugs while the other had done the weaving, and this past symbiosis provided the incentive to overcome hostility and resume breadwinning.

When it comes to the financial support of third parties for economic activities in such situations, we are arguably straying into the territory of development – and the way in which development is undertaken and supported can indeed play its part in conflict, for good and ill, as is now widely recognised. When (as in a case I heard of) a bull is given by an external organisation to a village on condition that it is to be available to inseminate the cows of all farmers there, regardless of ethnic affiliation, and this is done with the express purpose of promoting cooperative contact, this can reasonably be seen as a bridge-building intervention. It can also be seen as a somewhat manipulative, high-risk strategy, to which the 'do no harm' mantra could usefully be applied. Much has been written about the ways in which aid and development NGOs can help or hinder conflict transformation.[12] But increasing attention has been paid, within the conflict-transformation field, to the role of local businesspeople in helping to improve relationships between different groups in their area of operation – by those people

---

12. Most notably M. B. Anderson, *Do No Harm: Supporting Local Capacities for Peace through Aid*, Cambridge, MA: Local Capacities for Peace Project, 1996.

themselves, and by external organisations that are supporting and learning from them.[13]

External organisations have played facilitating roles in bridge building when there is insufficient trust for a direct approach from one side to another, supporting the establishment of sufficient trust between the parties for them to continue building bridges between themselves. In circumstances where there has been acute antagonism, and where anger remains strong, even the re-establishment of communication can take several years, involving painstaking 'good offices' work (acting as a quiet, unofficial go-between). Then mediation over specific issues may follow.

Bridges between civil society and government organisations

Some local organisations have built bridges with government institutions, such as the police, in order to work towards a common understanding of what peace requires. Other organisations have built bridges with local authorities, in order to find complementary ways of working for peace.

On occasion, a peace deal has involved the merging of armies, and external organisations have been asked to facilitate this inevitably difficult process.

Bridges between peacemakers

External organisations have also played a useful role in enabling people who are working for peace to meet together at a wider national or regional level, sometimes across societal or political divides, to provide each other with support (and to challenge one another), and to exchange ideas and encouragement, with the potential for future moral support and sometimes active cooperation. (This was one of the roles played by the CCTS and others when the wars in the former Yugoslavia were at their height.) Such opportunities can boost the morale of activists, confirming their vision for the future and making them feel that they are not alone.

External third parties can also be challenging, since feelings and perceptions will not always coincide, and some of the fears and tensions that are present in society at large will be felt in these meetings. But overcoming them often leaves participants all the stronger, and the recognition and understanding differences

13. J. Banfield, C. Gunduz and N. Killick (eds), *Local Business, Local Peace: The Peacebuilding of the Domestic Private Sector*, London: International Alert, 2006.

in analysis and goals is vital to peacemaking. Even groups and organisations that do not have the right context for active cooperation, or even sufficient common ground, can benefit from getting to grips with this fact while nonetheless reaffirming their commitment to working for peace.

Building solidarity networks

Many regional and global networks have been built for long-term solidarity, cooperation and learning. Those with which I have become familiar have been assisted by an international NGO that has friends and partners around the world or in a particular region. Once the network has been established, the international NGO has become simply a network member or, in the case of a network established in another region, has stepped out of any convening role and remained in connection with it only as a supportive friend.

Sometimes networks (which often grow out of shared experiences of training) run training courses for their members and arrange conferences and seminars to exchange learning, shape policy and plan joint action. I have seen the importance of the support that members of such networks are able to give each other, particularly in times of crisis, including visits, emails, money and lobbying, while local activists work urgently to make ad hoc connections and coalitions to prevent or stem a particular outbreak of violence. And their joint lobbying power within regional governmental structures can be considerable.

ADVOCACY

Popular advocacy and political lobbying play an important role in conflict transformation, whether undertaken by local individuals and groups or by national and regional organisations and networks.

Advocacy for justice and nonviolent resistance

All over the world there are organisations standing up for human rights, economic inclusion and political reform. Some groups do so on behalf of a particular community or section of the population that is being attacked, excluded or disadvantaged. The chronically unjust or otherwise violent treatment of one group or of the mass of a population has been described as 'latent conflict',[14] and addressing it can not only bring justice for those who are oppressed, but may prevent a wider eruption of societal or intercommunal violence.

14. Curle, *Making Peace*.

In places where freedom of speech is not tolerated, advocacy of any sort is seen as a threat by the authorities. Brave individuals who speak out are liable to be arrested, imprisoned, tortured or 'disappeared'. But at some point there may be wider mobilisation for public protest and resistance. Even then, those who have participated have in many well-known cases been severely punished for their courage. In some of these instances they have also, eventually, prevailed. It seems that, with the necessary persistence and sufficient numbers, popular resistance can bring down even the most controlling and cruel regimes. Consent is, in the end, necessary to stability.

When people take to the streets they do so not as organisations but as movements, though organisations (often small and dependent for any funds on their active membership) may have played a part in preparing and mobilising them. I would argue that this is a crucial organisational role in conflict transformation, and one that gets far too little attention. It is easy to see why: it is high-risk work for local organisations, and external ones may want to avoid seeming to encourage others to put their lives in danger. They may worry that their support will be used to discredit local activists. The risk involved is also likely to be unpopular with donors.

The activities of movements may express a political perspective with which international NGOs and external governments may not want to be associated. (There are exceptions to this – notably in post-communist countries where electoral processes and their outcomes have been decided with the help of large-scale demonstrations. The well-funded international support such popular action has received has indeed been politically motivated. Political judgements are unavoidable, but should be principled.) There may be concern that the action could become violent, and the strong principles of nonviolence constitute a challenge even to NGOs working for peace. Clearly, confronting violence and oppression should be carefully considered, and cannot be undertaken lightly; but in many cases it is essential to any transition to real peace. I will return to this issue in Chapter 6.

Meanwhile, activists around the world, often without external support or funding, and without being seen as working for 'conflict transformation', have resisted violence through boycotts and non-cooperation, demonstrations and publications. There have also been experiments in setting up constructive alternatives to prevailing systems, such as the 'peace zones' in Colombia, in which a community refuses to have anything to do with competing armed groups. These risky and courageous actions receive some help – not usually from large international NGOs but from smaller, struggling ones that are part of the international peace movement, which send volunteers as 'accompaniers' or 'monitors'. Their presence offers at least a degree of protection through the international visibility it gives both to resistance and to the human rights violations that it confronts.

Advocacy for peace

As the peace zone organisers would agree, when there is large-scale violence, the most urgent thing to be advocated and lobbied for is an end to that violence. Populations suffering from such violence can help to tip the interests of those who are organising it towards bringing it to an end, by making it clear to them that they are losing popular support (if they ever had any). Many local organisations, often with help from outside, are involved in work to influence public opinion in favour of peace processes, creating a 'peace constituency' that can bring pressure to bear on recalcitrant leaders.

Creating a peace constituency is likely to involve overcoming much fear and anger on both (or all) sides of a conflict, and the education of key groups and of the wider public is vital in this process.

Advocacy for participation in peace processes

Not only are peace constituencies needed; if the peace is to be a genuine one that meets the needs of all sectors of society, those different sectors need to be involved. Organisations in many parts of the world have advocated such inclusiveness, and have indeed, in some places, enabled some public participation, through regional forums or the inclusion of spokespeople for particular groups.[15]

UN Resolution 1325, on the right of women to be included in peace processes, has been used as a political lever by many women's groups around the world to strengthen their case for participation. When society has been through great upheaval and new constitutions are being drawn up, this is – in theory at least – a time of opportunity for change, both in social roles and in the way human rights are regarded. Women need a chance to see that their needs (and those of their children) are respected and their rights incorporated. Having a say now will help ensure that they have a say in the future. Minority groups who have not participated in the fighting will equally want

---

15. See C. Barnes (ed.), *Owning the Process: Public Participation in Peace-making* (Accord 13), London: Conciliation Resources, 2002.

to ensure that they have their say, and that a just position for them in the future society is legislated for in any agreement.

PEACE PROCESSES IN LARGE-SCALE CONFLICTS

Some peace processes take place at communal and intercommunal levels, are facilitated by local peace activists who do the kind of bridge-building work described above, and are eventually carried through by the parties themselves. The kinds of organisation we are considering here do not usually work at the level of direct and official negotiations between the leaders of conflicting factions in large-scale conflict, but they may well be involved in preparation for them.

Good offices and pre-negotiation processes

Even when no contact is officially countenanced, 'good offices' may be provided by go-betweens who carry messages and are used by the parties to test the ground. Where trust has been established, such people have in many instances (in Northern Ireland, for example) played a vital role in creating the possibility for negotiation – sometimes years down the line. Such work requires great patience and resourcefulness, the will to be of service without any kind of control, and great sensitivity to moments of danger and opportunity.

In other cases, internal and external organisations have provided venues and facilitation for behind-the-scenes talks between advisers and other influential people who are close to, and to some degree identified with, the leadership of the opposing sides. They discuss possible options for accommodation with those who will (or may) have an opportunity to inform the 'big leaders' and encourage them to negotiate. To do such work well requires skill, patience and good-will. And however well it is done, it may not bear fruit in the desired way, though doubtless there will be personal influences that may carry through into unseen or unattributable political effects.

Such opportunities sometimes take the form of seminars, in which broad discussion of relevant issues can lead into direct discussion of the case in point. Others take the shape of 'problem-solving workshops', in which a process of shared analysis is facilitated by trusted third parties and leads into an exploration of the different ways in which the needs and interests of the conflicting parties could be met. (Those third parties sometimes also have informal direct access to members of the top leadership.)

A great many such seminars take place, often over many years and without leading to any apparent breakthrough. In the end the decisions have to be taken by those who have the power to sign an agreement, and they are likely to be strongly influenced by their perceptions of their power to prevail over their opponents, as against reaching some accommodation with them. Often they seem to have unreal estimates of this power. Enabling them to see things more realistically is sometimes one of the things that those who offer good offices can do.

Such supportive activities, sometimes described as 'pre-negotiation processes', may well contribute to eventual settlements, or at least make it less likely that the parties will return to violence. If advisers and respected subordinates see no use in continuing or renewing violence, and consider a negotiated settlement as possible and desirable, this is likely to encourage decision-makers to pursue more peaceable options – the more so where there is a strong, popular peace constituency, whose representatives ideally have some access to those involved in the talks. (When those involved in high-level negotiations lose touch with their constituencies, there is a severe danger that, if a deal is made it, will lack the popular support necessary to carry it through.)

In cases where the conflict is centred on the 'integrity of the state', in relation to secession or independence, there is often a lack of experience and skill in negotiation on the side of the separatists, who may therefore need preparation – a particular form of capacity building: knowledge of the principles, processes and skills of negotiation. Gaining confidence in these areas may make them more willing to engage in talks.

Involvement with armed groups

There has been increasing recognition of the need to involve armed groups in pre-negotiation and negotiation processes, and NGOs, typically international ones, have in many instances helped them to prepare themselves as negotiators, as well as promoting engagement with them, as well as an understanding of what motivates and constrains them.[16]

Since it is, in the end, only those who have been fighting who can deliver an end to fighting, and since real grievances, as well as greed[17] (and a host of other factors) may lie behind their violence and need to be addressed, this must be regarded as positive. And

16. R. Ricigliano (ed.), *Choosing to Engage: Armed Groups and Peace Processes* (Accord 16), London: Conciliation Resources, 2005.
17. M. Berdal and D. Malone (eds), *Greed and Grievance: Economic Agendas in Civil Wars,* Colorado and London: Lynne Rienner, 2000.

there is no reason to assume that governments are always right and those who take arms against them always wrong – in their cause, at least, if not in their methods. Their aspirations may well be shared by a large sector of the population.

However, far more work needs to be done to enable *unarmed* groups to have their say. This is a key dilemma for peacemaking: how to get from war to peace without rewarding violence, whether it is the violence of the state or of factions rebelling against it; how to step outside the current system of power; how to give equal rights to those who so often experience powerlessness. That means a very high proportion of most populations: all those who are not physically strong and do not have weapons or wealth or influence. This will be the theme of later chapters.

RECOVERY FROM VIOLENCE[18]

Even when a ceasefire is reached and is followed by a settlement (which, alas, is not always the case), and that settlement is indeed implemented sufficiently for the fragile peace to hold and to be consolidated, there is a long way to go before a society can be 'at peace' – even acknowledging that peace will always be a relative term. Once there is sufficient confidence on all sides and security has been more or less restored, soldiers must be disarmed, demobilised and reintegrated, and we have seen that local groups may have a role to play in assisting that process, and may in turn be supported by external organisations.

War is an economic disaster, destroying infrastructure, homes and livelihoods, and material recovery is likely to require assistance from outside, which is never sufficiently forthcoming, and is arguably beyond the scope of the conflict-transformation field. Broadly speaking, it is the task of governments and major development agencies, though support for job-creation projects is sometimes given by international NGOs whose main remit is conflict trans-formation, precisely because livelihoods are essential to peace and the lack of them is in some situations a major destabilising factor. There is a tendency to focus on the need to find employment for former combatants (when they are male), so that they are less likely to return to fighting. This can be seen as making practical sense,

18. For a more extensive discussion, see Diana Francis, *Conflict Transformation: From Violence to Politics* (CCTS Review 9, Summer 2002), available at <www.c-r.org/ccts>.

but at the same time as rewarding violence and taking up resources that are equally necessary to the well-being of others. Moreover, it is likely to return women, who have in many cases been acting as heads of households, to highly dependent and subservient roles.

Competition for scarce resources also has an impact on the possibility of return for people who have been displaced by fighting (whether within or beyond existing national borders). It is difficult to create the necessary conditions of safety and confidence for this to happen, even when the returnees' homes are still standing and have not been taken over by someone else. Nonetheless, local organisations have sometimes played an important role in helping former neighbours to meet, mediating in unresolved and new conflicts, and helping to restore relationships. In some circumstances, international volunteers have accompanied returnees to give them confidence and offer unarmed moral protection – sometimes, if necessary, mobilising international support.

The establishment of inclusive and honest political processes, like economic recovery, is outside the core focus of conflict-transformation practice. However, like economic recovery and inclusion, it may in fact be integral to a peace process and to the demands that are brought to bear on it through lobbying, campaigning and popular debate. Local organisations and their international partners have sometimes been actively involved in such work.

Gendered roles and experiences

Violence against women – in particular sexual violence – is especially hard to address, since exposure of the crime often condemns the woman concerned to shame and exclusion. Such matters need to be handled with the greatest of sensitivity by parties who are acceptable interlocutors and who understand local norms and their impact, though in the last analysis this double cruelty – of not only being raped, but then so terribly punished for the fact – must be seen for what it is.

Most of the killing in wars, which is often accompanied by sexual violence, is still by and large done by men. Those who have violated others are also damaged by the experience as their victims, though their distress may be expressed in different ways. They have done and witnessed terrible things, not necessarily willingly (at least in the first instance). Domestic violence and suicide rise sharply when soldiers return home from war. I would argue that too little psychological work is done with former fighters to help them recover from their trauma, and also to make a moral assessment of what they have done. A powerful effect can result from their talking about it publicly, and this can enable a wider conversation to begin. I know of few but excellent examples of this (for instance, in the former Yugoslavia).

At the same time, the sexual violence done to women is insufficiently acknowledged, and its meaning and significance go unrecognised. The needs of those who have been only on the receiving end of violence – including the young and the old, as well as most women – must be given expression. I do believe that women's needs are gradually receiving more attention. I suspect that those of the young and old are not. In all cases, what is done is small in relation to the need, but much better than nothing to those who are helped.

Dealing with the past

This phrase, often shortened to DWP, has come into regular use in recent years. Most often it refers to the public processing of war crimes, or of the systematic human rights violations of a past episode or regime. This is increasingly seen as vital to the relative well-being of survivors of atrocities and their families, and to a new regime's integrity. Making known what was done by some and what happened to others is at the heart of such processes, and its rightness is little contested.

But the reality is messy. Victims are sometimes also perpetrators, for instance, and some perpetrators, such as child soldiers, began as victims. Moreover, despite the theory that there can be no peace without justice, for a while at least the latter is likely to give way to the former. As we have seen, it is often those who were to a greater or lesser extent responsible for the atrocities who are also involved in 'conflict settlement', and they will not sign up to a process leading to their own disgrace or punishment. This is part of the much wider dilemma of working for nonviolent (including just) ways forward within the context and rationale of violence.

This said, it is clear that the catalytic effect of movements of people demanding justice (as they have done in many places, often over decades) or the leadership of inspired and persistent individuals doing likewise can help bring about processes for 'dealing with the past'.

The relative weight to be given to truth, compensation and punishment is a matter of ongoing debate. The idea of 'restorative justice' is gaining ground (being in fact well established in the traditions of many cultures), in which wrongdoers are involved in compensating and helping to restore the well-being of the victims or survivors, thereby also restoring some of their own lost dignity and their place in society.

Psychological recovery and reconciliation

Violent conflict causes psychological damage, even to those who themselves have escaped material suffering. Many conflict-transformation organisations have worked to support recovery in individuals and communities, though increasingly focusing on social processes and eschewing Western models of individualised psychotherapy (which in any case fall outside their field of expertise). Helping communities to name (or draw or mime) and talk about what they have experienced (*if* that is culturally appropriate) can bring release, and enable people to feel less isolated as individuals and so face the future more positively.

In the right circumstances, such conversations can include people whom war has made enemies talking together about different experiences of the violence. Even where those experiences are different and unequal (whether morally or in terms of degrees of suffering, however defined), this can constitute an important step in restoring some kind of human relationship.

Reconciliation is an important concept, and represents a vast ambition – particularly after widespread violence. It is often one that is beyond the will or imagination of all but a few, certainly for many years after the overt violence has come to an end. But if a society is to move away from the likelihood of new violence in years to come, and to be at peace with itself, the ambition should be kept alive, and those who work for it with sensitivity, realism and courage have a vital contribution to make.

ONGOING LEARNING

All too often, those who are in the thick of practical conflict-transformation work are too busy to stop and think as seriously as they would like to, but almost all will recognise the importance of stepping back to reflect, as well as thinking as they go. As I have argued, structured opportunities for reflection, reassessment and adjustment (or at times more radical change) are vital to the quality of work done, and help to restore a sense of perspective. I will discuss evaluation more fully in the Chapter 3.

A variety of professional forums have been created around the world (CCTS being one of them). They can provide an invaluable opportunity (for practitioners who can occasionally manage to step outside their pressured schedules for a few hours) to reflect on their own work, to hear what their colleagues have to say in response, and to learn from accounts of their activities and dilemmas.

Through such processes, new thinking emerges that can cast new light on existing issues, some of which will be discussed in Chapter 3. It is vital that new insights bring a deeper understanding of the human realities and social and political complexities that make working with conflict so difficult, and hence of the potential for supporting forces for good. It is necessary to create a space where the self-promoting stance that appears to be necessary for dealing with donors can be relaxed, and where proper humility can take its place; where uncertainties, doubts, disappointments and questions can be voiced, and where participants can accept each other's help. It is easy to see that this is good and necessary for others; it is also good and necessary for us. I celebrate the fact that it happens – even though not enough – and that both practitioners and scholars have worked hard to put their findings into writing for others.[19]

Some university teachers and researchers in international relations and peace and conflict studies are also to some extent active 'in the field' – perhaps more so than in most academic disciplines. And some practitioners write articles and books that are used in universities. Sometimes they are brought into academic institutions as lecturers. I think it would be beneficial if the exchange and overlap were greater, and am heartened to see the practical nature as well as the academic excellence of many degree and higher degree courses, which give peace practitioners the opportunity to step outside their activities and reflect on it from a different angle, thinking about it in a more concerted way than is usually possible, and being nourished by the thinking of others.

INFLUENCING POLICY

Watching the organisations I am close to, and participating in ad hoc global conversations, I observe a growing urgency in the desire to affect policy at the political level, both nationally and regionally.

19. See, for example, CDA, *Reflecting on Peace Practice*, and W. Verkoren, *The Owl and the Dove: Knowledge Strategies to Improve the Peacebuilding Practice of Local Non-governmental Organisations*, Amsterdam: Amsterdam University Press, 2008. See also <www.centrepeaceconflictstudies.org >. I see this could be a problem. I don't want to go into a long digression. Take out the website if you think I can't have it just like that.

Peace practitioners are driven by concern for the particular realities with which they are so closely engaged, and at the same time are endlessly confronted by the impact of policy decisions that have thus far remained beyond the reach of their influence. Some of those working for conflict-transformation organisations have over the years come to be highly regarded by civil servants and politicians, on account of their long-term regional expertise. (Diplomats tend to come and go, and sometimes have little or no direct knowledge of the society in which they operate.) In conversation, they do their best not only to inform but also to persuade those who draw on their experience of how to understand events and what policies to adopt.

An increasing number of organisations have established ongoing programmes for engaging with national and regional institutions on policy issues. In the UK they meet not only with government officials and employees but also with the leadership of opposition parties, to try to influence the way they think about conflict and security. I am aware of similar activities in the US and of concerted policy work in Africa.

Such organisations also create channels of communication for their partners, with their governments, regional parliaments and other institutions, and the UN. Some have banded together in consortiums to increase their influence, and organisations or platforms have been created to link peace professionals with governments, to persuade them to take conflict transformation and its methods more seriously. Peace-related academics and university departments have also found opportunities to share their expertise. I believe there could be a more consciously symbiotic relationship between NGOs and universities, whose academic status can give them the kind of weight that is hard for some NGOs to achieve, while the close, hands-on knowledge of NGOs wins a different kind of respect.

This overview of the field is brief, given the scope of what it has attempted. It is necessarily general and impressionistic. But it was ground I felt it was necessary to set out, and I think I have been able to show something of what has been and is being done. I do not know what impression it will give the reader, but personally I am deeply impressed by much of the work I have seen, whether it is being carried out by local people to change their own situations, or by organisations dedicated to assisting them.

In any field there is work that is clear in its goals, carefully thought out, based on detailed information and good analysis, and conducted with efficiency, dedication and skill; there is also work that is sloppy, ill-conceived and of poor quality (and of course plenty that is somewhere in between). I may have been lucky but, in the field of conflict transformation, I have seen far more of the former than the latter.

3
Dilemmas and Limitations

People who work for peace do so within a global context that makes it very difficult to be both principled and effective. We are all caught up in the existing dynamics of 'unpeace'. This rather obvious fact sometimes makes the theories and goals that underlie our work appear unrealistic. It also creates seemingly endless dilemmas for the ways in which we work.

In this chapter I focus on some of the vexed issues that confront those who work for conflict transformation, all of which are in some way related to the question of power. I begin with the interrelated and apparently practical matters of partnership, money and evaluation. Then I move on to conflict transformation as such, discussing the complexity of trying to address conflict on the basis of needs and relating this to the question of power. I set out some of the difficulties of putting theory into practice, moving on to a broader discussion of our power (or lack of it) to make a strategic impact and the things that stand in the way of such success. The final section of the chapter is focused on the kind of work that I believe needs to be developed if we are to be more broadly effective.

PRACTICAL MATTERS

Conflict transformation is concerned with relationships and the exercise of power and responsibility. The principles of care and respect that inform our approach to these matters are relevant not only to the work we do, but to the way in which we do it. Thus the practical is never a matter of practicality alone – though principled behaviour is, arguably, the most practical kind in the end.

Power and partnership

As we have already seen, the idea of partnership is, at least at the level of civil society, central to international cooperation for conflict transformation. In CCTS we have often discussed what that should mean.[1] In the years running up to the NATO attacks

1. Clark, *Evolution*, pp. 11, 12.

on Serbia, we were very much aware of the nonviolent struggle of the ethnic Albanian population in Kosovo and the need to support those who were leading it. We hung back from suggesting ourselves as potential helpers because we felt we should wait to be invited by local activists, rather than put ourselves forward. This was an attitude we came to question, and I think regret, feeling that, even though the 'international community' had done nothing to support that nonviolent resistance, we should have been more active in the matter.[2]

If that was an example of over-sensitivity, some reticence on the part of practitioners in the West is entirely proper. Colonial history hangs heavy over us, and neocolonialism is all too real. Sometimes the rhetoric of partnership seems to understate the obvious: that outsiders, though they can often help, cannot establish peace in a community or country. But international NGOs necessarily have their own mission and agenda, their own analysis and viewpoint – and, if they are worth their salt, their own expertise and principles. And when they go to donors with a proposal, it has to be *their* proposal. They are the ones who will be held accountable.

This means in the first place that they must choose partners who they know to have a very similar agenda to their own, or at least one that is compatible with it. The same applies to local organisations that are being offered such a partnership. Those that I know certainly argue their own point of view and are, like their international counterparts, passionately committed to the work they do. But they also need the money that the partnership of an international NGO can bring. It is hard for them not to 'cut their coat according to their cloth' and adapt their programmes accordingly – as do international NGOs sometimes, when they wish to avail themselves of government funding; so this is another case of power asymmetry, with its inevitable tensions and distortions.

Many international NGOs are setting up their own operations in countries where they once worked through partnerships. This can be seen either as a consolidation of work and relationships, or as takeover or displacement. Which is true will depend on where decision-making power resides, as we shall see later in this chapter. It is hard for the key decision-making not to be located in the centre, and for that centre not to be where the international NGO is established. There is also a danger that small local organisations

2.   Ibid., pp. 13, 21.

outside the embrace of the international NGO are displaced as its local wing grows.

The impact of international NGOs on the 'ecology' of local civil society is clearly considerable, and doubtless has both positive and negative aspects. To raise these issues is not to point a finger of blame, but to acknowledge the difficult context in which people struggle to work together in a respectful and complementary way, in a true spirit of partnership, and the dilemmas that this entails.

Even the strongest partnerships are sometimes tested by events, at both personal and organisational levels. A change on the ground may bring about differing strategic or ethical assessments on the part of international and local partners. The local partner may want to shift from conciliation to advocacy, in a way that its international partner does not support (or that does not fit with the purpose for which funds were made available, which would have to be renegotiated); or a local partner may be drawn towards alleviating economic and other distress, while its international counterpart feels it cannot stray from its specific organisational focus on conflict. Such divergences will ideally be worked through until a common perspective is reached or an agreement is made to part. In practice there may be no such agreement, but only a unilateral decision on one side or the other.

These are not easy issues for either side. The international NGOs are often all too aware of their power and corresponding responsibility, and may find it almost impossibly difficult to end a partnership that no longer fits into their purpose in the region, while their local partners find themselves in a relationship of dependency which hampers their freedom of choice but which they cannot afford to lose.

The power of money

Established NGOs have offices to rent or buy, staff to pay, and costs to cover. Those who have founded organisations to work for peace in a particular way in a given context soon see that there is additional work to be done, which calls for additional income and new sources of funding. Sometimes they cannot get money for what they most want to do, but see a funding opportunity for work that is at least something similar, and which will help to cover core costs, so they opt for that (just as local partners may adapt their programme direction to suit their international partners). Or a donor might agree to provide funds on certain conditions – conditions that perhaps make little sense, but can somehow be worked with or around. And so the donor might become not only the enabler, but also a shaper – or sometimes distorter – of programmes.

Many organisations have difficulty in finding money to cover their general overheads. The only income they can generate for that purpose comes as a percentage of project funding. They therefore need to have plenty of projects running at all times. So financial considerations can become a factor in the search for projects – a far cry from the original CCTS idea of simply responding to requests for help.

Ideally, a programme or project in a particular place is a response, if not to a local request, at least to needs that have been carefully assessed with a potential partner or partners, rather than started simply because there is a likelihood of associated funding that will help an organisation to support itself. However, when needs come first and we are motivated to undertake a particular piece of work simply because we care about what is happening, and think we can help, the challenge is to find adequate and timely sources of funding – which may prove relatively easy or extremely difficult, sometimes impossible.

Even when there is a crying need for peace activities of all kinds in a given area, it may be that the presence of a plethora of organisations, which in theory should increase the amount of work that can be done, may bring confusion and create competition – for partners, for attention, and for money. In such cases there is a temptation for an organisation to 'talk up' the work that is being done, exaggerating its impact.

I have worked in places where the same key local individuals worked for several different international organisations. This gave them an income and meant that their skills and connections were well utilised, but it also made their lives frantic, and made it harder for them to set their own agenda and priorities. It is all too easy, without any ill intent, for organisational interests to intrude and distort those priorities, and extremely difficult for principled organisations (of which there are many) to know how to act for the best. These are difficult moral and logistical matters for all concerned, requiring good local knowledge, sound analysis, sensitivity about relationships and careful ethical judgements.

International NGOs, like local ones, are reliant on donors who do not always share their analysis of what most needs to be done. Governments and other large donors have their own strategies. They 'buy in' the services of NGOs to implement them, and have an electoral mandate to spend public money in the way they see fit. However, they may not have the best understanding of what their money could do, since they are often not so close to events or to the people on the ground. Since they have the biggest capacity to pay for programmes, this can, in practice, limit the effectiveness of action paid for from the public purse. Moreover, governmental bureaucracies limit the capacity of their own civil servants to act in ways that make a difference.

Evaluation

Differences of analysis and priorities notwithstanding, if our work matters, it matters that it is done well. Donors want to ensure that their money is well spent and organisations want to know that their work is effective. This is entirely proper, and evaluation is vital. But outcomes can never be guaranteed, and the efficacy or otherwise of what is done (as against its quality) is not easy to determine. The most important effects are not necessarily the easiest to quantify or attribute, and the greater the bureaucratic or organisational distance between the donor and the work on the ground, the harder it becomes for donors to feel or witness the quality of the work where hard indicators are impossible. This brings pressure to do what is measurable, rather than what matters.

Broadly speaking, we live in a climate of risk aversion, in which avoiding failure becomes a priority. Yet there is no way of predicting outcomes with any certainty in complex and changing circumstances. There can be no 'controlled' experiments. Unfortunately, some of the most important work is also the most risky – in that it may not 'work' at all, for one reason or another, though it might be justified by even a small chance of success. It is also realistic to recognise that, despite the injunction to 'do no harm',[3] the very initiatives that might do the most good could possibly do some harm, and that the cost of inaction is likely to be very high.

Movement towards peace is itself likely to involve conflict, as parties realign themselves and factions within factions compete for dominance. A promising peace process can occasion an upsurge in violence from those whose interests are threatened. Think of the 'Real IRA' in Northern Ireland and its murderous backlash against the peace process there. Did that mean that the peace process should not have taken place? It is vital to pay great attention to the risk of doing harm, but it is impossible to avoid it altogether. Still less

3.   M. B. Anderson, *Do No Harm: Supporting Local Capacities for Peace through Aid*, Cambridge, MA: Local Capacities for Peace Project, 1996.

is it possible to avoid the risk of failure to do good in the way one hopes for, and it is less possible again to prove the good done, in situations where the causes of change are not only complex but impossible to identify with any certainty.

A great deal of money is spent on evaluation exercises carried out by people who are in one way or another outsiders – sometimes generalist evaluators who are unfamiliar either with peacebuilding or with the country in question. While there are benefits in independence and an outside perspective, these may be outweighed by the difficulty an outsider might have in grasping, in the time available, the intricacies and the meaning of the work in question, or assessing the value of the opinions and information they receive.

Moreover, although it may be possible through such a process to evaluate the immediate effects of what has been done, it is far more difficult to weigh its strategic value. My experience is that, although one can reach a reasoned assessment of the way initiatives have been conceived and carried out, and sometimes a reasonable impression of their immediate effect on those directly involved, the wider impact of these things is hard to trace. On this question the most honest, intelligent and conscientious evaluators struggle to say anything with much clarity or conviction, and recognise the tenuous and speculative nature of their assessment. They see that there are many factors that affect the outcome of any initiative, while the context in which it is undertaken is unstable, and it is generally impossible to attribute changes to any particular cause.

The old argument about whether peacemaking is an art or a science perhaps has some relevance here. It may sometimes be possible and useful to count or measure things that matter within closely defined parameters, and this may contribute to achieving the best possible analysis and strategic thinking. But it is hard to factor in the quality of what is done, and when we are talking about people working with people, what works for one person may not work for another. What works for one combination of people may not work for another. The skill of peace work is not only in gaining knowledge but also in achieving understanding and feeling, and in helping to create useful understanding and the right kinds of feelings in others. Those things cannot always be measured, or even expressed on paper – nor can the subtleties of responsiveness or resourcefulness. Yet they may make all the difference to the effect of the work that is undertaken, and thereby constitute the quality of its implementation. So when we are trying to learn – as we must – about what works, we need to bear these subtleties and complexities in mind.

Another frequent dilemma in evaluating peace activities is weighing the importance of long-term work against the urgency of short-term interventions. Some work for transformation is absolutely necessary to long-term peace but will take decades, at least, to bear fruit. Work to 'deal with the past' comes into this category: it means not only finding a way to enable people to recover from particular anger and trauma, but also working to address the more general hostility between different sectors of society that probably existed before widespread violence erupted, and has now been augmented.

Such work is as necessary as it is daunting, if new cycles of violence are to be prevented. But who will fund it adequately and for long enough for it to have an impact? Money is found immediately and without question for military action, but the funds that are forthcoming for peacebuilding are typically disappointing, to say the least, even in the short-term, and unlikely to be sustained. ('Sustainability' is a euphemism for 'exit strategy', and is related to the myth that has been created that all work should be capable of becoming self-funding.)

A similar problem applies to decisions about the continuation of good-quality work that is apparently well thought out and as likely as anything can be to have some desired effect, but which in practice has had only very limited impact. Donors whose chief concern is with the big political picture are liable to become impatient, and even the organisations doing the work may come to doubt its utility. I have friends and colleagues working with courage and brilliance in situations where the large-scale conflicts they are trying to help address seem as intractable, and sometimes as deadly, as ever.

Should they all give up, locals and internationals alike? Or should they keep going because faithfulness matters, and because trying to do good and prevent suffering is a human obligation, because they do have the contacts and influence to make them potential contributors to change, and because if they give up they give the situation over to the unopposed forces of violence and chaos?

If we choose to persist, how can we hold ourselves accountable and be held to account? How can we think carefully about the impact we are aiming for and then consider, rigorously and productively, the value of what we do, looking for 'indicators' where they might exist, and finding alternative ways of thinking and of testing ourselves where they cannot? How can we maximise the chance that we will do no harm and at the same time do as much good as possible? How can we increase synergy without losing flexibility and account- ability? There will be no single answer to any of these questions. Perhaps the most important response is to keep asking them and to continue the endless process of careful and creative balancing in given situations.

POWER IN MID-CONFLICT AND POST-CONFLICT TRANSFORMATION

As I have already suggested, most of the effort in the conflict-trans- formation field has gone not into 'conflict prevention', but into addressing existing, open conflicts, demilitarising societies after violent conflict, and trying to restore manageable relationships. The scale of such work is, in itself, immense, and it takes place at many levels, as set out in Chapter 2. I will defer until Chapter 6 my discussion of the somewhat marginalised work of popular mobilisation to bring 'latent conflict' into the open and challenge the status quo.

'Popular mobilisation' immediately invokes the idea of power, while needs theory, which is central to our field and fundamental to our ethos, talks a different, seemingly unrelated language. For this reason and others, even within the 'conflict resolution' and 'post-conflict' stages of transformation that currently form the main focus of our praxis, it is in some ways problematic, as well as vital.

Needs, satisfiers and power in conflict resolution

Needs theory is at the heart of the non-judgemental character of conflict resolution – which, as we have seen, is a process in which the different parties to a conflict can reach an accommodation with each other of their own volition and, ideally, through a shared, cooperative process.

The idea of basic human needs as both the drivers of conflict and the key to its solution has proved its worth, in my experience, though perhaps more in terms of emotional than analytical understanding, or as a bridge between the two. The very fact of thinking about a conflict in these terms restores humanity to the process and to the way it is considered and experienced. The language of needs is the language of understanding and mutual recognition. It takes us beyond arguments about rights (and wrongs) and invites the parties into a relationship of mutual respect and care, rather than demands, and also into a place of shared vulnerability. However, it is also in many ways problematic.

I would question the practical utility of the distinction that is usually made between needs and interests, on the basis that needs are non-negotiable while interests related to them are not. I agree that the way in which needs are met can be negotiated, and that this makes room for flexibility and creativity. I do not agree that needs are in any practical sense absolute. Who could say that their needs were completely met or unmet? Who is to judge? What is enough in relation to need? As Shakespeare's King Lear cries out,

> O, reason not the need! Our basest beggars
> Are in the poorest things superfluous.[4]

We could say in this case that the apparent superfluity is associated with the beggars' identity needs. But agreeing that we all have needs of identity, security, autonomy and participation does not, practically speaking, get us very far. The challenge comes when we relate this idea to the perceptions of individuals and groups, and just what it is they think they need in order to be what they want to be. We are likely, often, to find ourselves questioning whether these 'needs' are in fact legitimate – and who is to be the judge?

As Max-Neef has suggested,[5] the same basic needs may have different 'satisfiers' in different cultures. One could argue that in many cultures the 'identity needs' of males require their total dominance over females. Without this, they may feel no dignity. In reply, it can be said that this should not be so, and that no human being can 'need' something that disregards the basic needs of half of their society for security, dignity and autonomy. In such circumstances men satisfy their 'needs' at the expense of women, and they do so because their power of dominance is structured into their culture and society, and exercised on a daily basis.

In political conflicts the language of need can help us to understand the motivation of those locked into current political units and systems. Prime ministers, presidents and governments, for instance, have both personal needs (often more influential than is recognised) and needs related to their institutional identity and function. These latter needs will be connected with the ways in which the relevant institution is perceived and the way in which it works. The personal needs of politicians will be interwoven with

4. King Lear, Act II, Scene 4.
5. M. Max-Neef, 'Reflections on a Paradigm Shift in Economics', in M. Inglis and S. Kramer (eds), *The New Economic Agenda*, Inverness: Findhorn Press, 1985.

those of the institutions they are associated with, and dependent on their performance within them. Though these two sets of needs can, at least in theory, be seen as separate, they will influence each other quite powerfully. It is highly likely that politicians will be affected, albeit unconsciously, by their 'need' to be seen – by themselves and others – as strong, upstanding, successful, and so on; but the effect of such personal agendas will be conditioned, at least to some extent, by their values. It may be that the institutions in question, and the ways in which they operate, are not in themselves very good, and 'need' to be changed if they are to meet the needs of those they claim to serve. Thus it would seem that, in the real world, there can be competing needs.

We can overcome these conceptual issues by referring to the notion of needs-related interests, or satisfiers, and focusing the debate on them. But as soon as we leave the broad generalities of 'identity', 'security' and so on (whose purpose is to anchor us in the universal), we are in trouble again. What about the interests of those whose role in conflict is determined by personal greed for power or wealth, and whose current power to hurt others has enabled them to pursue those interests? If they could be referred to therapists, whether medical or spiritual, who could help them to rediscover their 'true' values and deeper needs, it might make a difference. Maybe their encounter with 'the other' will be so powerful as to bring about some deep change in them and restore their humanity. Then we are talking about a very different form of power – the transformative power of processes, and the capacity of human beings to change each other.

Another apparent weakness of needs theory – which is not necessarily inherent, but which I have observed in its use – is that an assumption is made that, if only conflicting parties could see that they have the same human needs, the substance of their conflict would go away. But, if the need is for water and water is scarce, then, unless more water can be found, the interests of the parties will still conflict. Then the only hope would be that they might start to care as much about each other as about themselves – and, again, we would be looking for a spiritual solution rather than a purely rational one. I have experienced the benefit of exploring conflict through the framework of needs in generating the mutual recognition and empathy that encourage cooperative problem-solving. But unless this reaches the point where the 'different sides' no longer see themselves as such, or unless some solution can be found that removes the scarcity, agreement will be very difficult to reach.

To take another example: since, as in many conflicts, one group's sense of identity is rooted in the 'integrity' of the current unit within which they live, while another has an identity 'need' to separate from it and have a country of its own, the recognition of these different needs satisfiers – which has been achieved through various continuing dialogue processes – has not produced any mutually acceptable solution, even among those willing to be involved in dialogue. Very deep psychological and conceptual change would be needed to shift the focus on 'country' as a major satisfier. In the meantime, these conflicts remain unresolved. Moreover, they are not so stable as the term 'frozen conflict' would suggest and, as we have seen recently in Georgia, are at risk of being reignited or 'settled' by military action or threat from outside.

The notion of needs can lead us to a greater understanding of what drives different parties to a conflict, and what it will take to make them more or less content with any 'solution'. Used as a framework for dialogue, it can help people to understand each other and can generate a desire to seek the means of accommodation, while reducing the sense of 'otherness' and defusing the feelings and attitudes that tend towards violence. It does not remove the deeper philosophical, ethical, conceptual, political and practical issues that are present in any given conflict.

Nor does needs theory answer the question of how to generate the will to enter into a resolution process in order that needs can be discussed – or at least I have not seen it so applied. I believe it is indeed relevant to empowerment and mobilisation processes. To begin with, although the discourse of human rights and justice is very different from that of conflict resolution and needs, they can be directly linked conceptually.

The notion of human rights can be understood as the assertion that all human beings have the right to have their basic human needs met. The difference is that, whereas needs in a conflict-resolution process are to be mutually recognised between two or more parties as the basis for a cooperative process, in the case of a hopelessly asymmetrical and oppressive situation in which they are not recognised, they are to be championed and asserted as strongly as possible, by one party in relation to another. In good nonviolence theory the goal is still to find an inclusive solution: one that honours the humanity and needs of all. But that is in the future. First must come this assertive action that is not cooperative because cooperation is refused. Needs theory has to embrace this, just as the praxis of nonviolence can be enriched by needs theory.

Within peace processes that are underway, or in attempts to make them happen, the question of power is vital. All too often, there is insufficient will – or will that is insufficiently sustained – to end violence and resolve conflict. This means that, unless populations are to be at the mercy of their leaders' lack of will for peace, they must increase their leverage, whether that comes from their moral, persuasive power or from their capacity to withdraw political support and cooperation. War is in itself an oppression that needs to be lifted, and nonviolent mobilisation (of which more later) is as relevant here as in addressing latent conflict.

The challenges of demilitarisation and dealing with the effects of violence

Demilitarisation involves, first and foremost, the disarmament and demobilisation of fighters, their reintegration into civilian life, and their physical and psychological rehabilitation. It is a relative and selective term, since the 'normal' pattern is for national armed forces to be maintained, and sometimes to absorb those who have been opposing them, or for two armies to join into one. However, there can be a reduction in the numbers of people 'at arms' in a given area, and this may be given priority.

The rehabilitation of soldiers – putting their broken minds and bodies together again and finding them a place in civilian life – is, especially in poor countries, to say the least a hard task, and those who have been brutalised by fighting may find it difficult to adjust to civilian life. In terms of economic reintegration, an effort in this direction is likely to mean that they are given preferential treatment in opportunities for retraining and employment, because if they remain jobless they are liable to turn to crime or return to fighting. This is hard for those who may have equal need but who took no part in the fighting.

Former fighters are also liable to be violent at home, so that the hidden war of domestic violence is intensified.

Women soldiers find it extremely difficult to find a place in civilian life, having, from a social and cultural perspective, ceased to be acceptable as women, whether as fighters or as the victims of sexual abuse. And because of the relative powerlessness of women in most societies and the low level of their active participation in violence, typically their needs have a low profile in the theory and practice of demilitarisation and recovery.

It is remarkable that any degree of reintegration is ever achieved, given what war does to people. For instance, children who have been abducted and forced to kill are not easy for their communities to take back, and it is hard for them to become children again. The capacity of human beings to accept each other and pick up their lives again in such circumstances can only be wondered at.

The return of people displaced by fighting is another part of the theoretical normalisation process. Yet in many post-violence contexts, most of those who were displaced by war remain displaced, often for the rest of their days. There are many reasons for this. Their homes may have been occupied by others; they are liable to be unwelcome and still in danger in the place they had to leave; sometimes they may lack the resources to undertake the journey home. And since they are often unwelcome in their place of refuge, and regarded as political pawns by those in power, they often remain in camps or in buildings commandeered for their use, unwanted by anyone.

The hopes of displaced people of returning to their homes are often unrealistically sustained by their own longing, by the political agendas of those who are insisting – for territorial reasons – on their right to go back, and also (ironically) by the very theoretical and ethical perspective that regards return as a necessity. Those who choose to settle in the place where they have arrived and have the capacity to do so (including qualifications, health, seed money, sewing machines, initiative, and so on) are often the 'lucky' ones. The rest may languish for decades. I am not suggesting that these ideas about what should happen after a war are wrong. They are sensible and humane; but they are extremely difficult, and sometimes impossible, to achieve, and always costly; even when great efforts are made, the ravages of war will remain for generations.

'Dealing with the past' means addressing the damage done by violence in such a way that social and political relationships are brought to a point where they can be regarded as peaceful,[6] and where society has reaffirmed the rule of law. It has, as I have said, become a focal area for practice and theory in recent years, particularly since the groundbreaking processes of the Truth and Reconciliation Commission in South Africa.

Considerable agreement has evolved on the mix of ingredients needed in such processes to help people, both as individuals and collectives, to 'move on'. These include, for instance, that physical facts are known and, where possible, that it is known who was directly and indirectly responsible for them, that some public

6. A. Curle, *True Justice: Quaker Peace Makers and Peace Making*, London: Quaker Home Service, 1981, p. 37.

acknowledgement is made, and recompense is provided, whether as compensation or punishment, or both.

As suggested earlier, 'restorative justice' processes are being taken increasingly seriously in some societies (having existed in others, under other names, for aeons). They are designed to bring the perpetrator to the recognition of his or her wrongdoing and of the suffering that it has caused, and to make amends as far as possible, and in so doing to regain a place in society, so that relationships are restored.[7] (This is not, like other forms of conflict resolution, 'non-judgemental', but starts from a point where judgement has been made against one party in relation to another. This is also the case in 'victim–offender mediation'. The aim is still to respect and uplift the humanity of all concerned and, by implication, to meet their needs.)

We bring our own values to our theory on this, as on other things. In patriarchal (that is, most) societies, crimes against women and women's needs often receive low priority. Again, this is a cultural matter, but the theory of conflict transformation is founded on the value of respect and the assumption of human equality, and within that frame women's rights and needs matter as much as men's.

In some cultures symbolic acts may be used to restore relationships and, as we have seen, it is acknowledged that the things that will satisfy deep psychological needs in various cultures are – perhaps unsurprisingly – different. There may be more emphasis on collective purification than on 'justice', for instance, and an overarching priority may be placed on restoring community. While in one society it will be argued that this cannot be done without justice, this is not how it is seen in all cultures. No amount of 'justice' can restore well-being when lives have been devastated, but making sense and finding meaning can bring a degree of healing.

It may seem to us that honesty, recognition and reparation are the least that victims should be able to expect; but, like the reintegration of fighters and the return of displaced people, they are usually achieved, if ever, very belatedly. Even where there is a high level of awareness of the need, there is the dilemma that those who can deliver an end to the violence of war often require, in return, immunity from prosecution, and sometimes a place in the new government. This is another case of competing goods or needs, where justice is traded for peace, or at least postponed.

7. M. Liebmann, *Restorative Justice: How It Works*, London: Jessica Kingsley Publishers, 2007.

Moreover, as we have seen, in some situations the distinction between victims and offenders may not be so clear – people may be both – and collusion with violence may have been so widespread that to pursue 'justice' in a more than token or symbolic way is simply impracticable. In some circumstances, there would be no one left to run the country, no family in the clear (as, for example, in the former East Germany after the fall of the Berlin Wall, or in Iraq, where all Baath Party members were removed from their posts).

In addition, the ravages of war are so devastating, economically as well as psychologically, that the scale of what is needed exceeds what seems possible. Choices have to be made between the practical demands of the future and dealing with the past, in such a way that those who have been damaged can begin to contemplate it and coexistence is made possible.

None of this is new, and I am pointing not to a shortage of theory but to the reality of what violence creates. Theory must not be allowed to mask that reality – or the ethical dilemmas inherent in negotiating an end to violence, or the fact that the impact of tyranny and war is so bitter that it can never really be 'dealt with'. The dead cannot be rehabilitated, and many lives will have been irrecoverably damaged. Recovery is likely to take generations. The real shift that is needed is in our attitude to war and in our thinking about it: the recognition that it is always and everywhere a disaster; that we must deal with the past by resolving never to repeat it; that violence and peace are processes that are mutually exclusive.

Unless and until war has been abolished, mitigating its disastrous effects will remain a necessity, and excellent work is being done to learn from the experience that is accumulating.[8] But even more important and urgent is the work that needs to be done to develop theory on how we can demilitarise minds, societies and global systems in order to avoid the endless re-creation of violent histories, and to open up a very different kind of future for humanity. That is the most fundamental need of peacebuilding.

Dealing with the past remains an important concept and deserves wider application. If we want to build peace globally, and if global relationships are to be healed, there is a need to deal with the colonial past and the ideologically driven crimes that ruined lives and created lasting resentments and hatreds. Similarly, the structural injustices within every society, past and present, in relation to gender, class or caste, and identity or belief, all of which have made a mockery

---

8.   See, for example, the website of Swisspeace: <www.swisspeace.ch>.

of peace, need to be recognised as such and eradicated. This, like the settling of conflict, requires the ongoing, dogged activism of ordinary citizens.

MAKING A STRATEGIC DIFFERENCE

Given the complexity of the problems outlined above (to which a great many others could be added) it is perhaps unsurprising that we do not achieve as much as we would wish. In fact, significant and positive changes have been achieved at the local level through the hard efforts of committed people: silence broken, voices heard, violence refused or defused, bridges built, daily life made possible, ex-combatants reintegrated, extraordinary acts of forgiveness undertaken, new attitudes and patterns of behaviour established. Very often, however, big conflicts or systemic wrongs remain unresolved, even after many years of costly work by a great many individuals and organisations.

Coherence and scale

It is not only donors who are looking for change at that level – it is all of us; and it has to be said that, more often than not, we find ourselves disappointed and frustrated.

Donors, in their turn, must face comparable dilemmas.[9] Governments today are eager to give away large amounts of money in pursuit of their strategies, and are concerned to see their funds used to support coherent efforts that can lead to a consolidated impact. And it seems that they increasingly want to reduce the administrative work that is needed on their side, with its associated costs, by making a few very large grants rather than many small ones.

Theoretically, one way of achieving the desired scale and coherence – so obviating the need to liaise with a large number of organisations on a wide variety of projects and programmes – is to invite joint tenders from collectives of organisations. Such collaborative efforts are not always very comfortable or successful in their implementation. They may minimise some kinds of duplication and, from the organisations' perspective as well as the donor's, they offer the possibility of making a substantial contribution to a shift on the ground. However, organisations come into consortiums with their

9. For a discussion of donors' roles, see CCTS, *Funding Conflict Transformation: Money, Power and Accountability* (CCTS Review 25), November 2004, at <www.c-r.org/ccts>.

own pre-existing agendas, and are naturally concerned for their own interests. Effective liaison, let alone full cooperation, is also time-consuming, requiring very substantial groundwork; and it is likely to demand a degree of give and take that organisations that are used to making their own untrammelled decisions find irksome. The result is that the hoped-for degree of coherence and integration is not in fact achieved.

An alternative approach is for organisations, where possible, to enlarge their own programmes in order have a greater impact: to 'work to scale'. The person from whom I first heard that expression is the director of a UK-based international NGO, who explained to me that in his organisation they had taken a decision to try to relate the scale of their work to the scale of a conflict. They had done so because they refused to accept an apparent inability to have a strategic impact. He did not accept that simply 'cultivating one's own garden' was all one could do, and his organisation was committed to making a strategic difference. This meant pushing beyond existing 'comfort zones' and working at every level and in many places across a country or region to address both the root causes of the conflict and the consequences of the violence. The organisation maintained a focus on the kind of work that seeks to address violence in relatively direct ways 'on the ground', by supporting local people and building their capacity to make a difference, while also, whenever possible, working directly with people at or near 'the top'.

When asked how the impact of even such ambitious programmes could ever be traced, he argued that, if you could make a visible difference in a village and could then extend that to 40 villages, you might begin to see similar results from similar efforts, which would confirm the connection between activities and hypothetical results – and would perhaps also represent a cumulative shift that might have a visible impact on the large-scale process.

He described the very serious ways in which his organisation tried to ensure that what it did was as good as it could be, by constantly evaluating and reflecting, holding itself accountable for the quality of its work, enabling its ever-growing number of partners to become more professional in what they did, accompanying them directly through the placing of top managers in local offices and through frequent visits from its head office. The senior manager in a local office was almost always an expatriate. One major reason for this was the need to have someone without any vested interest or affiliation at the top, so that the organisation was trusted locally by all sectors of the population; but of course this policy had other implications too, and the ultimate supervision came from the centre, which set the standards.

The director was aware that this had taken his organisation a long way from its earlier emphasis on having a 'light footprint' in a place, and also aware of the organisational 'liability' that such a wide and deep commitment to a region entailed, if taken seriously. He insisted on the need to 'be professional' (working to as high a professional standard as possible), though he said that his attitude on this was liable to raise the hackles of some colleagues, and agreed that it could have the effect of excluding uneducated people, at least from the organisational structure. At the same time he put a great deal of time into visiting the organisation's local offices, and its contacts and partners at every level, in order to avoid or at least reduce any sense of remoteness; the frequent visits of central programme staff were designed to keep the communication close.

I was impressed by the careful and honest thinking and the determined commitment revealed in this interview. I was convinced that a serious attempt was being made to address the problem of how to have an impact at the wider level: one that could provide important learning, not only for this organisation but for others too. This approach combines local groundedness and a high level of reliance on the work, skills and insights of local people with the accountability and 'quality control' of a body directly accountable to donors; it is internally rigorous, and has the power to create a cohesive programme on a relatively large scale.

On the other hand, by moving from partnership to direct employment, this model vests great power in the international NGO, and control lies outside the countries in question. It could be argued that the hierarchical nature of this structure is just a more explicit version of the power asymmetry that is such an issue in the partnership model, and that it may be a more effective one. However, the fact is that the overall vision is owned by the international NGO, which then supports, influences, and in some measure directs local action, which becomes the instrument of an external purpose. If this approach works best, maybe egalitarian angst is a luxury and a distraction. But in the long run a transfer of power would seem essential. And if 'professionalism' is needed on the part of all staff in such a system, it is vital that this is directed towards intensified capacity building, rather than used as a pretext for 'losing' those who do not fit the label.

Wider considerations

The thinking outlined above is an intelligent and serious response to the limitations of current praxis. There are, I believe, many reasons why it is so hard to transform large-scale conflict. Conflict transformation is, by its own definition, multi-levelled, involving the great mass of 'ordinary people', uneducated as well as educated, whose support, or at least compliance, is needed for governments to govern. It also requires the sincere efforts of those governments themselves, who often need to put at risk their own reputations and careers and set aside the rhetoric of decades, which has been the source of their power. As suggested above, there needs to be a sustained will to resolve conflict.

Where those at the top can retain a degree of control that they find tolerable, their motivation to reach a settlement is often insufficient for them to shift their position. To become peacemakers they would need to become the humble servants of their people, rather than pursuers of their own power. I do not think it is too cynical to say that this would represent quite a leap from current reality, in many if not most cases.

In a context of civil war or insurgency, unofficial armies or insurgents also develop huge vested interests that make accommodation and demilitarisation deeply unattractive, and indeed frightening. There are therefore plenty of reasons why leaders, official and otherwise, are not drawn to peacemaking. They stand to lose their status, income and sense of identity if the fighting ends, and their followers may fear future unemployment and marginalisation.

Despite an enthusiasm on the part of practitioners for analysing 'levels' of society and 'tracks' in peace processes, the grassroots population in most countries is hard to reach on the scale that would be desirable. NGOs, however radical and egalitarian in their thinking, are often run by members of an educated elite. The lack of education that excludes a large proportion of the population in many countries from any meaningful engagement in public life supports theory asserting the need for widespread 'conscientisation', but in the meantime its absence renders the realisation of grassroots involvement next to impossible. And even where the divisions between the educated and uneducated are not so extreme, the gulf between the culture and aspirations of public-spirited intellectuals and others remains a wide one.

In most situations, of course, the populace does not constitute one single mass, but is divided (whether by clan, religion, ethnicity, history or politics). Then lack of education and miserable living conditions make those affected ready prey for political manipulation, resulting in ongoing or sporadic intercommunal violence. Where governments are weak, territories vast and populations complex, it is not easy for intercommunal violence to be kept always at bay, and if its risk is to be reduced a radical improvement in living conditions and education will be necessary. Transforming problems of this magnitude is beyond the scope of NGOs, though they may help in given situations and spheres.

Where international attention is attracted and the pressure of public opinion persuades outside governments to bestir themselves diplomatically, whether bilaterally or through the UN, this can increase the likelihood that the conflict may be addressed and resolved in some way (as seemed possible at one point in the case of Tibet, but appears less hopeful at the time of writing). But there are so many conflicts and human rights abuses going on at any one time that most continue without any adequate concentration of international attention or effort.

It does seem extraordinary and shocking that people who happen to live in some countries enjoy lives of relative safety and prosperity, while those whom fortune has placed elsewhere live in squalor or great hardship, and are also liable to suffer terrible violence. It is shameful that the resources required for waging war are never lacking, while those that would be required to build peace are so woefully inadequate, and that the few grow ever richer at the expense of the many. It is even more shameful when wars fought in the name of peace or democracy, which result in untold misery of every kind, are in fact driven by hegemonic interests and the desire to control resources, as I shall discuss towards the end of this chapter.

Structural change and people power

In the light of all the factors listed above, the 'failures' of conflict transformation seem unremarkable. However, they must lead us to consider what more we can do to mobilise for change: radical change, in which the gulf is bridged between the governing and the governed, so that informed electorates, pressure groups and partners hold governments to account, and governments in turn begin to put their people first. For that, 'people power' will have to become an established element in public affairs, rather than being seen as something that occurs at exceptional moments, and we will need to take it far more seriously. Top-down decisions may be able to make certain things happen relatively quickly – but peace is not a matter of fiats, but of minds and hearts, too, and of the distribution of power. What seems efficient in the short term may not be effective in the long term.

Despite the popularity of the idea of 'conflict prevention', the kind of long-term, radical work it implies is not, as I remarked earlier, so much in evidence. I suspect this is because of the motivating power of immediate crises, as against that of structures and underlying causes, and also because of the difficulty in showing that slow, patient work on the latter has 'worked', since it is not possible to demonstrate that violent conflict would have happened and has been prevented.

The deepest-rooted changes, the processes of growth and transformation, are also very slow, and governments, influenced by their own precariousness and transience, feel the need to show immediate results. Where they do decide to act (rather than to ignore a situation), they tend to favour the quick (and usually temporary) fixes of 'realpolitik', often involving the exercise of violence by external parties or the brokering of unprincipled deals, frequently between those who are equally 'guilty' and undesirable in relation to the needs of their people. Such interventions tend to result in a progression from one corrupt or despotic regime to another.

A peace process needs to have enough power behind it to succeed (as well as a sufficiently fair wind, and no terminally disruptive cross-currents or obstacles). But do we see power as vested primarily in the numbers of 'ordinary' people who are rooting for peace, or in the high-ranking control of those at the top, who are thought able to deliver it? Most of us, for reasons of political philosophy or inclination, will be more interested in one location of power than the other, and will have a corresponding argument and examples to support our preference. However, both kinds of power are needed to secure an end to violence and build a peace that deserves the name, and that will last.

The theory (and I believe the reality) of conflict transformation is that the process of negotiation, when it is conducted in a respectful and cooperative atmosphere, can tap into the humanity of the military leaders who are involved and transform their relationships and perspectives. (It is clear that most insurgencies are ended through some kind of political accommodation. How long will it be before the recognition that this is so will lead to acknowledgement that there is a need also to use a conflict-resolution approach with those labelled as terrorists, or at least with the communities from which they come?)

As I have suggested, it is more likely that serious negotiations will take place if there is popular pressure for them to do so; and leaders cannot make peace without popular backing. The necessity of accommodating the needs of their erstwhile adversaries must be balanced by the need to satisfy their own people. The existence of a wider peace constituency will help to ensure that the politics beyond the talks will be supportive of any agreement, and that it will not be blocked by a popular backlash.

The violence that is endemic in Palestine/Israel is arguably continuing because the Accord that was reached after the Oslo peace process did not have popular backing on either side. It was not honoured by Israel, which continued to expand its settlements and to tighten its stranglehold on Palestine. Nor was it accepted by many Palestinians as a sufficient outcome, after so many years of misery and struggle, with the consequent growth of Hamas and its power-struggle with Fatah, and of attacks on Israel.

This Middle East conflict illustrates not only the importance of having a popular constituency for any agreement, but also of the ineffectiveness of 'conflict resolution' processes where there is insufficient power parity to produce a settlement likely to be seen as just by both sides. What is to be done to address the power asymmetry? It cannot be rectified by violence. Even if that were desirable, the military power of US-backed Israel is too great. All that Palestinian violence can do is inflict harm counterproductively, giving Israel a pretext for new assaults and violations. If there were a concerted nonviolent *intifada*, international backing would be much more difficult to withhold, and this would have the best chance of making a real difference.

It seems, however, that most governments are unwilling to fund popular mobilisation for change. I know of several cases where bids have been made and refused. There are doubtless many and complex reasons why government departments would be reluctant to fund movements that challenge other governments. Some are related to their own alignments and the way they will be perceived, others to their fear of further destabilisation. If they were willing to act on principle and work with the consequences, they could offer support not only financially but also in the form of messages and statements or the provision of incentives – but they might have to put their own interests second.

As suggested in Chapter 2, destabilisation is not so far from the agenda of the big powers when they are keen to see a shift in power that will strengthen their own hegemony. They have in the past used violent processes, but the West was clearly delighted by the different examples of nonviolent 'regime change' that brought about the disintegration of the former Soviet bloc and, more recently, the removal from power of Slobodan Milošević by the 'Otpor' movement in Serbia and the mass action in Ukraine and Georgia, where pro-Western governments were brought into office. Where the status quo is deemed to contribute to a country's hegemony, or at least not to disturb it, and where there is no public outcry, most governments are likely to opt for the status quo and avoid interference in the affairs of another state.

Preventing or ending violence often demands more fundamental change in a society than the replacement of one regime with another. It may therefore involve conflict and turbulence. While 'conflict resolution' is felt to be stabilising, movements for change are, by nature – in the short term – destabilising; and short-term results are needed, politically. The self-motivated and self-determining dynamics of 'people power' do not generally fit with the agendas of the big ruling powers, and the energy of popular movements is too volatile to be amenable to waiting for months for the adjudication of others. Nor, if it is to retain its own essence, should it be dependent on it.

But it is not only governments and other donors that are nervous of movements. Most international NGOs want to be seen as politically non-aligned, in order to have access, trust and influence in all quarters. Yet at the local level what is needed, very often, is to take a stand, to challenge the powers, to resist, to be disobedient, to negotiate for particular things, while respecting the needs of one's fellow citizens. Upholding peaceable principles and the dignity of all can be a threat to vested interests.

With or without help from outside, people do mobilise for peace and against injustice – protesting against slaughter; marching to capital cities to demand that talks are seriously pursued; organising opportunities for parties to come together; resisting the competing violence of paramilitaries, whether of governments or insurgents; diffusing incipient conflicts at the community level; and helping to establish relationships that can resist provocation and build trust. But it is my assessment that, unless their action somehow chimes with an 'international' agenda, they do these things without the benefit of major support, or even attention.

There are some organisations and individual trainers who specialise in training for 'people power', sharing their knowledge and international experience on 'applied nonviolent action'. Globally, the work of supporting nonviolent resistance to oppressive violence is undertaken mostly by organisations that also resist war, because they reject all violence. They see the development of nonviolent assertiveness as a necessary moral concomitant of this rejection, having no wish to be passive in the face of cruelty or exclusion.

The US has a strong history of nonviolent action for change, and has contributed a great deal to the theory concerning it. Several US organisations are doing substantial work to spread the ideas of nonviolence[10] and to support popular movements committed to it. They have been accused of being instruments of Western imperialism, as well as of left-wing subversion – but, as they argue themselves, people power comes only from the will of the people.[11] No real peace can be imposed, from outside or from above. Any notion of democracy has the people, the *demos*, as its foundation, though people's participation may take forms unlike those of Western democracy. People power is essential in challenging tyranny and injustice, addressing power asymmetry, and creating new realities on the ground. The greater it becomes, the more governments will genuinely have to govern with consent. But people power, too, must be ethically motivated and focused, respecting democratic principles, if it is to deserve the name of nonviolence.

For 'conflict prevention' to become a reality, far greater popular activism will be required. The way in which a peace agreement is reached between conflicting parties, and who has a voice in that process, will greatly influence the kind of peace that is produced. Active engagement by different people's groups and organisations will help to ensure that it is *their* peace. And a concerned, active populace, practised in nonviolent assertiveness, will be a strong guarantor of positive peace, and indeed could be seen as an essential aspect of it. All of us need to be concerned for the awakening and empowerment of populations, including our own. It is in them that the power to build inclusive and stable peace resides, and nothing of lasting worth can be done without them.

There are indeed some excellent examples of ways in which 'the people' have involved themselves in peace processes.[12] This kind

10. See, for example, P. Ackerman and J. Duvall, *A Force More Powerful: A Century of Nonviolent Conflict*, New York: St Martin's Press, 2000, and accompanying videos.
11. See S. Zunes, 'The US, Nonviolent Action and Pro-Democracy Struggles', at <www.fpif.org>.
12. C. Barnes (ed.), *Owning the Process: Public Participation in Peacemaking* (Accord No. 13), London: Conciliation Resources, 2002.

of action must grow. By the same token, popular movements to prevent governments from going to war are equally important. If conflict transformation is to be globalised, the growth of people power and peace constituencies in countries that launch wars is a necessity – and we all need to be involved.

Activism, professionalism and popular involvement

I believe that, in the West at least, the conflict-transformation field is populated largely by people with a background in movements, who have turned from voluntary 'activists' into professionals – partly because they needed paid employment, and partly because they wanted to make a real difference, rather than simply campaigning to little apparent effect. Most have therefore lost touch with their knowledge of how movements work, and have been caught up in the 'professionalisation' that is part of the managerialism that seems to have spread from the private economy into societies at large. While it has its strengths, and can provide a counterbalance to self-indulgent fervour or sloppiness, it also has a deadening effect and tends to become exclusive.

If the power of 'ordinary people' is to be brought into play, it cannot be done through NGOs, in the sense of relatively small, professional organisations working through paid staff. It needs movements. Small organisations can exist without money in the bank, meeting in people's homes and relying on the activities of volunteers to carry out their purposes. Unless there is external funding, if a movement needs coordination by a central organisation, however modest, its members or participants need to give money out of their own pockets to sustain it. External funding is often hard to come by because movements are by nature political, in that they are designed to challenge and change the establishment, which is in control of most of the money.

Because people's experience of politics is often so negative, there can also be a wishful assumption that they can somehow be excised from action for peace. Yet it is essential to engage with public systems and public life, and vital to have some kind of a political analysis, albeit it with a small 'p', because without it our actions may be naive and their outcomes avoidably different from what we intend, or lacking in the kind of 'bite' or 'leverage' that we are looking for.

Neither autocracy nor the skeletal democracy of representative government sits easily with the idea of popular action for change. Those NGOs that are involved in advocacy, in education, or in work to change social relationships can, in my view, be seen as to a degree political, and it is argued by some that, since they are unelected, they are unaccountable and that their unmandated work for change is thus undemocratic. Others, of whom I am one, believe that collective voices and movements are a part of healthy democracy, providing the ongoing engagement with 'the system' that keeps it responsive and holds it to account.

However, in many parts of the world there is no widely established tradition of social movements. Family and clan loyalties and systems are, for many people, all-encompassing. The words 'society' and 'citizen' do not have equivalents in every language and culture. They are the constructs of a particular worldview. And in other places activism is a novelty because the state has always controlled and provided everything. It follows that the mobilisation of what I would refer to as 'social movements', through the kind of loosely organised, minimally structured, unpaid activism that is familiar to me, is a model that is not universally applicable.

Sometimes religious affiliations and networks provide connections that transcend communal boundaries, and may also house movements (as was the case, for instance, in what was East Germany, where the churches provided a home for all sorts of dissident groups). But in many places the idea of making a major, ongoing commitment to unpaid activity of a broadly social nature is not widely considered an option. Work done for an NGO (particularly an international one) is likely to be well paid in comparison to other work – if such exists – and in most cases it is carried out with commitment and diligence. But without any tradition of voluntary work for 'causes', and in hard economic conditions where making ends meet is a struggle, it is hard for most people to envisage making time for unpaid activism.

The sad reality in most countries is that the bulk of the population are too preoccupied with day-to-day living even to try to participate in the larger decisions that affect them. Institutions of various kinds may lobby politicians and exert some influence – whether overtly, honestly and for the common good, or covertly, dishonestly and for their own ends. A proportion of the general public may from time to time rise up in large numbers to demand change, sometimes with NGO stimulus, but this state of activity is likely soon to lapse and be replaced by the usual quiescence, leaving the frustrated few lifelong activists to continue in apparently fruitless fidelity.

The absence of real grassroots people within NGOs, in particular, and in some cases the gradual institutionalisation of what may have begun as activism, are exacerbated (as was suggested in Chapter 2) by the fact that most donors are unlikely to finance organisations of any kind that do not have professional, qualified staff and, in particular, accountants. I heard a heartbreaking story from an African woman colleague who described the village group that had begun the work in which she was now involved. No-one had a degree, no-one was used to handling money, but their work was vital, and they were in control of it. Then someone put them in touch with a donor, who was keen to support the work but had stipulated qualified staff and professional accounting as a precondition. Now not one of the original women was involved.

Women, gender and power

Since in many societies girls are often excluded from education, or have fewer and poorer educational opportunities, such professionalisation is liable to have a disproportionate effect on women, who in those societies are also the regular victims of daily violence – often sanctioned by law – and are largely excluded from power and public participation. This hidden war, covering a large part of the globe, needs to be seen as such and addressed at least as seriously as other, localised wars.

Of course 'gender' and 'women' are two different things. But in the current gender dispensation women, the numerical majority, are a power minority, and are often assigned the roles of servants and victims. Of course there are differences in this respect between one society and another, but when we talk about the great progress that has been made over the last century in terms of gender equality, we should not forget that, for many of the world's women, nothing has changed. Nor should we ignore the role of sexual violence in war, or the particular ways in which war and its consequences are experienced by women.[13]

The Islamophobia that has grown since 9/11 and the wars subsequently launched by the West have fed extreme, repressive forms (or perversions) of Islam, and have added political sensitivities and complications to women's work and its profile in affected societies. They have strengthened the forces of religious and cultural patriarchy and have left women caught between concern for their own rights and freedoms and the wish not to be out of solidarity with their own 'side' in relation to Western bullying and disrespect.

13. For moving examples of these, see L. Vušković and Z. Trifunović (eds), *Women's Side of War*, Belgrade: Women in Black, 2008.

In some places the lot of women improved for a while, only to deteriorate again as one dominating, controlling system was challenged by another, and women became – as so often in war – the emblems and victims of the struggle for mastery. This has happened in Iraq and in Palestine, where women's freedom has been greatly curtailed and violence against them has risen sharply. Rape continues to be a weapon of internal war – for instance in Sudan and in north-east India. News of sexual crimes against women by UN troops in the Democratic Republic of Congo caused some apparent shock, but rape has always been one of the hallmarks of military violence.

Although women far outnumber men in peace work, the pattern of male dominance in key positions often prevails in organisations. But that may be changing. Moreover, many women's organisations have been established. UN Resolution 1325 has provided a lever for women to insist on having a voice, and has helped them to win funding for mobilisation. There are some excellent programmes to support this work and to help them access funds.

I do, however, hear disturbing accounts of the negative impact of 'gender mainstreaming', which is meant to ensure that the gender dimension of all work is explored and addressed as a matter of routine. The danger is that, in practice, it may mean no more than the ticking of boxes in strategic planning frameworks and funding applications. And since the funds no longer get earmarked for gender work or for women's use, some work that might previously have been supported no longer is. It seems also that, in general, more funds are allocated to work in the 'security' and 'institution-building' sectors, and less to the kind of community-based work in which women often take the lead.

We are faced here with the dilemma already referred to: that, in efforts to escape from the immediate violence of war, it is hard to avoid privileging the power of male-led violence, by virtue of the attention those leaders receive. This is reflected in the relative absence of women, whether as parties or third parties, from top- or high-level negotiation processes, despite the progress made in building civil society's role (including that of women) in wider peace processes. And when it comes to the third-party roles of NGOs in peace processes, here too most of the work that is done with political and military leaders (who are almost always men) remains male-dominated. There is a largely unspoken assumption (probably correct) that men will take other men more seriously. It is crucial that work be done on rethinking gender constructions and relationships, not only in women's groups but also in mixed and men-only settings, so that dominant models of masculinity are re-examined and male–female identities and relationships reconsidered. I will argue in Chapter 4 that a shift in understanding on masculinity is central to a shift away from the culture of war.

Gender and culture are inextricably linked, but special pleading about culture that excuses violence against women and the wanton constriction of their lives has no moral basis and denies their full humanity. We all bear responsibility for our cultures, not as we have received them but as we choose to live in them. We can perpetuate them or we can change them. All of us, women as well as men, need to pinpoint and then to break the cultural link between constructions of masculinity and the idea of dominance, expressed in men's 'conquest' of women and their glorification through military violence: the notion that the archetype of manhood is the warrior hero, whether he is armed with a spear, toting a machine gun or piloting a B52 bomber. Until we break this link and unmask war, finally, as the brutal, inhumane and destructive institution that it is, any progress we make will be limited and fitful and all of us, male as well as female, will suffer.

CONFLICT, STATES AND GLOBAL SYSTEMS

In this penultimate section I want to consider matters that are beyond the scope of most organisations concerned with conflict transformation practice, but which must be part of a wider view of violent conflict and its transformation.

Conflicts often do not limit themselves to state boundaries. Sometimes, as we have seen, those boundaries are the focus of the conflict. Moreover, local conflicts are often subject to forces that are beyond the sphere of influence of even the most extensive, intensive and professional endeavours of NGOs, local politicians, or local citizens.

States are increasingly being challenged by forces within, and shoring up 'failed' and 'failing' states is a major preoccupation of the Western powers. As the sphere of environmental, economic and even legislative control of all states shrinks, some cling more tenaciously to their monopoly of legalised violence. Yet a state's military sovereignty is often dependent on military alliances, or is challenged not only by groups within its borders but by groups and states outside them.

Many states were created by conquest and bear little relation to the way people within and beyond them think about their lives and connections. Where their jurisdiction is contested, there often seems no way out of the impasse. The recent recognition of Kosovo as a new state by those whose military power created it as such is an uncomfortable exception to their own usually rigid rule that state boundaries should not be changed except with the agreement of all parties. But several new states exist de facto, in defiance of the jurisdictions from which they seceded. While the state continues to be *the* recognised unit of self-determination, many 'peoples' will continue to struggle, with or without violence, to establish their own boundaries, and these conflicts will remain intractable.

This is but one example of the way in which any particular 'conflict writ large'[14] is in fact writ even larger than this term usually suggests: it is subject to norms, influences and interventions from way beyond the boundaries of the state or states within which it is occurring. So however much one worked 'to scale', say, in Georgia, or in Israel/Palestine, and however good that work might be, unless one were able to engage the big powers whose hegemony or strategic interests were at issue in those places, its impact would always be subject to their influence and behaviour – which often means, in effect, blocked or nullified.

The shadow of global struggles for dominance is cast across every region, making attempts at conflict transformation seem puny, and constantly disrupting and reversing progress and sharpening divisions. Russia is motivated by its determination not to be further threatened at its boundaries, feeling increasingly encircled by NATO. For years the US has been determined to keep Israel as its bastion in the Middle East – seeing it, for instance, as a possible proxy in its standoff with Iran, though Barack Obama's arrival on the world stage might have a significant impact on these global relationships.

India and China vie for influence in Burma (Myanmar). India has been seen as a potential influence for good there, but suffers from chronic 'insurgency' in its north-east (fuelled by weapons from its neighbours) and, in view of China's growing strength, seeks border cooperation with Burma. These considerations affect the way it seeks (or does not seek) to influence Burma's internal politics.

Meanwhile, the Sri Lankan government has won, for a while at least, its decades-old war with the LTTE through a sustained and

---

14. CDA, *Reflecting on Peace Practice*, Cambridge, MA: CDA Collaborative Learning Project, 2004.

pitiless military onslaught. This 'victory' was aided by weapons from China and Pakistan (and, in the name of combating terrorism, also from the UK government).

The 'war on terror' has had an extremely adverse effect on relationships in many places, with the US pressurising the governments of other countries (the Philippines and Pakistan, for instance) to crack down harder on insurgents rather than trying to address internal conflicts constructively. Other governments have used it to justify their own renewed attempts to pacify those who oppose them, and peace processes (as in Sri Lanka) have collapsed. The wars and human rights violations of the US and its supporters also gave a twisted kind of moral cover to Russia for its excesses in Chechnya and its lack of democracy at home. Similarly, the 'horizontal' proliferation of nuclear weapons that continues to threaten global safety and stability is justified by the ongoing possession of nuclear weapons by existing nuclear powers.

Such lines of action do not create security and stability: quite the reverse. Democracy, or politics by active consent, which positive peace requires, cannot be imposed, only lived – and today it needs to be global. At the same time the fabric of a democracy is created by the participatory activities of individuals and groups. So there *is* no large-scale peace without local peace, and at the same time large-scale peace will remain elusive unless we focus also on global peace and begin to transform global systems and relationships.

FACING THE GLOBAL CHALLENGE

I have no doubt that making small differences is worthwhile. Nor do I doubt that enough small differences can make a large difference, and sometimes do. I accept, moreover, that nothing in life is permanent or secure. All things, good and bad, are transient. I shall continue to believe in conflict transformation as something that is possible at every level.

I know that, despite the chaos of seemingly uncontrollable forces and the unpredictability of their impact on each other, we do have agency, and that the choices we make will have an impact at some level (though not necessarily the one we intend, or to the extent that we want). I shall continue to be inspired and heartened by the acts of kindness and generosity and the courage and commitment of those who work to stop violence and build peace, and to hope that, little by little, their influence spreads.

When I think of the people I have worked with, when I listen to colleagues in every part of the globe who are changing their own communities, when I hear of the small contributions that have helped wars to be settled and communities to live together, and when I think of women's work to challenge gender roles and domestic violence, I see how important this work is. Much has been achieved, both by heroic actions and in seemingly mundane ways.

The pool of people who have developed their thinking and skills in this work is now substantial in many parts of the world. There is decreasing need for people to travel half-way across the globe to train others, though of course there are places where leadership and skills are in short supply and the people can benefit from the support of others, especially those who have had to struggle in similar circumstances and have successes and insights to share. We need each other's inspiration and support. We need to know that we are part of a global movement to mitigate violence and transform it – a movement to create peace where we live, and for a peaceful planet.

Recognising and nurturing this already-existing and growing potential is important in itself. Building on our growing knowledge will make us stronger and more effective. We have found that it is possible to find commonality across societies and cultures – humane values that can be shared and translated into action in different ways, but for similar goals. There is no real discontinuity between the micro and the macro. Systems and cultures do not exist independently of people and their thinking, behaviour and choices. Everywhere people are capable of kind and constructive behaviour as well as greed and cruelty. Societies can change, and some people make it their business to see that they do. The night is certainly not devoid of stars.

But I also want to join the NGO director cited above in refusing to tolerate our field's apparent inability to have a strategic impact. He is right in thinking that we need to work on a bigger scale, growing our capacity and involving ever more people in the work of peacemaking. In thinking about this question I have returned again and again to the notions of structural and cultural violence. People's actions can and do have an impact on these, either entrenching or changing them. Changing the way people think is fundamental. Action is education, and education is action.

But at present the culture of violence poisons all our societies. It corrupts our thinking and our relationships. It is entwined with the global system of military and economic domination that is the apparently unstoppable big tide in which our small counter-current is often overwhelmed: the world of business as usual, of the 'necessity' of war as an institution, of massive military spending while people die of hunger and poverty. It is at odds with the most fundamental values of conflict transformation: respect and inclusiveness, participation and cooperation.

The culture of violence continues to find expression in the brutality of intercommunal violence in Orissa or Kenya, in the callous repression of protest by the military government of Burma, in the demolition of homes and killing of whole families in Gaza and in the suicide-bombings that blow up Israeli citizens in bus queues. It is also embodied in school shootings in the US and knife crimes in the UK. It is glorified in video-games and films, and played out in domestic violence in homes across the globe, and obscenely justified in the 'shock and awe' of invasion and in the global arms race.

The conflict-transformation field, although it makes increasing efforts to influence the policy of governments on specific conflicts, does not, in the main, challenge militarism itself, nor take seriously enough the global culture that makes it seem acceptable. I believe this seriously reduces the chances of its making a strategic impact, leaving the system of militarism and the thinking that justifies it deeply entrenched. My argument is that military forces and structures, whether those of states, armed factions or terrorist networks, must be central to what conflict transformation sets out to address and transform.

In the following chapter I will present a radical analysis of the worldviews that are implicit in the dilemmas I have discussed in this chapter, and which will do much to decide our future, suggesting that a profound shift is needed in our approach to power and the human condition.

4
Peacebuilding and Pacification

Having devoted my first three chapters to conflict-transformation practice in the recent past and the present, I will now take a broader, more conceptual and analytical look at the global context: the big sea in which the little conflict-transformation boat is bobbing precariously and making slow progress.

In doing this I will outline what I see as two very different orientations to life and the systems and policies that they produce. I will argue that, although they are everywhere intertwined and one will never displace the other, the balance between them and the ways they are expressed will need to change if we are to make any major and lasting impact on the violence currently besetting the peoples of the world, and to achieve real progress in building positive peace.

PEACE AND MILITARISM

In the last chapter I suggested that there is already a global movement of people who come from different backgrounds and cultures yet nevertheless hold common values, and in their own ways carry forward the work of conflict transformation. Such work, as I argued in Chapter 1, is based on the assumptions that equal respect should be accorded to all and that cooperation for inclusive solutions is more effective for good than the endless struggle for domination and win–lose outcomes.

But the values of conflict transformation and of the kind of peacebuilding it envisions, though they are present in all cultures, are often undermined and overshadowed by radically different ones, which tend (perhaps unsurprisingly) to dominate. Here lies the heart of the dilemma: How can a value system that wishes to avoid domination avoid being dominated? How can inclusiveness include the non-inclusive? So although the work of conflict transformation receives support from high places, and 'conflict prevention' and 'the peaceful resolution of conflict' are promoted by governments, those governments usually spend vastly more money on building and maintaining military forces.

Some rich nations spend astronomical sums on waging wars in other countries, using violence on a grand scale and fuelling the desire of others to be 'in the same league' – that is, to achieve enough destructive power to be less susceptible to bullying (and perhaps better able to bully).

Militarisation of this kind results from the embedded structures and culture of militarism, which is first and foremost the militarisation of the mind:[1] the entrenchment of a worldview that sees all things military as playing a key role in collective relationships, and embraces military power as a route to dominance and control. It is this militarisation of minds that makes fitness to be commander in chief an acid test for a US presidential candidate. It is this that makes governments opt for military 'solutions' that are in fact tailor-made for catastrophe. It is this that allows them to spend obscene amounts of money on destruction rather than well-being: an estimated global total of $1.2 trillion per annum[2] on arms and armies, while millions lack adequate food, medicine and education. It is this that hides otherwise evident contradictions, and prompts the grieving mother of a murdered youth to tell a newspaper,[3] as evidence of how peaceful he was, that he was going to join the army cadets.

'Demilitarisation' is a term usually applied to situations in which there has been armed conflict. In such contexts the need for it is apparently self-evident. But the wider prevalence of militarism and the need for the demilitarisation of global thinking and relationships seems less obvious – perhaps because this form of militarisation is so all-enveloping and profound.

Recent years have been marked by military interventions by Western powers, with the objective (whether declared or not) of achieving regime change and hegemony. In such contexts the term 'peacebuilding' has been used by them to indicate the things they then want to see happen. But these invasions have been followed by notional settlements only, without an end to hostilities, so that the term begins to invite scepticism and becomes difficult to associate with local self-determination. Similarly, the word has acquired military connotations that sit uneasily with its core meaning, and are related to the notion of security. 'Security', in turn, has been

1. See H. Clark, *Demilitarising Minds, Demilitarising Societies* (CCTS Newsletter 11, Winter 2001), available at <www.c-r.org/ccts>.
2. A. Shah, 'World Military Spending', article published on their website by Global Issues, available at <www.globalissues.org/articles>.
3. The *Metro* (London), 2 September 2008.

militarised to mean (more often than not) armed protection and control and the establishment of a newly-fashioned state's monopoly of violence. And this is predicated on the approval and 'assistance' of those powerful outside governments whose capacity for violence is taken to give them the right to support, control or remove a regime.

The word 'human' has usefully been added to 'security' to counter this militarised notion of it. In the situations I have just outlined, other aspects of human security – for instance, continuous power and water supplies; the rights of the female half of the population to participate fully in their own society; the possibility of earning a living; and the rights of the population as a whole to benefit from the country's wealth – are addressed woefully inadequately.

Protection from lawlessness and violence would, I am sure, come high on anyone's list of human security needs. But it is usually assumed that it is military violence that must be the means of achieving that security, which in practice does not end militarisation but reinforces it; it certainly does not facilitate the restoration of relationships and mutual accommodation that can provide the basis for the building of lasting peace.

I would argue that this kind of approach should be seen not as peacebuilding, but as pacification, and that it arises from a radically different worldview, as suggested in Fig. 4.1,[4] which will be explained and then discussed under a variety of headings. One side represents peacebuilding, as approached through the attitudes, assumptions and choices of conflict transformation; the other side represents the pacification model.

TWO WORLDVIEWS

In Fig. 4.1 I have represented the idea that people's orientation towards others is fundamental to their approach to life: whether they see themselves and others as bound together in a relationship of interdependence, of needing each other; or as obeying the so-called law of the jungle, in which they must 'eat or be eaten'. This starting point provides the pivotal orientation for social and political life, opening out like a fan and leading to very different notions of peace and of how it can be achieved. As I see it, peacebuilding, as understood within conflict transformation, begins from the worldview in which interdependence is the point of departure, orientating people and institutions towards peacebuilding as

4.   First published, in an earlier version, in CCTS Review 30 (March 2006).

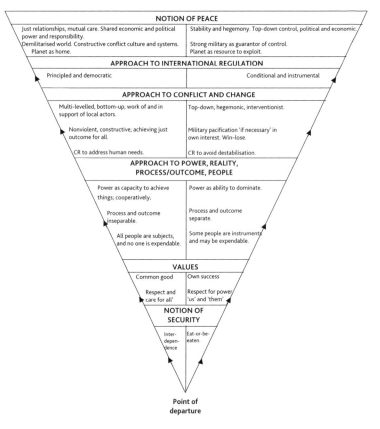

NOTION OF PEACE

Just relationships, mutual care. Shared economic and political power and responsibility. Demilitarised world. Constructive conflict culture and systems. Planet as home.	Stability and hegemony. Top-down control, political and economic. Strong military as guarantor of control. Planet as resource to exploit.

APPROACH TO INTERNATIONAL REGULATION

Principled and democratic	Conditional and instrumental

APPROACH TO CONFLICT AND CHANGE

Multi-levelled, bottom-up; work of and in support of local actors.	Top-down, hegemonic, interventionist.
Nonviolent, constructive; achieving just outcome for all.	Military pacification 'if necessary' in own interest. Win–lose.
CR to address human needs.	CR to avoid destabilisation.

APPROACH TO POWER, REALITY, PROCESS/OUTCOME, PEOPLE

Power as capacity to achieve things; cooperatively.	Power as ability to dominate.
Process and outcome inseparable.	Process and outcome separate.
All people are subjects, and no one is expendable.	Some people are instruments and may be expendable.

VALUES

Common good	Own success
Respect and care for all'	Respect for power 'us' and 'them'

NOTION OF SECURITY

Inter-depen-dence	Eat-or-be-eaten.

Point of departure

Figure 4.1   Two Worldviews

cooperation, while the worldview that sees life as a matter of eating or being eaten leads to what I have termed 'pacification'.

An orientation to life that is grounded in the notion of interdependence will lead to the values of respect and care for all, while a sense of life's being a matter simply of the 'survival of the fittest' will lead to the primary value of success for oneself or one's own group. If one's understanding of relationships is based on a sense of interdependence, and one's primary goal is the well-being of all, power will be conceived chiefly in terms of the ability to achieve that goal cooperatively, through the pooling of resources. In the eat-or-be-eaten model, it will be understood as a contest for control or domination.

I would argue that the interdependence model brings with it a sense of reality as complex and shifting, as a matter of relationships and processes in which an 'outcome' is simply a moment in something that continues, rather than something fixed. On the other side, reality is something to try and fix, or at least control, and is therefore viewed hierarchically, in the sense of 'being on top' of things. These contrasting approaches have huge consequences for how conflict and change are understood and treated. On the right-hand side conflict tends to be understood as a binary affair, whose sides are in themselves monolithic and framed by those who have positioned themselves to control them. On the left-hand side conflict appears multifaceted – a complex of different actors and issues that cannot be controlled, but can be worked with.

From the perspective of the eat-or-be-eaten side of things, if the status quo is conducive to 'business as usual', conflict must if possible be prevented; but it must be waged vigorously if that is seen as necessary to the protection of entrenched interests. Either way, it is a matter of control, and violence may be thought necessary. People are instruments of goals, and as such are expendable.

From the 'true peacebuilding' perspective on the left, conflict is seen as potentially constructive, and often necessary for changing the things that are unjust. Constructive conflict seeks solutions that address the rights and needs of all who are involved. Violence goes against the value of inclusive respect for people and for life, so nonviolent methods must be used. Coercion, if and when it is used, must be temporary, and must not inflict lasting harm. It should open the way to dialogue. True peacebuilders will be broadly positive in their approach to international bodies and regulations, since these are potentially instruments of cooperation . However, they will want to see the principles of fairness, nonviolence and inclusion – the hallmarks of positive peace – applied to the structure and workings of these institutions.

Pacifiers, on the other hand, will be unwilling to be fully committed to bodies and regulations that could compete with their own interests. Their approach to them will be conditional, and they will tend to use them when doing so will serve their own ends (as we saw in the run-up to the Iraq war, when the US and UK tried to 'persuade' other countries to support the invasion, and went ahead without a UN resolution when they failed).

The notions of peace that emerge from these two tendencies are, unsurprisingly, very different. Those who see the world through the lenses of interdependence understand peace as grounded in – even consisting of – what Adam Curle calls 'peaceful relationships':[5] those characterised by justice, mutual care and the cooperative exercise of power and responsibility. And from this standpoint a peaceful society would be informed by a 'constructive conflict culture'[6] that was translated into customs and institutions, and that excluded the use of violence.

On the pacification side, peace is understood in terms of hegemonic stability, hierarchically managed, which in the first place meets the economic and political interests of those who control it, though its beneficiaries may seek to justify it in terms of 'trickle-down' benefits for others. Conflict should not rear its ugly head: it must be kept down or extinguished through the monopoly of violence.

From the peacebuilding perspective, positive peace will include a caring approach to other species and to our planet, which together constitute our wider family and our home. On the pacification side, the planet is a resource to be exploited, and the universe is out there to be conquered.

At the heart of this analysis lies the question of gender. These two approaches bear a direct relationship to the way gender is constructed (rather than to genetic differences between the sexes). In the constructions of gender that are globally dominant, femininity is associated with softness and mutuality, and masculinity with the power to coerce and control. Masculinity equals machismo, and its archetype is the warrior. These cultural constructs involve the glorification of violent strength and male domination over women. It is no accident that war has been associated with the violation of women. (All too often, women have accommodated themselves to their lot and joined in the perpetuation of these constructions, by the way they raise their children – male and female – with dire consequences for both.) The issue of gender (like that of militarism itself) is so huge, pervasive and complex that, paradoxically, it easily becomes invisible. But until its profound importance is taken for granted and incorporated at the heart of our theory, and until it is addressed in serious and radical ways, we shall be unable to move from pacification to peacebuilding.[7]

Fig. 4.1 and the ideas it represents invite all kinds of criticism, the first of which may be that it is in itself polarising and confron-

5. Curle, *True Justice*, p. 37.
6. Francis and Ropers, *Peace Work*.
7. See the works of C. Cockburn – for instance, *From Where We Stand: War, Women's Activism and Feminist Analysis*, London: Zed Books, 2007, and Francis, *Rethinking War and Peace*.

tational, inviting a contest between these two orientations, and so contradicting the spirit of 'true peacebuilding'. When this was first pointed out to me I found it ironic and discomfiting. I later remembered Michael Billig's thesis that thinking always involves arguing, setting one thing against another,[8] and I choose to frame this apparent contradiction as a 'paradox' (and therefore something to be accepted and enjoyed). That does not, however, let me off the philosophical hook, and indicates real tensions and challenges.

There is another fundamental objection to be made, which is that this kind of dichotomising is deeply misleading, because in practice all these approaches and tendencies are mixed together. These two orientations are not really discrete, either in themselves or in their expressions in policy and practice. Rather, different institutions and people will tend more to one than the other, and most – probably all – will combine them. I accept that; but at the same time I believe that thinking about them as fundamentally different orientations, each with its own logic, can be helpful. I would argue that the mixtures and contradictions between them should give us serious pause for thought, in the first place to help us to anatomise the way we all think, and in the second place to consider from a different angle the goals that we have and how we might be most likely to achieve them.

ADDRESSING VIOLENCE: DILEMMAS AND ETHICS

Those engaged in pacification often wear peacebuilders' clothes, covering themselves with the benign language of 'humanitarian intervention', 'peacekeepers', 'peace enforcers', 'force', 'strength', 'liberal interventionism', 'security', 'normalisation', 'regime change', 'nation-building' and so on. 'Peace is our profession' says the army. Similarly, the ugliest elements of pacification are hidden by the airbrushing-out of casualties in opposing armies and civilian populations. Yet many soldiers have a serious moral commitment to what they do; and genuine peacekeeping, whether it is carried out by soldiers or by civilians, can create a space for peacebuilding.

On the other side, all of us who work in the world of conflict transformation and are committed to peacebuilding are, whether we like it or not, caught up in the world of pacification. Some of us work alongside armies, and many of my colleagues will feel that I have divided things in too sharp a way, believing that there is a

8. M. Billig, *Arguing and Thinking*, Cambridge: Cambridge University Press, 1987.

necessary role for the military. They will, for instance, refer to the 'responsibility to protect' and will argue that 'peace enforcement' can be necessary, for the general good.

Both those engaged in pacification and those who work for true peacebuilding are confronted with the dilemma of uncontrollable violence and situations in which they fail to find any effective response. And the lack of any kind of positive peace (the goal of peacebuilders) is often the ground for the kind of escalating disturbances that both pacifiers and peacebuilders fear, and that need to be addressed. This may involve conflict, if only of a nonviolent kind. At the same time, conflict is a disruptive and risky business, and is sometimes wrong-headed and unnecessary. Most of us dislike it for good reasons.

In the currently dominant paradigm of eat-or-be-eaten, greed and grievance are two sides of same coin.[9] Some may fight because war makes them rich, and some may do so because they suffer from the greed of others. The sad reality is that most of those harmed by violent conflict had no interest in it – they only suffer from it.

Ethical systems usually give a high place to altruism, and 'greed', by definition, is a pejorative word, whose only association with ethics is negative. Part of my subtext is that peacebuilding is more ethical than pacification; but I can see that altruism is not the exclusive domain of the left-hand side of Fig. 4.1, since the eat-or-be-eaten perspective might involve courageous loyalty to one's own, as well as being expressed in a more expansive commitment to humanity. But in this case the scope of altruism is limited, and its impulse and direction, one might argue, distorted or limited. The collective that is the object of such partisan altruism could be seen as an extended version of the self.

Yet partisan allegiances are also part of conflict transformation, as people mobilise and take action for change, disturbing the apparently calm surface of the 'interdependence' model. Here we have the double paradox that pacifiers hate conflict but embrace war, while peacebuilders (in my analysis at least) hate war but embrace conflict. Since we live in unpeace, radical change is essential if we are ever to get beyond fire-fighting, and this will necessitate 'constructive conflict'.

At the same time, it is clear that a degree of stability is necessary for lives to be lived and for new forms and patterns to emerge and become established. Can we shake up social arrangements at

9.   Berdal and Malone, *Greed and Grievance.*

the same time as building them? Stability can in any case never be absolute, since its maintenance requires continuous effort and adjustment, and change is continual. Moreover, the process of active participation is fundamental to peace, which is why it needs to be understood as an ongoing process rather than a fixed state.

Security (which, of course, can never be permanent) does imply a tolerable degree of stability, if – and this is a big if – the existing situation does meet people's needs. But 'stability' achieved by dominatory methods is inherently unstable. The pressure-cooker effect renders it so. Stable governance requires consent.

As we have seen, conflict transformation is concerned with addressing the causes of conflict, actual and potential, which may mean bringing hidden conflict into the open when it is only latent, confronting oppression and injustice nonviolently. This involves taking sides on what is at issue, assuming a moral position, and entering into what can be seen as a competitive power dynamic. The daily violence of severe economic or social exclusion, or chronic direct violence in streets or in homes, is as much in need of an effective response as an invasion or a terrorist attack. And, as with any kind of violence or conflict, the goal will be to achieve the inclusion of all in a just outcome.

How can violent power be countered when power disparity makes dialogue impossible? How can a space be created for the negotiation of peaceful relationships? What kind of power can be deployed by the apparently weaker side? Coercion cannot itself build peace, but in some circumstances and some moments coercion may play a role in creating the space for peace to be built. Within the framework of transformative peacebuilding, where a marginalised group would not otherwise be listened to or where coercive (or lethal) power is used or threatened by another, coercion can be one element in creating a route to dialogue and creating the circumstances for future cooperation and positive peace.

Is there a role for violence in building peace?

As I have suggested, 'humanitarian intervention' is not without its supporters in the world of conflict transformation; indeed, it has gained new momentum under the current banner of the 'responsibility to protect'. In the past, the primacy of state authority had been accepted as precluding external interference; but more recently, and rightly, there has been a growing concern with the responsibility of human beings to stop terrible things being done to each other. Surely there are situations in which the processes of peacebuilding and conflict transformation are impossible, and where decisive action is needed?

But what is described as 'humanitarian intervention' is usually nothing of the sort.[10] Militarism is part of the eat-or-be-eaten paradigm, and military action is rarely taken for purely humanitarian reasons – particularly by the powers with the greatest military resources, which often collude with some of the most corrupt and despotic regimes. In cases where there is no vested interest to motivate serious intervention, humanitarian disasters – both chronic and acute – are regularly ignored, or addressed in shamefully inadequate ways.

Furthermore, the effect of military assault and invasion (inhumane in themselves) is not usually to build peace. Unless the task is to police a peace that is already more or less in place (as the UK did in Sierra Leone and the US did in Liberia), and to do so by agreement, there will always be the serious risk that 'decisive force' is not in fact decisive, and a high chance that the intervention will become an ongoing war. Even in the short term, violent intervention may only intensify the violence against those whose protection is the declared aim of the exercise.

Thus, as I have pointed out elsewhere,[11] and as BBC reporter Bridget Kendall noted recently,[12] the killing of Albanian Kosovars, despite the impression so often given to the contrary, rather than being stopped, was in fact hugely escalated in response to NATO's 'intervention' – and was followed, in the true spirit of warfare, by the 'ethnic cleansing' of Serbs, Roma and other minorities. Military 'solutions' in Kosovo and East Timor followed years of neglect and failure to give serious support of any kind to those resisting tyranny – whether by diplomatic persuasion, preventing weapons from reaching the oppressors, or creating economic incentives for change. The outcomes of invasion in both cases, many years on, remain depressing in many ways (quite apart from the high levels of violence, including rapes, that were suffered by the local population at the time, along with the other ills of occupation, such as the displacement of local actors and the distortion of the economy).

'National security' is the other banner under which military invasion is justified. It is hard to imagine that security can in fact be furthered by such means, and there is plenty of recent evidence

10. See Francis, *Rethinking War and Peace*.
11. Ibid.
12. BBC Radio 4's 'Today' programme, at the time of Radovan Karadzic's arrest (21 July 2009).

to counter that claim. Equally, it is unlikely that terrorism can enhance anyone's safety. Both war and terrorism are attacks on the security of human beings, and are profoundly unjust and destructive in their impact. Victory in either case is not only unpredictable but necessarily pyrrhic. In the words of Yugoslav graffiti, 'To the victor go the spoils, and the spoils are a heap of ashes'.

All the arguments that are marshalled to justify war gloss over its hideous reality: death and mutilation on a massive scale; bereavement and trauma; destruction of habitat, livelihood and infrastructure; displacement; and lawlessness – with the privatised violence of kidnap, murder, rape, domestic assaults and the further disempowerment of women, new feuds and power struggles, hatred, and despair. This is hardly the stuff of peacebuilding.

Citing Bosnia, Edward Luttwak argues that what he would describe as half-hearted military intervention cannot work, but will leave behind a situation in which war could start again at any time. His logic is that, without real and determined national interest expressed in a fully imperial way – that is, as a complete takeover – there cannot be a new and lasting regime; and if there is not the will for such a takeover it is better to let local forces fight through to a decisive victory.[13] This is pacification par excellence; but it does not necessarily work, even in its own narrow terms, as is woefully clear in Iraq and Afghanistan, which may be seen as sufficiently imperial test cases.

Peace and democracy cannot be imposed by guns and bombs, but only built through practice. To try to crush violence with greater violence is to sow the seeds not of harmony and cooperation, but of more violence to come – even if, for a while, that violence is hidden behind house doors, where the sexual violence that is part of the fighting continues within families. Furthermore, future violence cannot be ruled out: those who have lost may in time regroup and begin to fight back in new ways. There has been no accommodation or building of trust because a win–lose outcome has been brought about by invasion, which has not resulted in locally owned peace, but has given another vigorous spin to the wheel of violence.

In situations brought about by violent intervention, 'peacebuilding' becomes a post-violence exercise, rather than a step in the process of conflict transformation. When, as in Afghanistan, pacificatory action has been taken and a programme of peacebuilding is declared, international organisations that are devoted to conflict

13.   Edward Luttwak on BBC Radio 4's 'The World Tonight', 15 February 2008.

transformation can find themselves in a difficult moral position. The situation that has now been created cries out more than ever for peacebuilding. Yet this peacebuilding will be contaminated, in local eyes, by its association with invasion and occupation, and the ongoing violence will make it very difficult. Any work to try to achieve it can also be seen as supplying a fig-leaf to cover the naked aggression of war, lending credence to its justification and making future wars more likely. This is a dilemma for NGOs, whether local or international. It can be compounded when the funding for proposed peacebuilding work actually comes from the governments that have directed the invasion.

Moving straight from war to peacebuilding is like trying to step from a boat to distant dry land without any kind of bridge. In conflict transformation, the post-settlement stage of peacebuilding is based on the capacities for peace developed in earlier stages of the conflict and through the resolution process. When 'regime change' has been brought about by war, there has been no resolution process, only 'winning', and local capacities have been destroyed or swept aside. In such circumstances of extreme discontinuity, the social and political fabric is torn apart and the foreign presence, both military and civilian, occupies centre-stage.

I have witnessed this in Kosovo, where most old colleagues, if they were lucky, were given 'bit parts' in the new show, working in humble capacities in international organisations, and were 'let go' once those organisations began to cut staff. In the few cases where former activists have been drawn into elevated positions following an invasion, they have consequently been lost to grassroots leadership, cut off from their former colleagues, to operate in a context that is still highly militarised.

For peace to be built, it is necessary for conflicting groups to negotiate the means of coexistence, and for military factions to be dissolved or converted into political parties. Military occupation is unlikely to promote demilitarisation and genuine accommodation of this kind, and in the end it is only local people who can build and sustain peace.

Terrible violence continues in Africa (especially in the DRC and Sudan) and lives continue to be devastated, despite the efforts of the African Union, with some support from other countries or from the UN. Indeed, the conflicts are so complex and state structures so weak or irrelevant that it is hard to see how any top-down solution could be applied.

Even if we wished to do so, we would not have the capacity to deploy forces to protect human rights around the world. The UN is only as strong and well resourced as its member-states can or will make it. Nor would such a pax Romana, or perpetual military pacification, constitute the kind of global peacebuilding we need, even if emergency protection is sometimes necessary. Genuine peacebuilding and effective human rights protection need to be home-grown, even where they need support, and will thereby be far more effective than military measures.

Can people power meet the challenge?

Rather than thinking about more and bigger armies, under whatever command, we should be giving serious attention to capacity-building for peace and human rights around the world. When we see an abject population driven hither and thither by violence, we should be asking ourselves some profound questions about their powerlessness and vulnerability, and the ways in which these are reproduced. It is precisely peace*building* that is needed, not 'peace enforcement' – which is a contradiction in terms, particularly where 'enforcement' is carried out violently.

In such circumstances, participatory peacebuilding would need to include the most basic elements of development, with empowering education (including new thinking on gender) at the top of the list. For there to be positive peace, in the sense of general well-being and peaceful relationships, there is a need for transformation: personal, cultural and structural. If the rich nations that are able to help are to have any moral legitimacy internationally, or indeed the capacity to help support such a transformation, they too need to transform their own social attitudes and economic and political policies, and to take peacebuilding seriously, for what it is.

But surely, sometimes, coercion will still be needed? As I have outlined above, I believe that the power of violence to make good things happen is fictional, though its capacity to coerce through pain and destruction, and through the threat of them, is all too real. Yet there remains the question of how to stop bad things happening for long enough to be able to do good. Can nonviolence do this?

If the principle of not harming others is adhered to, and if the goal of nonviolent coercive action is the good of all (including those who are currently being confronted), there is no contradiction in principle between nonviolent coercion and interdependence. I am not convinced that nonviolence is ever truly coercive, or indeed that it needs to be. Its power lies more in its psychological than its physical effects. So-called 'direct action' (such as occupying seats in a segregated café, or damaging the control panel of a bomber aircraft) is indeed direct in its nature, but its power for change is not restricted to its nuisance value, but extends also to its symbolic power. In both cases, to be sure, there is an economic cost involved, but the opportunity of presenting a justification in court, of raising public awareness and of pricking consciences is far more important.

Non-cooperation with wrongdoing is a key principle of nonviolence, and it is the most powerful tool of 'direct' or supposedly coercive action. It may express itself visibly, on the streets. For instance, rulers may be deposed by the sheer force of the numbers of people demonstrating their unwillingness to accept their rule by surrounding a parliament. But their power lies not so much in keeping politicians out or in, as in winning over others so that they too withdraw their support. Governments can govern only with the consent (whether active or passive) or their people. Withdrawal of labour can, in itself, bring a regime to its knees. As we have all too often seen, removing a ruler or a regime does not in itself build peace, but it may create an opportunity for peace to be built.

Although, by definition, nonviolence does not inflict violence in any direct way, given that it carries real power, it is essential to its nature and necessary to peacebuilding that it is harnessed for purposes that are respectful, caring and inclusive, and that it is employed in a manner that is assertive rather than aggressive. The question of 'just causes' and related issues will be discussed, among others, in Chapter 6, where I will reflect further on the power of nonviolence and take a radical look at the very notion of power. I will underline the argument I have already suggest here – namely, that coercion, though it may in extreme cases be crucial, nonetheless has a limited role to play, and that confrontation itself may often be the least effective means of transformation.

Disarmament and demilitarisation of existing security systems

One of the reasons why nonviolent action requires such courage is the large quantity of armaments in existing systems, both official and unofficial. The world is awash with weapons. This is the current reality: one that needs to change, with all that this means for the arms economy. Currently, nonviolent assertiveness has to take place in a militarised context. This means that a process of disarmament must be one goal of global conflict transformation. In the meantime, is it possible for people's security to be protected, when necessary, by unarmed forces, whether they are operating at home or abroad? (I will discuss in Chapter 6 the risk incurred by nonviolent activists who choose to assert their own and other people's rights in the face of violent systems and in violent situations.)

I am old enough to have seen the gradual increase in the use of firearms by police that has taken place in my own society: a trend resisted by older police officers. Even now, most policing is carried out by unarmed officers, and I believe that most of my fellow citizens, like me, feel safer if they see unarmed rather than armed police on the streets. When, as happens occasionally, an armed person is holding a victim hostage, the police almost always disarm that person and release his (or occasionally her) prisoner unharmed without resort to arms. It seems probable that those carrying out criminal activities have themselves carried guns more often, as police practice has changed. If this is accepted, it is clear that it is necessary to de-escalate and reverse the trend, however difficult that may be.

I would suggest that both in countries that are 'at peace' and in places where a transition is needed from armed violence to established peace, it is possible to offer protection without resort to lethal weapons. Unless police, like armies, are to become involved in shoot-outs, their power lies very largely in the respect in which they are held, the consent of the majority in upholding their power, and their skill in defusing aggression and persuading miscreants to submit. Playing their role in this way will entail some risk, but so does engaging in shoot-outs, and there can be no doubt that there is greater readiness to shoot an armed person than an unarmed one.

Occasionally, those who are charged with maintaining order and security may resort to immobilising those who threaten them, or who become a threat to themselves or others, by using the physical restraint techniques they are trained in. Can immobilising weapons play a role in peacekeeping or policing, without causing permanent harm either to people or to relationships? This is a knife-edge question for me. When I watch a nature programme on television and see a huge and dangerous animal felled instantly by a tranquil-lising dart, recovering later with no apparent ill effects, I wonder how we can have developed the ability to do this with other species and not our own – as if their well-being mattered more to us (in these contexts, at least).

I know how easily non-lethal but highly coercive weapons can become instruments of tyranny by police, and how much pain they can inflict. Perhaps research would be useful into possible means of humane disabling in highly exceptional circumstances. However, for those circumstances to be highly exceptional and for the object of the research to be sincerely compassionate, it would be necessary for the norms within which such use was contemplated to be nonviolent. And I believe that this would need to be seen as an interim objective within a more radical disarmament process.

This whole uncomfortable interface between pacification and peacebuilding requires serious, committed attention from all those who wish to shift our global systems and culture from one paradigm to the other. Practitioners of nonviolence around the world will have much to offer to the building of knowledge and thought in this area.

PEACEBUILDING AND INTERNATIONAL RELATIONS

States that are internally democratic and peaceful (relatively speaking) can be the least democratic and peaceful – the most prone to pacification – in their external relations. This seems to escape popular notice for much of the time, because it is so familiar a pattern, so hidden by comforting and rationalising language, and because its effects occur so far from home. As I have already noted, the mode of operation of the US and the UK within the United Nations points to a desire to use and manipulate it for their own purposes rather than to cooperate with others, in a consensual manner, for the good of all, and to uphold the rule of international law. Our preference for unilateral military action over global solidarity and cooperation puts us at odds with democracy, just as our policy of nuclear armament contradicts our insistence that other countries should not acquire or develop nuclear weapons.

The culture that prevails within our democratic systems is mixed. Our governments can be seen both as agents of control and as vehicles for cooperative action. The way multi-party democracies work, however, is often highly antagonistic. Politicians gain ascendancy by undermining the credibility of others, rather than by offering realistic and principled policies that people are likely to support. Election campaigns have the rhetoric and bitterness of wars.

Within governments, different tendencies often predominate in different departments. For instance, in the UK the Department for International Development (DFID) is influenced by peacebuilding, while the dubiously-named 'Ministry of Defence' (MOD) can, generally speaking, be located on the pacification side. (The Prime Minister's Office will have its own style and focus, determined by the incumbent of the day.) Foreign policy, as pursued by the Foreign and Commonwealth Office (FCO), takes a diplomatic rather than a military approach. Establishing constructive relationships is an important part of its work, sometimes with recommendations for exerting influence through the use of 'sticks and carrots'. The FCO can thus be seen as straddling the two sides of Fig. 4.1. Doubtless, these differing tendencies could be attributed to departments and positions in other governments, as well as to different intergovernmental institutions, both regional and international.

Foreign policy, as its name suggests, is predicated on the notion of one state in relation to others, those others being seen and described as foreigners. We are 'us' and they are 'them', and our interests come first. This formulation fits into the 'pacification' side of things, though I am sure that those responsible for it also take interdependence or mutual interests seriously, in some instances and relationships, if not all. But there is the rub: mutuality of interests in this context is conditional on particular circumstances, rather than being seen as universal.

The ethical norms and goals implicit in a more radical understanding of peacebuilding and conflict transformation are not at the heart of UK foreign policy. In this the UK is, of course, not alone. Doubtless, most if not all governments reassure their people that their foreign policy is designed to further national interests. In any case, in the UK at least, the rhetoric of self-interest has traditionally been regarded as a vote-winner. The announced intention some years ago of the then-Foreign Secretary Robin Cook of pursuing an 'ethical foreign policy' had an air of novelty about it, but was followed by disappointment and cynicism on the part of those who longed for such an approach.

Whether a majority of the electorate would currently support a truly ethical foreign policy is another matter. The notion of 'enlightened self-interest' has the appearance of offering the best of both worlds and of leaning towards the notion of interdependence. Nonetheless, national interests prevail, albeit sometimes disguised as humanitarian or global ones, and on occasion combined with genuine (if not overriding) concerns of a more altruistic nature. Truly enlightened self-interest would be founded in the notion of interdependence, and would not be in any way at odds with a truly ethical foreign policy.

In its current publicity, the FCO advertises policy goals on conflict that are to 'counter terrorism, weapons proliferation and their causes; prevent and resolve conflict'. But these policy goals are either disingenuous in presentation, or surprisingly lacking in insight. The

UK government is determined to retain and 'modernise' its own weapons, including nuclear weapons, thereby helping to perpetuate the arms race and providing the incentive for other countries to join in. The UK is one of the world's major arms exporters, imposing only very few restrictions on itself, in the most convenient of ways. It is also a country that has seemed second only to the US in its willingness to engage in violent conflict, creating enemies around the world. These pacificatory policies run counter to other more constructive behaviours, and suggest rather little attention to the notion of interdependence.

The UK government supports some genuine conflict-transformation initiatives and programmes. However, its current key phrases are 'prevention'; 'mitigating, winning, resolving'; 'stabilisation'; and 'consolidation'.[14] The presence of the word 'winning' in this collection is both honest and significant, making it clear that the thinking behind the words is related to perceived national interest and the UK's own possible involvement in the conflicts in question. It suggests that, where national interest is involved, UK action on conflict is in sharp contradiction to the values and methods of conflict transformation. 'Prevention', 'mitigating' and 'stabilisation' indicate that the (presumably) violent conflicts of others are undesirable, whereas ours may be fought and won. ('Losing' is of course not part of the picture.) 'Resolving' is, I imagine, therefore, intended largely for the conflicts of others.

If conflict resolution is indubitably right for others, why is it not always right for us? Whereas it is easy for a disinterested third party to see that a 'win–win' solution may be desirable from a broader perspective, when it comes to one's own conflict, if there is a likelihood of all-out victory this will tend to be seen as preferable to a solution negotiated in a process predicated on equality and give-and-take. That is indeed the logic of working 'in the national interest'. If it is to be countered, then ethics need to come into play more forcefully, and the notion of interdependence, with all that it implies, must be brought to the fore. (Renaming 'foreign policy' as 'international policy' – and meaning it – would be a good beginning.) The understanding of national self-interest requires radical re-examination and debate, both public and academic, around the world. It has gone unchallenged for far too long.

14.   See the paper commissioned by the UK Government's Global Conflict Prevention Pool and authored by Nicole Ball and Luc van de Goor, *Promoting Conflict Prevention through Security Sector Reform*, London: Price Waterhouse Coopers, 2008.

STATES AND THE LIMITATIONS TO THEIR SOVEREIGNTY

While local peace needs to be built primarily by local inhabitants, it is increasingly evident that security anywhere is dependent on security everywhere. Peacebuilding cannot, in the end, be piecemeal: it needs to be a global process. The most direct impact from global unpeace is that of hegemonic interference by big states in the affairs of smaller ones, whether through invasion or more subtle forms of military or political action.

As we have seen, wherever NGOs are working to support peacebuilding and conflict transformation they are aware of the influence of powers and forces that are beyond their scope. Yet by and large (though with notable exceptions) they continue to try to address internal conflicts as if their outcome were in the power of local actors alone. All over the Caucasus, for instance, the hand of Russia is seen at work (as is the influence of the US), but there is little engagement with Russia by international NGOs working in the region, and there has until recently seemed to be an increasingly confrontational or distant relationship between many Western governments and Russia. Moreover, governments that are themselves involved in hegemonic activities are hardly in a position to wag fingers, and are unlikely to be heeded when they do.

Ironically, however, while big states constantly interfere in the affairs of smaller ones, and peoples secede and seek new statehood, the notion of sovereign and inviolable states is pivotal in the eat-or-be-eaten view of things, and is associated, as we have seen, with holding a monopoly on violence. Normally speaking, this monopoly is represented by a state army.

The 'international community' (that informal and shifting alliance dominated by the powerful) is extremely reluctant to countenance the creation of new states, or to see any weakening of the state concept – presumably because of the threat this would pose to the stability of the current system. In the case of Kosovo, for instance, while a de facto separate entity was created militarily, without negotiation, the issue of the territory's final status remained unresolved until 2008, when Kosovo's independence was unilaterally declared – with the support of some states and the disapproval of others, who pronounced the declaration illegal. The 'frozen conflicts' in Moldova, Georgia and elsewhere are influenced by the desire of current power-holders to maintain the status quo rather than entertain the risks of throwing old assumptions into question and precipitating the disintegration of states – their own or others'.

This fear is understandable. But the 'freezing' of conflicts has so far failed to deliver the kind of stability and consensus necessary for peacebuilding. 'Frozen' conflicts are inherently unstable. Our attachment to the notion of the nation-state proves unhelpful in the many situations where old borders and entities – often highly artificial and imposed – have been and continue to be the focus of costly conflict. It blocks the evolution of more viable, flexible and acceptable units of identification and governance, impeding the way to peace, and should therefore be rethought.

FEAR, CONTROL AND FUTURE SECURITY

Greed is not the only motivation for the drive to control, or that lies behind the tendency towards pacification. Fear arguably goes even deeper, and underlies the eat-or-be-eaten approach. That is why so many citizens of the US place such emphasis on presidential candidates' fitness to be commander in chief, as against their character and gifts for leadership, dialogue and governance. Perhaps the knowledge of our own vulnerability and mortality lies at the root of all our struggles for identity and control. (Surely, acts of 'senseless' violence, like starting wildfires or gunning down children in school, are a response to feelings of powerlessness. Destruction is so easy, and its effects so readily apparent.)

However that may be, fear and frustration at our lack of control are blocks to the kind of creativity we need if we are to enjoy and cherish life and each other, developing the understanding and the sources of power that will enable us to meet our own and others' needs. Clinging to our belief in the power of violence to protect us and make our will prevail is like clinging to a comfort blanket that does nothing to cover our nakedness; in doing so, moreover, we in fact sustain a vast, deadly and pervasive complex of killing mechanisms that make all our lives less, not more, safe. Can we kick the habit of fear and place our faith in each other's capacities for empathy and resourcefulness?

There are global, structural threats to future peace that go beyond the deadly effects of militarism, and can be viewed through the same lenses of interdependence and self-interested competition. Economic dominance and injustice not only militate against peacebuilding, but cause immense resentment and perpetual instability that no amount of pacification can begin to address. The lack of any economic democracy and the decrease in political control over increasingly vast, transnational economic interests mirrors the controlling and reactionary relationships both between nations and built into global political structures.

Security, in this context, should be understood broadly as 'human security': all that is needed for physical and mental well-being. It is abundantly clear that a large proportion of the world's human occupants have a big deficit of it in every respect: their dignity is disregarded, their autonomy denied, their participation blocked, their lives and livelihoods threatened. Those who are utterly crushed by their lot and denied even the tools for thinking are indeed pacified – that is, made passive. But those who have enough education and space in their lives to think a little, and the determination to act, will not submit forever to such inequities and the sense of humiliation that they bring. One precondition for peace is respect – in attitude and in action. Those of us who live in countries that are now dominant must realise that our assumed cultural superiority, our easy justification of our actions, and our endless double standards are felt as a daily outrage by others. Peacebuilding at the local level cannot address such profound asymmetries. Global peacebuilding must do so. The perpetuation of resentment makes no one secure.

Perhaps there is some hope to be found in the new rhetoric of politicians and the surge of public awareness about the need to tackle global poverty. But real action on that front would mean acceptance of lower levels of consumption by those of us in relative wealth. Truly enlightened self-interest is likely to require a different understanding of human security and well-being. One thing that could help us to respect each other as equals is the fact of our common, global peril: the environmental crisis that could overwhelm us all. If we are not prepared to cooperate on a truly global scale to address this common threat to our security, we will be driven ever further apart, with disastrous consequences. If this does not persuade us of the reality of our interdependence, as participants in one ecosystem, then probably nothing will. The shift in global economic (and therefore, inevitably, political) power to the global South and East is also a wake-up call to those who have taken for granted their own perpetual dominance, making the cooperative model immediately more attractive.

SHIFTING THE CULTURE AND BRIDGING THE DIVIDE

There is a prevailing, global assumption that conflict must have winners and losers, and that, when it comes to vital collective interests, violence is likely to be the most effective means of winning.

This belief in the efficacy of deadly force manifests itself in the military metaphors that pepper our everyday language and find their apotheosis in the 'magic bullet'.

This cultural tendency towards pacification is expressed in the fact that we have the military edifice to match it, which in turn consolidates the culture. Globally, we have highly developed systems and resources for military responses and far weaker ones for responding in other ways. In global terms it is plain from public spending patterns that conflict transformation is, relatively speaking, a hobby, while maintaining powerful military positions and exercising military strength is a very serious business. Even countries that are, from the military point of view, small fry spend an inordinate proportion of their GNP on weaponry and armies.

Though violence is presented as a 'last resort', in fact it never is, since alternatives are barely thought of – and certainly not resourced and developed. Since the machinery of violence sucks up such vast wealth and attention, most governments fail to build up sufficiently strong policies and strategies for avoiding it, or the means of achieving security in other ways – ways that do not replicate violence, and that might be effective for security and peace.

At the same time, there are governments, such as those in Sweden and Canada, that have for some years been pushing in quite another direction. They have not divested themselves of all traces of militarism, but they have begun to rethink the role of armies, have put a substantial proportion of attention and public funds into support for conflict transformation and peacebuilding, and have contributed to a reduction in the flow of arms and bans against landmines and cluster bombs. They have resolutely remained free of nuclear weapons, and have encouraged multilateral processes to de-escalate the arms race. This other trend – based, I would argue, in a stronger sense of interdependence and mutuality – should give us hope that the tide can be turned away from pacification and towards global peacebuilding, based on the principles of interdependence and common security.

The pivotal assumption of interdependence and the related value of unconditional respect for fellow human beings (as moral equals, if not equally moral) require clear ethical choices. Although human nature and all of our societies embody both cooperative and competitive tendencies, the capacity for moral choice enables us to privilege one over the other in our personal, social and political thinking and aspirations. Ethical judgements must, by definition, be practicable, which must mean that they take account of both tendencies. These tendencies are not exclusive to particular people, groups, institutions or cultures, and many of us who have strong ideological commitments to one side may have equally strong personal tendencies towards the other. (I hope I am not alone in this!) We might also do well to examine our own organisations and practices, and consider how consistent they are with the values we hold and with our peacebuilding values.

At the systemic level, we need to recognise that people often work from one perspective in an organisation that we would see as largely informed by the other. They may choose to work there because they believe that to do so will offer them opportunities to make a difference or work for change in the system. They may see us as potential allies and look to us for support. We, in turn, need them. It is they who may be best placed to begin the work of transformation.

One of the dangers of clear moral thinking and strong moral views is that they can lead to self-righteousness and intolerance. In Brecht's words, 'Even anger against injustice makes the voice grow harsh.'[15] As a peace movement activist, I am acutely aware of the frequently strident harshness of our collective voices. This is not just paradoxical: it is contradictory; and this kind of advocacy is counterproductive. Communication is a two-way process, and if we have a message we want it to be heard. Ears will close themselves to insulting messages and attitudes of moral superiority (quite different from moral judgement).

I believe that we should assume a level of good-will on everyone's part, and try to communicate at that level. We will need each other's knowledge and experience if we are to flesh out our own analysis and think creatively about how things could be done. I would not for a moment suggest that all government policies are malign – even less that all those who work to formulate and implement them are lacking in care, commitment and passion, or that support given to initiatives for conflict transformation and peacebuilding are all self-serving and cynical. Rather, it is as if the left hand and the right hand are working in very different ways.

But the impact of the aggressive military policies and actions described above runs counter to, and threatens to overwhelm, these positive initiatives, and undermines their integrity. Government policies and actions that ignore the long-term, global impact of

15.   From a translation of Bertolt Brecht's *An die Nachgeborenen*.

this kind of violent power are bad ones. We need internationalist, humanitarian policies that contribute to global demilitarisation.

We need to face up honestly to the dilemmas and challenges that confront us all as we work for peace within the current dispensation, and to develop an ongoing dialogue between those of us working within the two different paradigms and anywhere in between. We must, for instance, grapple with the issue of nonviolent leverage (such as the use of incentives and sanctions) within the paradigm of interdependence and respect.[16] Is it possible to exert such power effectively, in such a way as to foster constructive relationships rather than creating greater hostility and resistance? What gives laws legitimacy within the context of global interdependence, and how is the rule of law to be upheld?

We need to wrestle with the relationship between ethical judgement and the tolerance of difference, knowing that reconciliation may in practice involve living gracefully and creatively with tension and disagreement. We need to find out what is essential and non-negotiable within the reality of competing goods.[17] And while each of our countries has a remit to act for the well-being of its people, we need to explore how 'enlightened self-interest' can be related more fully to the notion of interdependence and mutuality.

If we are to build peace, we need to relinquish our reliance on bullets – 'magic' or otherwise. We must escape from the dynamic of enmity and put our faith not in commanders in chief, but in the human kindness that still manifests itself in so many day-to-day attitudes and actions and in the civility that almost all of us, regardless of culture, consider vital to our own dignity and identity. We need to extend the founding principles of our ordinary social lives, which demand at least civility, to our global, political relationships. We must identify and develop sources of power (both for parties to conflicts and for third parties) that build rather than destroy relationships, and shift the emphasis from controlling violence to building cooperation and community.

All this will require philosophy and imagination (including the emotional imagination of empathy), creativity and intelligence. 'Facts' will take us only so far. There is no map, and no certainty. The way we value different things and formulate moral priorities is not the province of 'hard knowledge'. It is, in the end, a matter of

16.   See Conciliation Resources, *Accord Policy Brief: Incentives, Sanctions and Conditionality in Peacemaking*, London: Conciliation Resources, 2008.
17.   Isaiah Berlin, 'My Intellectual Path', *New York Review of Books*, 14 May 1998, pp. 53–60.

how we understand our lives as human beings, and how we create meaning within them. It is, I believe, a spiritual matter. Eat-or-be-eaten means in effect that might is right. It is no motto for the sociable human animal, whose evolved nature is capable of altruism and finds meaning in it. It is through our capacity to cooperate with each other that we have flourished as a species. Our propensity for domination has brought misery and injustice to each other, and extinction, or the threat of it, to other species. As applied to other species and to the earth, it has brought great wealth and security to some of us, along with poverty of spirit and the ill health of over-consumption and pollution. Now it threatens our future well-being, and even our survival. It is only through cooperation that we can build a future for humanity.

5
Caught between Two Systems:
Co-option or Transformation?

In this chapter I want to relate the broad, conceptual analysis of Chapter 4 to the world of conflict-transformation practice. What are the implications for us, the questions we need to address? Can we take a collective stand on violence? Can we do more to support nonviolent action for change? What hinders us, and how can we proceed?

CONFLICT TRANSFORMATION AND REALPOLITIK

At present it is hard to imagine that ideas and processes based largely on cooperative power and a commitment to inclusive solutions could have any influence in a world where might is right, and where all must be for or against the West. One policy-related group in the UK circulated a response to the violent conflict between Georgia and Russia over South Ossetia in August 2008, calling for 'lasting resolution of the conflict based upon a mutually acceptable outcome meeting the legitimate needs of all parties involved'.[1] But the bodies it was appealing to do not operate on the principle of what would be universally recognised as the 'legitimate needs' of all, but on the basis of their own self-interest, as they see it.

As I suggested in Chapter 3, the 'basic human needs' concept used in conflict resolution is hard to apply in the world of government politicians. The needs they should be addressing are those of their state, as they understand them, but those needs will be perceived and prioritised (or not) in the light of their own personal and political needs. The 'realm of states' and the 'realm of societies', as Ropers refers to them,[2] operate according to their own very different norms and, in either case, what constitutes a legitimate 'satisfier' of a fundamental need is always difficult to agree upon. This could be

1. Confidential personal communication.
2. N. Ropers, *Peaceful Intervention: Structures, Processes and Strategies for the Constructive Regulation of Ethnopolitical Conflicts*, Berlin: Berghof Research Center for Constructive Conflict Management, 1995.

a useful line of thought, as applied to states, but in the current international climate it is in the nature of states to guard jealously the right to make those judgements for themselves.

When politicians from other countries or from international bodies wish to intervene constructively to help put an end to violent conflict, those that are most mighty are often the least acceptable as third parties, when the aim is genuine mediation. The countries involved are more likely to be effective facilitators of a settlement if they do not have a strong vested interest in the outcome, and if they desist from sabre-rattling or other forms of threat.

Those large military powers best equipped for the politics of eat-or-be-eaten are themselves at risk in the eat-or-be-eaten dynamic. Often they prove incapable of imposing their will by violence, or pay an unacceptable price for doing so. Russia's war to crush the Chechens was hugely costly, and its adventures in Afghanistan did not pay off – just as the US's attempts to impose its hegemony in Vietnam was a disaster; like those in Iraq and Afghanistan.

When those who think they can pursue their aims by military means find themselves unable to do so, they are likely to end up seeking a negotiated settlement. (Even the current occupiers of Afghanistan and Iraq have found themselves negotiating with at least some of those they have been fighting.) And after long wars of attrition the good offices of others may be sought or accepted. In such circumstances, even NGOs may find themselves involved, as well as those acting on behalf of third-party governments.

Sometimes armies seek help in developing their capacities for working together, or for minimising the violence they use in situations where they see that this would be advantageous. Is such work simply oiling the wheels of an essentially pernicious system, or does it provide an opportunity for sowing the seeds of alternative approaches?

And can 'power mediators' ever be persuaded that obtruding their own interests into the process, rather than offering good offices in a genuinely disinterested and impartial way, does not in fact bring about the stability they desire? (Results in the Middle East should convince them that it cannot.) Can they, even more ambitiously, be persuaded to accept the ethical case for setting their own particular agendas aside and working for the common good? Can those who choose to pursue their interests by war be brought to recognise that they could be more successful without it?

At present, although the militarily, economically or politically powerful apply sanctions and incentives to weaker powers, there is no means of similarly 'persuading' or controlling those who exert their power in these ways against others but see themselves as above such 'regulation'. The big powers, with their ambitions and antagonisms, are an ongoing threat to global 'peace and stability', and themselves are guilty of the lawless and destructive behaviour and violations for which they berate each other. How can they be transformed?

The only way in which they could be persuaded to submit themselves to any process of genuinely collective decision-making would be through a radical reorientation from the dominatory to the cooperative approach – conversion to the philosophy and praxis of interdependence. This might at face value seem unlikely, but it must be attempted, and the deep threats that affect them as well as others, together with the rise of new global powers, may induce them to focus more sharply on the issue.

Such change would be more likely if populations, instead of rallying behind their leaders when they have taken them into a military disaster, as the Georgians initially did with Saakashvili, were instead immediately (ideally, pre-emptively) vociferous in denouncing them. A global peace constituency needs to be built. I believe that this is, little by little, beginning to happen, and the militarist–nationalist culture is beginning to weaken; but there is a very long way to go.

The values and logic of conflict transformation are clearly at odds with those that are dominant in the world of 'realpolitik', and our little boat of conflict transformation is constantly being torpedoed by the politics and actions of military control. Yet, despite our conflict-prevention rhetoric, our overriding concern has been with helping to address immediate violence, and our efforts have gone into fire-fighting, picking up the pieces, and assisting with recovery. Moreover, while at one level it 'works' to stay away from the big issues, it also keeps us stuck in our fire-fighting role. I believe that to ignore the radical questions when we work with others is not only short-sighted and shallow, but represents a failure to deepen both our impact and our learning.

Our collective failure to challenge the system lies in our inability thus far to take a stand against war as such, and to give adequate attention to the need for nonviolent answers to structural violence: the chronic violence of oppressive and unjust regimes, or of exclusion and marginalisation.

VIOLENCE AND NONVIOLENCE

In my division between pacification and peacebuilding, I situate violent coercion firmly on the side of pacification. Most conflict-transformation NGOs would say that their role is to support nonviolent ways of addressing conflict. Yet few NGOs explicitly and unequivocally reject all violence. In relation to discussions of policy, they might argue that they do not have opportunities to open up such broad issues, but only to focus on specifics – whether those are the specifics of particular mechanisms or approaches or the specifics of a particular conflict. In the short term, maintaining a relatively narrow focus increases their chance of making some progress.

Furthermore, many practitioners are themselves unconvinced of the case against all military violence, and are therefore more comfortable concentrating on the practical task of reducing violence in particular circumstances. Within the CCTS we have sometimes touched on these issues, comprising as we do both career peacemakers and radical war resisters. Sometimes we have published articles that represent different perspectives. But more thoroughgoing discussion is needed in our field – more exploration of the overarching values and philosophies that we bring to our work. There seems to be a reluctance to take positions that would seem to put us beyond the pale of mainstream thinking and the world of political power. As one organisational director told me recently, 'We tend not to talk about ethics in our policy discussions.'

In recent years, as we have seen, there has been a growing consensus that state sovereignty should be relativised according to an international 'responsibility to protect', no longer precluding 'humanitarian intervention' when gross violations of human rights are being carried out within state borders. This has increased the debate within the conflict-transformation field.[3] Most of those involved are not pacifists, but are distressed by the violence and inhumanity they see, and want them to stop. But will the currently dominant powers and structures ever make it a priority to protect the vulnerable? In most instances of violent conflict, violent intervention from outside to stop it (as against joining the war because you have an interest in it) is not even contemplated.

Where claims are made that interventions are humanitarian and democratic in their purpose, as I argued in Chapter 4, their effects

3.   See, for example, A. Pleydell, 'Never Again: The International Responsibility to Protect' and D. Francis, 'Pacifism and the Responsibility to Protect', in *CCTS Review* 31 (June 2006), at <www.c-r.org/ccts>.

have been dire. Have good, inclusive, united and stable regimes been established in Kosovo, Afghanistan and Iraq? Quite apart from the massive violence of the invasions and occupations, the status of Kosovo remains contested and the Serb enclave continues as a fortress; Afghanistan is experiencing ongoing violence and chaos; and Iraq remains tense, divided and violent. Regardless of the reasons for these invasions, their failure to bring even negative peace suggests that not even massive military violence can be relied on to quell the violence of others.

The failure of 'peacekeeping' – in Rwanda and the DRC, for instance – illustrates the fact that, where there is no peace to keep, peacekeeping cannot work. I would argue that the current military system is designed to protect and advance the prosperity and control of the powerful, not the weak. The only thing that is sure about military intervention is that it will kill people. It not only inflicts new misery on beleaguered people, but lays the ground for new violence in the present or future.

The presence of occupying armies (even in UN uniforms) is not calculated to make women or children safe. It normalises violence and gives it a respectable face. Gandhi said, 'When [violence] appears to do good the good is only temporary – the evil it does is permanent.' The repercussions of violence continue for a very long time, and when attempts are made to lay new foundations the ground is full of the roots and seeds of hatred.

NONVIOLENT PEOPLE-POWER

There has been strong evidence in recent decades for the power of people to change a political landscape. Just as the collapse of the Soviet empire was not predicted to occur in the way it did, so in Nepal, after years of Maoist insurgency against the powers of the monarchy and its army – during which time all kinds of programmes were backed by various external governments without bringing about a cure – an unpredicted popular uprising ended the monarchy and brought about free elections (which, ironically perhaps, led to the creation of a Maoist parliamentary majority). Whether the future of Nepal will be peaceful and prosperous is not clear. The point is that people-power had a decisive impact, not as a function of someone's programme but in an unpredictable fashion, arising from local social and political dynamics.

Nonviolent resistance can also fail to achieve its goals, and at a high price, as we saw in China in the events that culminated in the deaths of student protestors in Tiananmen Square or, much more recently, in Burma, where the protests were led by Buddhist monks. In both of these cases the action of the protestors was non-violent, and in both it was met with harsh repression. (In China the demands of the students were clearly too ambitious in relation to their support, and in Burma the monks were left too exposed when the wider population was intimidated.) But the hold of tyranny in both countries is the weaker because of those protests; the liberation movements will return. There is no violent alternative that would be less costly and more likely to succeed.

The regime change that was achieved in many places by 'people-power' could not by itself bring positive peace without fundamental, long-term work for social and political change, but it could at least make way for it. As I suggested in Chapter 2, I believe we need to pay more attention to the potential of political movements in conflict transformation. This is an issue particularly for Western NGOs working for conflict transformation, for whom it may feel 'natural' to link directly with organisations that correspond most closely to themselves. But with greater will and creativity it should be possible to move beyond these effective boundaries, as some already do.

In Chapter 2 I mentioned the work that is done to protect activists in dangerous circumstances. This work is not on a scale that can answer the need for larger-scale protection. Can nonviolent forces ever play such a role? I suspect that there is no way in which human beings can be made secure from the psychopathic tendencies of individuals or ideologies or crowds gone mad, and that the only real protection is to demilitarise minds and societies. Yet, at the same time, I believe we can do far more to develop nonviolent capacities and systems for both change and protection, so that people-power could be more readily effective, more intentionally mobilised, and more grounded in the values and ethos of nonviolence.

RESISTANCE TO NONVIOLENCE

Questions of impartiality and ethical judgement

In Chapter 2 I named some possible reasons why 'mainstream' organisations for conflict transformation are reluctant to be associated with movements (as against NGOs). Supporting nonviolent action for change is seen as taking sides, and our field wishes, by and large, to avoid this. There is a valid and serious reason for nervousness in this regard. If we wish to be trusted in non-partisan roles, which in many cases are our strength, we cannot be seen to ally ourselves with any particular party or constituency.

But in some circumstances being partisan for a cause might be exactly what we should be doing. Supporting those who are resisting human rights violations, whether on a minor or a grand scale, is one way of exercising the responsibility to protect. Surely it might fall within the brief of conflict transformation? What would human rights organisations and those trying to uphold democracy have wanted of us in Robert Mugabe's Zimbabwe? If conflict transformation includes addressing systemic violence, how can those committed to it avoid supporting nonviolent assertiveness and protection?

I believe that the tendency within the conflict-transformation field, in the West at least, to make a sharp distinction between human rights work and conflict transformation needs to be rethought. Depending on our role and the stage of conflict we are seeking to address, the two may be absolutely compatible – and indeed overlapping, or interdependent. Human rights are essential to 'conflict prevention' and to 'dealing with the past' (in which ethical judgements are not only unavoidable, but implicit). It is only in one restricted phase of conflict transformation – that of conflict resolution – and within that restricted phase only for those who are acting as impartial third parties, that such judgements are problematic.

Although, when we are involved in third-party work in which our impartiality is of the essence, we may need to maintain a distance from those acting to hold one party to account, the trust in which we are held is, paradoxically, likely to be closely related to our known values, and consequently to an implicit moral position. And in some conflicts the most important role for us might be involvement in or support for action to challenge and resist the violence of a government.

Even if Western NGOs, in order to preserve their perceived impartiality and keep their own standpoint out of the equation, have good reasons to avoid direct involvement or solidarity with nonviolent action, they might find it within their field of activity to help groups with 'capacity building', in the same way that they might help prepare an armed group for negotiation. In some parts of the world there is perhaps little organised activism to support; and when there is, activists perhaps do not identify NGOs as potential supporters. Maybe they see them as part of the system. I believe we could and should make our solidarity more visible.

Of course, not all movements that avoid violence in their action have objectives that we would support. When they do not, we may or may not wish to help them build their capacity, depending on the degree of our disagreement with their goals. But it must be borne in mind that those who have a sense of grievance and know of no other way to express it are liable to turn to violence.

Questions of risk

I suspect that, despite our theory about conflict and change, we are not only reluctant to compromise our impartiality, but also (properly) wary of action to confront structural violence and bring hidden conflict into the open – afraid that it could make things worse rather than better. (Maybe we are also aware that most major donors will be unwilling to support interventions that lift the lid off conflict, rather than turning down the heat or pressing down the lid.) Is the notion of conflict transformation simply too idealised and unrealistic? Is it in fact better to 'stabilise' an unjust situation than to risk a conflagration?

There is no moral principle that will relieve us of the responsibility for making such judgements, case by case – no general answer to the question. War is so horribly cruel and destructive that to risk it is to risk a very great deal. But is there any evidence that nonviolent resistance leads to war? Keeping the lid on a very oppressive or unjust situation is unlikely to work in the long run. Until the heat is reduced by measures addressing the unmet needs that underlie such conflict, it is better to create channels for challenge that can lead to change, rather than to tighten the lid and wait for an explosion. Nonviolence training can help prepare people to mobilise effectively and to spread the values and discipline of nonviolence, so increasing the chances of success and reducing the likelihood of a violent response by giving it no pretext. (Even in demonstrations that are largely nonviolent, demonstrators often respond to police action by losing their nonviolent discipline and start throwing stones or burning cars, which only encourages repressive violence.)

Nonviolent resistance to oppressive systems certainly involves risk to those who are active in it; and the more unjust the situation, the more cruel any backlash is likely to be. We may hesitate to promote such resistance because we are unwilling to encourage others to take risks with their own lives, particularly if we will not share in those risks.

One of the principles of capacity building for nonviolent action is that it should enable people to examine a range of options and consider very carefully the likely impact and cost of any of them, to weigh the personal risk and likely consequences, and to explore the different ways of reducing the risks and mitigating the impact of counter-violence or repression. But would such careful consideration nullify our moral responsibility for any grievous consequences for action that we had, if not instigated, at least inspired?

This too is a serious question. But do we adequately weigh the likely costs of inaction? What are the risks, as well as the actual costs, associated with uneasy inertia? What is worth risking for positive peace, and who makes the calculation? Here we return to those early questions about partnership, and at this point it seems clear that, where much is to be risked for the sake of the future, it really must be those who have the greatest stake in that future and take the greatest risk who make the decisions.

However we weigh these issues, if we have any sense of global community in our commitment to transforming conflict, I believe there needs at the very least to be solidarity in thought and action. Even if we are not involved in movements for change, we should be informed about them and seek to understand their role, and its implications for our theory and practice.

When movements arise in regions where we are working, or when we hear of people who are already finding ways to resist (and there always are such people), we can meet with them and establish what help we might be able to give them (if any), or in what ways we might complement their efforts. It may be that we will be asked to pool our knowledge with theirs, exchanging perspectives, which could help their action to be strengthened and become more effective. It might also turn out that seeing what they are doing changes the way in which we go about our own work.

The world of nonviolent activism and the world of conflict transformation have been semi-detached for far too long, and many activists could benefit from, and add to, the knowledge base of nonviolence. Our field has sometimes allowed itself to be a complement to war, rather than a challenge to it, and (ironically) this is partly because it is uncomfortable with the assertive, sometimes confrontational energy and risk of nonviolent resistance. How, if at all, can that energy be made more safe and conciliatory, and how can we learn to take risks responsibly? For we must do so if conflict transformation is ever to be recognised as *the* answer to conflict, and not as an adjunct to war, and if peacebuilding is no longer to be confused with pacification.

ETHICS AND CULTURE

While NGOs may encourage others to explore nonviolent options, they rightly do not wish to be seen as assuming any kind of moral superiority, and thereby risk alienating those with whom they work. Those who have been caught up in violence may have no principled opposition to it. They may want to address it because of the particular circumstances in which it has been used, or because of its impact; or they may want to try something else because it has not produced the desired results. It would ill behove anyone who was not in that position to produce glib moral certainties.

Yet it is my experience that making one's own moral philosophy and ethics known to those one works with need not be felt by them as judgement. On the contrary, being open about these things can make one vulnerable and thereby deepen trust, taking discussion to a deeper level that transcends the dynamics of a specific conflict. Of course, we cannot always be holding such wide and deep discussions. Responding to the particular, urgent needs of an existing situation must at times be a priority. At the same time, I have noticed repeatedly that facing up to the ethical implications of the human costs of war can play a role in motivating groups that have been engaged in violence to try and bring it to an end. Ethics are also central to the messages that peace constituencies convey to their leaders, and they lie behind those notions of human needs and inclusive solutions that are at the heart of conflict resolution and conflict transformation.

When I began my international work, there was much discussion of 'culture' as a cause for wariness, particularly among Western NGOs. It was correctly pointed out that it was impossible to discuss conflict in a way that was independent of cultural norms. This was an important and interesting debate, but what emerged from it for me was the insight that, although there can indeed be cultural differences in the way people think about conflict, in how behaviour is likely to be interpreted, and in the weight given to particular issues, in most cases these differences need not constitute too great an obstacle to communication and cooperation, if due care and sensitivity are applied.[4]

4. This view is seen as over-optimistic in, for instance, N. Rouhana, 'Unofficial Third-Party Intervention in International Conflict: Between Legitimacy and Disarray', *Negotiation Journal*, July 1995.

I have discussed these issues in some detail elsewhere,[5] and much else has been written on the subject. My argument is that it is power disparities that make culture such an explosive issue: the implication that Western norms are *the* norm, and that Westerners are the experts. This turns gaps in knowledge and mistaken assumptions into emotional dynamite. The good news is that the 'experts' are all around the world, and that the tectonic plates of global power are shifting. What is needed now is a cooperative understanding of power that renders the old asymmetry meaningless.

Humble and sensitive partners, educators and facilitators, whoever they are, will know that they have much to learn from those they work with, and will not assume that things work everywhere as they do 'at home', wherever home is. If they ask questions rather than giving answers, that will remove much of the danger (though one does need to know what questions to ask – and questions, too, reflect assumptions). Those who offer their services as facilitators or mediators need to listen carefully to local colleagues for guidance about norms and perceptions; but openness about themselves will, in the context of assumed equality and expressed with sensitivity, help to build mutual understanding rather than obstruct it.

Culture plays a vital role in conflict. The challenge for all those who work to transform it is to tap into those aspects of a particular culture that tend towards respect, compassion and cooperation, and to re-examine those areas that encourage cruelty and glorify violence. This task is one for all cultures. We can perhaps help each other to identify truly humane values that can be our touchstone. The global transformation that is needed must overturn the 'normality' of war and break the association between militarism and masculinity. It must privilege kindness and cooperation above all else.

Some of us need to ask ourselves whether we only export conflict transformation, or whether we work for it at home. Maybe we, too, live in a place where nonviolent action is needed to challenge a violent status quo. For those of us who live in places where violent conflict is a present reality, this is unlikely to be a question at all: they are likely to be involved in action that is costly and important. But for those of us who work for the many international NGOs that are dotted around the West, who see around us largely peaceful streets and whose daily lives are relatively secure, the challenge may be to confront the violence that our governments export, as well as the hidden violence at home.

5. For example, in Francis, *People, Peace and Power*, pp. 59–82.

If we are fully committed to supporting people in other countries who are facing daily danger and hardship, we may find such work for change at home either of less immediate importance or very difficult to combine with our full-time work. If, however, we are able to engage in the life of an active citizen directly, where we live, this experience will be felt as real solidarity with colleagues elsewhere. It will also give us first-hand experience of an aspect of conflict transformation that we may have known little about, so equipping us with vital additional knowledge to bring to our work – and greater authenticity as partners.

It may be that we are held back from wholehearted engagement with nonviolence by our own ambivalence. Both the ethical and practical issues related to it call for open reflection and debate among us. We cannot yet present a united front to policy-makers, but we can instead include them in the discussion. Avoiding these fundamental issues leaves the big picture and the big policy levers untouched.

SIGNS THAT THE SYSTEM CAN CHANGE

The work for conflict transformation that has been done to date, both in promulgating its thinking and in putting it into practice, has helped many people to build their sense of interdependence and their power for cooperative action. These activities and the changes they have produced are small in comparison with the many facets of 'the system', and the multitudes of oppressed and disempowered people. But I believe that the seeds sown and the precedents created by transformative action around the world have greatly multiplied the capacity we have for wider transformation. We now need to raise our eyes to that wider horizon.

If our small contributions were the whole story, there is no doubt that they would still be worth continuing, but there would also be grounds for discouragement. However, according to the Freirian doctrine that undergirds all training for conflict transformation,[6] there is already present in any society implicit knowledge of how people can deal with each other on the basis of interdependence, because most of us do it in our daily lives, in whatever societies and systems we live and work in, despite any tendencies we may have towards controlling or dominatory ways of thinking and behaving.

Moreover, the cost and futility of violent power struggles have borne down on so many societies, with such force, that for many

6.   P. Freire, *Pedagogy of the Oppressed*, London: Penguin, 1972.

the myth of violence's power for good has already been shattered. The information revolution makes the reality ever harder to avoid. In the West there is a growing movement against war, which is increasingly seen as inhumane, uncivilised and counterproductive – and it is linked to the growing awareness of the urgent need to address global poverty and exploitation, and to curb the greed and heedlessness that lead to the plundering and spoiling of our planet. There is a yearning among many for a more principled and caring way of living.

Alongside this awakening of moral understanding and concern, examples of citizens' refusal to submit to tyranny are growing in number. In some cases the resistance seems short-lived, but in others it leads to surprising – and surprisingly swift – change. It demonstrates the capacity of unarmed human beings for courage, and flags up the possibility of collective impact. Even where resistance appears to have been crushed, it signals the transience of even the most oppressive power and heralds change to come. Thanks to modern technology, it will become known around the globe and contribute to the transformation of global assumptions and the growth of a global counterculture.

Civil courage of this kind can be an inspiration to those who want to oppose war (a particularly virulent form of tyranny) and build support for peace. It affirms those of us who believe that peace processes should, by definition, include popular participation. Those involved in popular movements for change might in turn be strengthened by insights and skills from within the repertoire of conflict transformation.

There is a global women's movement that refuses to see strength and autonomy as male prerogatives, and that brings a different energy into the world of civil action for change, whether that is focused on the human rights of liberty and participation, on economic justice, on environmental protection, or on ending the wars that threaten all of these. This all-too-slow but still considerable and exciting shift brings new energy, perspectives and possibilities.

As a field of practitioners, we should be ready for our own transformation – open to new ways of seeing things, and to developing a more thoroughgoing conceptualisation of the relationship between gender and peace. The difficulties we face in achieving women's participation in political processes, and the wider challenge of operating effectively within current realities while working to change them, will not go away in a hurry. And women are not the only ones who are marginalised by current models and systems of power. We need a deeper understanding of this dilemma and more informed strategies for addressing it. We also need to strengthen our theory and practice in relation to participation. At the same time, we can be inspired by the pioneering work that has already been done.

Working at this interface between power politics and conflict transformation is the most difficult and necessary thing we can do. We must somehow bring them into one frame, building a rounded understanding of what peace requires.

When crises happen, there is room only for mitigation of disaster. We can focus on conflict management and list the things that need to be done to try to bring the carnage to an end. We can even try to insist that the underlying relationships should be addressed once the violence has stopped. But unless we get to those deeper questions, we will be falling far short of our responsibility to contribute in the wider political world.

If we are to be true peacebuilders, we must face up to a challenge from which we cannot escape: the need to discover or create the means of upholding those things that are agreed by societies at every level to be for the common good, whether agreements take the form of recognised custom, legislation, or treaty. This is the point at which peacebuilding meets pacification, and cooperation meets control. If the cruel and lawless destructiveness of war is to be overcome, we need to put immense effort into developing our own concepts and strategies of power – including, on occasion, non-lethal enforcement. We also need to devise and 'sell' the cooperative and ethical concepts and systems necessary for deciding what needs to be enforced, and by whom. All this will mean changing both minds and hearts (our own included).

DIALOGUE WITH DONORS

The practical work that now being done to transform conflict, despite its limitations, is good and necessary. It is also the source of our experiential knowledge of what is possible and transformative – our evidence that relationships based on interdependence are fruitful for human flourishing. And it is through such practical action that we begin to change the conflict culture, and thereby to address the big picture.

However, given the current policy focus in international relations, which is largely on 'security', how are we to find support for the kind of transformative peacebuilding that we want to do, both 'on the ground' and in terms of demilitarising the minds of policy-makers?

How can we avoid co-option through financial dependency; being seduced into second-best work because that is where the money is; becoming morally and politically compromised by associating with war efforts; being told who we can and cannot work with; being stifled by overwhelming, top-down managerialism and commodification and the demand for quick and provable impact?

A colleague of mine was recently present in a meeting organised by a consortium seeking to influence government policy, which involved both NGOs and civil servants. He challenged a claim that the government in question was a 'real market leader in security sector reform', referring to its track record in Palestine as evidence of this. He observed that the view from Gaza would be quite the opposite. He received no support whatsoever from the floor at the time, though a number of people thanked him afterwards for what he had said. As he noted, he – a freelance consultant – was probably the only person there who was completely independent, as civil servants had to look after their jobs and NGOs were mindful of their grant-dependency.

Those who have had the good fortune to be funded by grant-making trusts that share their values and orientation will have experienced something very different, especially when those trusts have accumulated real expertise of their own: a real partnership, with personal contact, continuity, open communication, give and take, participatory evaluation, and mutual influence.[7] Although such donors do not have so much money at their disposal, what they have is likely to be far better spent, precisely because they work so effectively with their grantees. Is it possible that the big governmental donors could work in similar ways? Is it foolish to imagine that NGOs could develop cooperative relationships with them?

We too are interdependent. Donors need us as we need them. Or do they? Might the big ones decide that if we will not angle our work towards their agenda, they will find other organisations that will? I would suggest that a dialogue needs to be instigated with government departments and civil servants, to explore the current relationship between them and their grantees, and the impact of their current policy. For the importance of that dialogue to be recognised, there would need to be solidarity between funding recipients, actual

7. For an excellent discussion on donor–grantee relations, see J. Prager, 'The Funder's Perspective', and B. Walker, 'A Grant-Seeker's Perspective', in *Funding Conflict Transformation: Money, Power and Accountability*, CCTS Review 25 (November 2006).

and potential, for mutual protection and to maximise their voice and leverage.

At the same time, it is important to recognise that there are many within government circles who will share some, if not all, of our thinking, and who are already 'on our side'. The system may be quite largely inimical to our ideas and ways of working, but it is still operated by people. Interestingly, it seems, for instance, that despite the current emphasis on formal evaluations, decisions about grants and their continuation are often based more on intuitive judgements and personal assessment,[8] which suggests – among other things – a degree of personal engagement. Perhaps these civil servants realise that short-term evaluations cannot be a good guide to the likely benefits of long-term and necessarily uncertain undertakings, and draw instead on their own knowledge and judgement (including intuition).

Unfortunately, rapid staff turnover in government departments makes it difficult for those working in them to develop relevant expertise and relationships. This must be frustrating for them, as well as for others. Can we create circles of confidentiality and trust, as we do in other dialogues, in which such problems can be shared and real learning and change can take place?

The current donor–client relationship does in practice include some honest exchange, with civil servants (and through them their governments) drawing on the expertise of those whose work they fund, simply because they respect and need it. But they work within an ideology and a political framework that puts the kind of wider analysis that I have been discussing beyond the pale. No doubt those who have access to them are able to be frank, sometimes, about the impact of particular government actions or pronouncements in relation to specific situations and events. I trust so. But do they ever find themselves in a position to question the underlying values, assumptions and relationships that inform the policies on which those actions and statements are based? And if not, are they in effect colluding with them?

Do we also collude with false assumptions about results when we comply with requests to claim likely impacts for our work, despite being aware that it is impossible to know what its outcome will be? Is it not time to insist that, while we can and should explain our rationale for proposing a certain line of action, relating it to theory that has grown out of experience (ours and others'), and while

8.   See Prager, 'The Funder's Perspective', p. 5.

we can assess the quality of our work and its immediate effect, its more distant and (from the donor's point of view) more important repercussions will probably never be known, though they may be surmised. This would help us to work honestly together, and to learn what can really be learned about what works, through observation, both closely and broadly focused, and the insights that sometimes come unlooked for, if we are alert, through some chance piece of evidence. Such an approach would facilitate true accountability.

Whatever the difficulties, we have a responsibility both to retain our independence and to locate funds. We should also, in the name of democracy, be in favour of governments that develop policies and seek to implement them. If we do not like those policies, we should seek to change them. At the same time, we can seek to develop sources of funding that involve the direct participation of ordinary people, and help to create and express solidarity (as one or two NGOs have already done). This may be the best way of funding support for movements.

All that said, the challenge of presenting a coherent and clearly argued case for programme funding is a good catalyst for checking assumptions and reviewing the rationale for work that is already underway or being contemplated. Without donors, the work of 'professional' NGOs would not be possible. If donors and their beneficiaries share the same goals, they will have a shared interest in planning and evaluation systems that maximise efficacy. I will return to this issue towards the end of the next chapter.

6
Building the Praxis of Nonviolence

In this chapter I will focus on those aspects of conflict transformation that are usually described as 'nonviolent action': standing up for what is right and opposing violence, whether endemic or acute, structural or direct. The assumption tends to be that, when violence of any kind is acute, there is little that can be done by nonviolent means to address it and to begin to transform the conflict. But if conflict transformation is to offer a way forward in situations that are most in need of it, it has to do better than that. It has to be able to find and to widen the space in which constructive action is possible, in order to address human needs and stand up for human rights.

I begin this chapter by summarising the case for building the theory and practice of nonviolent people-power in conflict transformation, and by setting out the forms of social and political violence that it needs to address. Then I review a range of situations in which citizens can act nonviolently, the dilemmas associated with such action, and the role of NGOs and governments in supporting it and helping to bring about nonviolent change. Finally, I discuss the building of capacity for nonviolence, including the roles of analysis, strategy and evaluation, and what lies beyond logic.

PEOPLE-POWER IN CONFLICT TRANSFORMATION

In sociopolitical conflicts, conflict transformation is about the transformative power of non-military processes to address latent conflict and, in militarised situations, to transfer influence from military to civil actors. I believe therefore that we need to give our concerted attention to the sources and capacities of nonviolent power to resist and displace violent power and to transform the systems and culture, the people and behaviour, that use and sustain it.

It is recognised in conflict transformation that it is important that 'the people' – in particular those who have had no part in the violence – should be able to have a voice in peace processes once they are underway, and in some cases they have managed to have some input.[1] Sometimes, moreover, a 'peace constituency' – a vocal part of the populace, representing many more and bringing pressure to bear on their leaders – can exert considerable influence in persuading the military and the politicians that a negotiated settlement is needed, thus helping to set a peace process in train.

How can citizens assert their rights more widely in the face of violence, whether it is the violence of oppressive systems, of war, or of invasion? How can governments fulfil their duties without resort to violence – particularly the mass, indiscriminate violence of war? What are the transformative processes through which these things can be achieved? At what levels can they be undertaken, and by which actors? How can we, in our field, act, within the spaces currently available to us, in such a way that we open up those possibilities, rather than confirming the status quo and perpetuating the power of violence, whose only power is, by definition, to harm and destroy (the power of blackmail)?

If power is the ability to create something, to make something happen or to influence or change something or someone, this may be achieved in many different ways and through many different kinds of relationship. Military power, as expressed in military systems, capacities and action, is widely seen as supreme in coerciveness. But military power cannot compel people to do things. If it 'succeeds', it either prevents them from doing something by killing, injuring or otherwise immobilising them, or it persuades them to do things (or not to do them) by threatening them with injury or death.

It can never make people do what they are determined not to do. Certainly it cannot force them to think differently or effect any positive, essential change in them. It cannot therefore be seen as transformative, in any positive way, of the actors in a conflict. As often as not, it fails also in its power to crush the violence of others. But the power of militarist culture is to make military power seem effective and acceptable, and thereby to promote the building and strengthening of military systems and the habitual recourse to military action.

As I have argued, militarism is the enemy of democracy, being its antithesis, making violence, not the people's will, the ultimate arbiter and guarantor in public affairs. By the same token, the strengthening of democracy through wider and more active participation in public affairs, in whatever social context, will be needed to displace

1.   C. Barnes (ed.), *Owning the Process: Public Participation in Peacemaking* (Accord 13), London: Conciliation Resources, 2002.

military power. While in any society there are courageous people acting for change, in most they are a small minority. This needs to change. But although in wealthy countries the problem may stem from the apathy that can result from comfort, or a general mistrust of politicians (important issues in themselves), in others the overwhelming obstacle to participation is tyranny of one sort or another, exerted through violence.

There is a strong existing literature on nonviolence, civil resistance and civilian-based defence.[2] What I am calling for is a concerted effort in the field of conflict transformation and peacebuilding to incorporate this thinking and to change and develop it in the process. Violence is the problem we want to address, directly, structurally and culturally. Most particularly, we want to displace the use of violence as a means of addressing conflict.

I suggest that we could do this in a more concerted, determined way, deconstructing the notion that there have always been wars (which there have not),[3] and therefore always will be, and looking instead at all the other ways in which human beings can and do deal with each other, and at the values, institutions and customs which already exist and can be developed, or can be devised to displace the uncivilised institution of war. This, surely, must be part of our task, even as we struggle to help remedy the effects of the current dispensation.

As we have seen, peacebuilding – whether preventing war by addressing structural violence, or moving on from war – is not given the resources that war soaks up. In Afghanistan, for instance, at the time of writing, the UK aid budget is less than 10 per cent of military spending. This is typical of a global pattern in which aid and development money is dwarfed by the resources given to the military. If we took 'conflict prevention' as seriously in practice as we do in theory, the ratio would be reversed.

This under-resourcing affects our sense of what it is possible to achieve through non-military means, and this limitation of our vision is expressed in our theory and discourse. If we take seriously the prevention of war of all kinds, we must resist being drawn into focusing most of our peacebuilding attention on international

2. A useful overview is provided by M. Kurlansky, *Nonviolence: The History of a Dangerous Idea*, London: Vintage Books, 2006.
3. See J. Keegan, *A History of Warfare*, London: Pimlico, 1994; R. Kelly, *Warless Societies and the Origin of War*, Michigan: University of Michigan Press, 2000; E. Boulding, *Cultures of Peace: The Hidden Side of History*, New York: Syracuse University Press, 2000; and Francis, *Rethinking War and Peace*.

policy and post-war processes, and develop the theory and practice of nonviolent assertiveness at every level and in every context. We must also see how demilitarisation (global as well as local) can be treated as part of war *prevention*, rather than being regarded as a post-war activity.

FORMS OF VIOLENCE

There are many different forms of violence that take place within the overall system of violence, all presenting severe challenges to those who would transform conflict nonviolently. I will discuss some of them, briefly, here.

Invasion and occupation

Military violence has been used to invade and occupy other countries. It is taken for granted by all but a few that military invasion (of one's own country, that is) should be met by counter-violence or 'military defence'. Instant capitulation is regarded as shameful, though where there is an overwhelming power disparity there may in practice be very little resistance.

In any case, if the invading side succeeds in overwhelming initial resistance, occupation will follow. This will be an infringement of the rights and liberties of the local population, and is likely to be accompanied by harsh or restrictive treatment. Counter-violence or insurgency will draw further violence, and all too often the civilian population will suffer at the hands of occupiers and resisters alike. The ongoing conflict will be costly to all involved. It cannot deliver victory to both sides. A negotiated settlement years down the line, when all have suffered and lost, is usually the best outcome that can be hoped for. In the meantime, again all too often, those who resist occupation violently will have split into factions, bringing yet more violence to a suffering people.

Internal warfare and intercommunal violence

Civil wars are fought between governments and separatist or revolutionary movements. Sometimes independence movements split into factions that fight each other, like those that fight against occupation. Allegiances in such violent conflicts are often shaped by matters of identity, related to tribe or ethnicity, religion or politics, or a mixture of all of these; but they often relate also to a sense of marginalisation, oppression or exclusion, or to the ambition (financial or political) of leaders. Again, civilian populations are severely affected. In some circumstances, the breakdown of political processes is so profound that the situation becomes one of violent chaos. Such situations can last for decades, causing unimaginable human misery.

There are also briefer, more localised episodes of intercommunal violence, usually focused on identity but often taking place in situations where there is a high level of dislocation or deprivation and so, in part at least, resulting from wider structural violence. So it was in Northern Ireland, where the violence between Republicans and Unionists took place largely in poor areas, while the lives of the middle classes were, on the whole, not so directly affected. So it is with the other 'identity' conflicts that erupt around the world – whether in Kenya, where the catalyst for the violence of 2008 was a contested election result; or in the Indian state of Orissa, where poverty and a shortage of land have created tense competition for resources, or, at different times; in British cities, where shortages of work and housing spark trouble between established populations.

Typically, when violence erupts it is quenched, or more often suppressed for a time, by state coercion, often involving violence. Is there an alternative to violent action by police or soldiers? Can unarmed citizens act to protect the vulnerable, cool the heat, and restore people to their right minds, in order to create a space in which to address the underlying perceptions and problems? Civil society groups played a vital role in stemming the violence referred to above in Kenya and in Orissa, working to address the problems before and after the violence of 2008. The tragedy is that, very often, the work that could have prevented such outbreaks of violence is neither recognised nor supported.

Structural violence

Gender violence is one form of structural violence that is globally endemic. Violence against females of all ages by men is 'normal' in many societies, and gets worse during and after war. Furthermore, when women are beginning to organise and make their voices heard, violent conflict often destroys the fruits of their endeavours, wiping out the results of decades of struggle. Often, too, extremist groups within a society respond with violence to women's advocacy, and in the home the price women pay for speaking out can be high.

Violence against others who are not part of the 'prime male' group is also endemic in many societies. Children are often abused on a regular basis, along with others who are considered weak or are in some way dependent. In parallel with this kind of violence against physically vulnerable groups comes violence organised around race, caste, sexual orientation, religion, and so on.

Structural or systemic violence can take many different forms. It is directed against particular sectors of society by 'the system', whether simply as a matter of fact or also by law, and consists (to use Galtung's words) of 'avoidable insults to basic human needs'.[4] These include direct, bodily attacks, along with deprivation, exclusion, and tyranny of different kinds. Systemic violence, I would argue, should be seen to include the ongoing wars that are sometimes waged for decades, inflicting great harm on populations, which suffer extreme deprivation and misery as a consequence.

Those who suffer can seek redress from those in power, but since those in power have their own reasons for what they do, unless they undergo a change of heart, or see that there might be a price to pay for maintaining the status quo, or that they themselves might have something to gain from change, they will not alter their policy or behaviour.

If this is the case, those who suffer can mobilise for violence against their oppressors, leaping straight into armed conflict and joining violence to violence. But since physical violence is the means of perpetuating structural violence by enforcing subservience, any action (even nonviolent) to expose and resist it 'invites' physical assault of one kind or another. So the violent resistance or 'insurgency' will be met with a military response from the state. Both sides will not only mete out violence, but risk violence of all kinds against themselves. Their response to this risk will be to try to minimise the degree of violence to which they are exposed, and to make their own violence as painful and costly as possible to the other side.

It is impossible to predict who will gain the upper hand. Deaths in horrifying numbers will be accepted on both sides, often without the cost-effectiveness of their own violence being called into question. The violence may continue for decades, with no clear winner, causing countless deaths and much suffering, and the seeds of violence are endlessly re-sown. Yet, such is the power of the myth of violence's efficacy that somehow this abysmal track record fails to deter those who choose violence, and the 'risk' of death is taken for granted. But in wars between governments and insurgents, as in other kinds of war, unarmed civilians are also exposed to this risk, without any choice in the matter.

4.   J. Galtung, 'Cultural Violence', *Journal of Peace Research* 27: 3 (1990), p. 292.

NONVIOLENCE

From military to civil action

By definition, violence is harmful. It hurts, damages, violates and kills. I have already argued its futility. But once it is in train it is hard to break its cycle, to refuse to pay it homage and escape from its dynamic.

Escaping from the misery of violent conflict through negotiation without in some way rewarding violence is, as we have seen, difficult, if not impossible. In processes where two or more hitherto violent parties negotiate an end to their violence, they make concessions (or refuse to do so) on the basis of the relative strength of their remaining power to harm each other – often because they have reached a 'mutually hurting stalemate' and are powerless to achieve their ends through violence. When high-minded go-betweens work with them to prepare or facilitate negotiations, or if they have themselves 'seen the light', they may manage to focus on reaching an agreement that caters, as far as possible, for the needs of all. But it will still be the perpetrators of the violence who are deciding the future (unless terms are in practice imposed by a third party more powerful than either of them).

It is highly desirable that a settlement be agreed by local actors – but in the last analysis the power to end a war is in the hands of those who have been fighting it, or those under whose orders they have done so. Assisting armed groups to negotiate peace is therefore important. But this leaves civilians (who are often caught in the crossfire or who become 'collateral damage') dependent on the fortunes, whims and 'needs' of the different military actors. Their own needs for autonomy and participation in the things that most affect them are disregarded.

In theory, at least, soldiers can refuse orders, lay down their arms, and go home. They are war's victims as well as its perpetrators, and many would leave if they could. In practice it is likely to be very difficult for them to do so. Their participation may have resulted from kidnap or some other form of coercion. Helping people to resist conscription is important work, and deserves far greater attention.[5] But what about those who have not been involved in the fighting – only afflicted by it?

5. Here we should honour the work of War Resisters International: <www.wri-irg. org>.

Civilian defence against invasion and occupation, about which much has been written, is based on the notion of non-cooperation. Since an invading force will be incapable of running the country that has been invaded unless its citizens report for work as usual and hand over vital information, careful preparation for such a scenario and wide commitment to collective non-cooperation would render that country so inhospitable and unmanageable that controlling it would be impossible. Such preparation should do as well as any weapons system to deter potential invaders, or encourage them to find a way of leaving.[6] To be effective, however, such non-cooperation needs to be widespread and determined, and commitment to it needs to be voluntary if the spirit of unity and nonviolence is to be maintained.

In civil war or intercommunal violence, non-participation in that violence is the first step of resistance. Civilians can play the role of whistle-blowers and bridge-builders, acting both as a peace constituency and as peace-brokers (as they did in Kenya and Orissa). They can offer each other, and others, protection from violence by opening their homes to those at risk, keeping watch over each other, and having systems in place for rapid communication. They can witness to their belief in nonviolence, humanity and human rights both spontaneously in a given moment, and in coordinated ways, with others, acting as catalysts to change the mood of the crowd or the public at large. They can build external support for peace, whether through public statements, diplomacy, or practical aid (given carefully in order to avoid harm and help rebuild relationships). They can also create intercommunal committees and other such venues for constructive political exchange. (These things are part of a 'regular' conflict-transformation menu.)

Women will be involved in all these activities. In addition, they can and do campaign tirelessly for the right to be regarded as equal human beings, with all that this entails. They can offer each other the protection of solidarity and seek it from outside, so that when they speak out they do so in the spotlight of international attention. Vitally, women are sometimes able to offer protection to those under attack by acting as human shields – for instance, encircling homes or encampments (as was done by Naga women in Manipur at the beginning of 2009). Paradoxically, their traditional place in society may make public violence against them less likely than against

6. See, for example, G. Sharp with B. Jenkins, *Civilian-Based Defence: A Post-Military Weapons System*, Princeton: Princeton University Press, 1990.

men when they make themselves vulnerable in this way. (More generally, it is one of the insights of nonviolence that, although it exposes a person to harm, vulnerability can also be both touching and disarming at a human level.)

Reluctance related to nonviolence and risk

The idea of nonviolent defence against invasion is almost entirely ignored, even within the field of conflict transformation – which, for historical reasons, has focused largely on 'internal conflicts'. If we are to apply conflict transformation at the global level, this will need to change. Since militarism in national defence is so embedded in the public consciousness, beginning to take non-military options seriously will be a huge step.

Within current conflict-transformation theory and practice, as outlined in Chapter 2, bridge-building and conflict-resolution processes are seen as vital, and the role of peace constituencies to support them is also fully accepted. The areas of nonviolent activity that are relatively neglected are those focused on the needs and rights of a particular group, or of those who are challenging the policies and actions of governments. As we have seen, to support such action is to step outside organisational impartiality or, in the case of governments, beyond current diplomatic policy. Moreover the actions themselves are liable to incur violent reprisals, and this risk may be seen as unacceptable.

So, although there is widespread recognition of the need to address the latent conflict of injustice, deprivation and so on (and, in theory at least, governments may sometimes act on 'early warnings' in such cases), the idea that populations themselves should mobilise to act on their own behalf is really not widely or fully accepted. With the types of bridge-building and peace-constituency activity that take place when war is in progress, risk is already reality, yet the action (albeit non-violent, and indeed often risky) is seen as tending towards risk-reduction. In the case of 'latent conflict' or 'structural violence', it is perceived to increase risk, both of violence against the activists and of a more general escalation of the conflict.

These qualms are not readily dismissed. Who decides what is, in fact, unjust enough to be described as structural violence, and to warrant the dangerous business of disturbing the status quo, risking one's own life and disrupting the lives of others? One person's sense of oppression may be seen by another as an ill-founded notion of grievance, whipped up by demagogues for their own purposes. Is the probable cost of the proposed action, to all concerned, likely to be justified by the good that it might achieve?

When the assessment of any harm that is risked is careless or avoidably inadequate, the action cannot be regarded as fully nonviolent. Still, it is highly unlikely to have the catastrophic and far-reaching impact of war or terrorism, and inaction carries its own risks, and often known costs. I would argue that it is the responsibility of all members of a society to make moral judgements about systems, attitudes and actions within that society, standing up for what is right and exposing and rejecting cruelty and injustice. The ethos of nonviolence requires that this should be done with care and respect, without an assumption of personal or collective moral superiority. Without such an assumption of social and political responsibility, however, it is impossible for positive peace to be built and maintained.

Given that, as we have seen, culture cannot fail to be part of the picture, and that some things are accepted by the mainstream in some cultures that in others would be abhorrent to most, how can cultural bias be avoided? We cannot escape the need for a frame of reference, and mine here is that of conflict transformation and its fundamental values, which I have named as respect, compassion and inclusiveness. I believe that these are the values that our interdependent humanity requires.

It is always possible that our 'right' may not be right. However self-challenging we may be, there will be things that we fail to see, or that we see in ways that others would not recognise. That is an additional reason why it is so important to find non-lethal ways of fighting for causes and choose methods of struggle that are as respectful and compassionate as we can make them.

Civil courage

There is no chance of avoiding risk in dealing with violence, whether violently or nonviolently. The principle of not doing harm, can be applied to one's own behaviour, but cannot prevent harm being done by others. This takes us back to the ethics of risk-taking. I use the word 'us' deliberately. We cannot countenance for others what we would be unwilling to do ourselves. Mercifully, though, many others have been there before us. People living in dangerous places do develop levels of courage that are hard for the more protected among us to imagine. They do not, in my experience, take risk lightly. They want to live. They hate pain. They feel fear. But they are drawn on by something stronger: by their passion for justice, their love of people or their sheer refusal to submit to tyranny. They are driven by the power of their will to make a difference, to effect change. They persist in spite in spite of the risks and hardships they face, and precisely because of the violence of the situation.

What people in such situations need to do, and in many situations have done to the best of their ability, is to accept that they are vulnerable, but also do their best to minimise the risk that goes with their insistent assertiveness; to form support groups and networks, building trust and solidarity; to begin with small actions, to learn what works and find their balance; gradually and carefully to develop networks of trust through which to spread information; to use these networks to enable quick, surprise actions that convey a clear message and end before the authorities can attack, and to establish safe contacts in the media who will protect their identity.

Ideally they will be inventive about how and where to meet – doing so, for instance, in private homes, or in very small groups in churches or mosques. They will be constantly but carefully recruiting, taking care to integrate newcomers. They will take seriously the need for personal and group preparation, sharing fears and weighing risks, strategising, role-playing, practising quick decision-making, learning how to calm themselves and others, how to reach out to the humanity of the other. They will debrief after any action to process what they have been through, both rationally and emotionally, and to learn for the future. They will take time to celebrate values, hopes, solidarity, courage and achievements; they will grab every chance they can to laugh. They will support each other practically and promise care for the family members of anyone arrested or killed.

Over many decades, Latin America developed a powerful praxis of nonviolence, having witnessed the best of civil courage in response to the worst of violence – whether the violence of economic deprivation, or the armed violence of the state against its citizens and the counter-violence of armed groups. They learned to combine conviction and hope with imagination and logic, courage and persistence. Women were at the forefront of this resistance, speaking out against torture and disappearances and for truth and human rights, in the face of the most extreme threats. Many were killed, but others took their place. This is a very different model of heroism from that of the warrior hero, but one that should be even more inspiring. I believe that in our search for meaning we need this level of courage and altruism to aspire to, even if most of us feel it is beyond our reach. But courage need not be expressed through violence.

Although the risk of death, the possibility of 'laying down one's life', is taken for granted in warfare of any kind, when the question of risk is applied to nonviolent resistance, the response is very different. For instance, the South African Sharpeville massacre, in which 69 unarmed protestors against apartheid were shot dead and 180 injured, was seen as a valid and indeed necessary reason for nonviolence to be abandoned in favour of armed struggle. Yet there was an initial and massive nonviolent response, and in the end it was the popular uprisings by civilians that rendered the system unsustainable.[7]

The usual response to the certainty of violent assaults of all kinds in violent conflict is to prepare for them. Soldiers are trained to be 'unnaturally' courageous (as well as brutal), to overcome the natural fear of deadly violence. That natural fear is such that two soldiers with guns would be able, in most circumstances, to control a crowd that could easily overwhelm them if even a few of its members overcame their fear of being shot and took the risk of moving to disarm them. And although there are plenty of cases in which soldiers have indeed fired on unarmed civilians, there are also some striking examples of their refusing to do so, and sometimes joining them. Their humanity and sense of commonality, often directly appealed to by protestors, have overcome their desire to obey orders or their fear of the consequences of disobedience.

What would have happened in Burma if, even after the deadly action against the monks, more people had kept pouring onto the streets? I believe that eventually the people would have prevailed, and that the regime would have been changed. (Needless to say, if I had been a Burmese citizen I too would probably have stayed at home, overwhelmed by fear, defeated, and amazed at the no-longer-imaginable courage of past days.) That such a regime was shaken was in itself a vast achievement, and civil society has since grown in strength. Recent history – of the Soviet collapse and of regime change in the Philippines, Nepal and Bangladesh – has shown

7.   Even the role of economic sanctions has been brought into question. Recent analysis suggests that they were not as effective as those who imposed them like to think, and that in fact, in terms of external pressures for change, it was wider geopolitical shifts that contributed more decisively to the waning of the National Party. Inside the country it was the ANC's ability to make the country ungovernable through a variety of forms of non-cooperation that was decisive. See Conciliation Resources, *Accord Policy Brief*.

just how great the power of unarmed people can be. How much greater, how much more principled and disciplined, could it become if its potential were to be more widely recognised and included in capacity building?

Does this mean that we should be putting at least some of our efforts into training ourselves and other civilians for physical heroism, in the way that Gandhi did? I believe it does, though if we live outside the place in question we should do so only if invited. (Local trainers will always be the most appropriate for such work, though training outside the country may be helpful in some instances.) Given that we currently live in a world in which violent assault is sanctioned both culturally and politically, if we want to make the shift to nonviolent ways of addressing violence and dealing with conflict, the role of action requiring extreme civil courage is a necessary one. If most people find military training and lethal action and exposure normal, why should training for civilians to face violence seem so outlandish? Furthermore, the reality is that most people caught up in violence have no adequate violent power to get the better of those who use violence against them, so that this is the only kind of preparation that is realistic for them.

In places where repression was severe, it would be very difficult to arrange such training – certainly of the scale and intensity that would seem to be required. Yet there have been cases where a courageous few have prepared themselves, through their own practice of resourcefulness and acts of personal courage and resilience, to act as catalysts for mass action, designing it in such a way as to minimise the risk to those who participated and at the same time to maximise its impact.

There can be no doubting the power of violence to do terrible things to people, but it is not the only kind of power. The power of refusal, of non-cooperation, is immense. It is what robs violence of its power to do other than destroy. It can make governance, even tyranny, impossible. It can close down an administration and an economy. If soldiers disobey orders they can remove the destructive power that is a state's tool of control. What is needed is the knowledge, strategic coherence and preparation that can make sporadic resistance so strong that it can provide the basis for peace.[8]

8. V. Dudouet, 'Nonviolent Resistance and Conflict Transformation in Power Asymmetries', in M. Fischer, H. J. Giessmann and B. Schmelzle (eds), *The Berghof Handbook for Conflict Transformation*, Berlin: Berghof Research Center for Constructive Conflict Management, 2008; and V. Duduouet, 'Cross-border Nonviolent Advocacy during the Second Palestinian Intifada: The International Solidarity Movement', in H. Clark (ed.), *People Power: Unarmed Resistance and Global Solidarity*, London: Pluto Press, 2009.

I believe that, in its bid to compete with the power of violence, nonviolence has sometimes been cast in a rather macho mould, seeking some kind of equivalence with military power, and emphasising nonviolent means of coercion and counter-coercion.[9] This is indeed important, but even more so is its power to touch people and to provoke change – as the nuns did in Manila when they gave food and cigarettes to the soldiers whose tanks they were blocking. Although resistance may be necessary, outreach is vital if there is to be transformation, rather than a locked struggle for control. The powers of thought, of the emotions, the imagination, and the will are unquenchable, except by death; and since they are infectious, they may well survive even that. They are what motivate and mobilise.

The symbolism of the iconic badge of War Resisters International, with strong hands breaking a rifle, could be complemented with something to represent a different kind of energy – perhaps a flower pushing up through concrete.

Real, deep and lasting change must be chosen, embraced. Coercion cannot accomplish this. What can change the way human beings think and react? In the short term, quick thinking; opportunism; synergy; intuition; surprise; humour; emotional disarmament through some step of outreach; awe at another's courage; the awakening of pity or empathy; a sudden recognition of commonality, of the self in the other; the sense that one's own dignity is recognised; the respect embodied in an appeal.

A fellow trainer once introduced me to the aikido approach to energy, in which one takes and works with the energy of the other, rather than trying to counter it. This seems something worthy of experiment, and I sometimes notice myself achieving something of the kind. To put the idea in another way, it means getting in touch with the negative or hostile feelings of others and redirecting them. It can also mean connecting with the positive potential in the other: a capacity for empathy, a deep code of honour, or an instinct to protect.

As suggested above, apparent powerlessness can be an advantage. Vulnerability makes people less threatening to others, and can therefore decrease the likelihood of their taking action against them. This is why women can sometimes 'get away with' things that men cannot. Being vulnerable is not the opposite of being strong;

9.   See the works of G. Sharp, including *The Politics of Nonviolent Action*, Boston: Porter Sargeant, 1973.

it can be accompanied by assertiveness, creativity, and the power of communication.

The intuition that enables some people to act in just the right way at the right time is something we cannot fully understand, but we have all experienced it, whether at first- or second-hand. I have seen extraordinary cases where a process about to collapse has been turned around by just such power: by someone who has felt instinctively exactly what was needed to arrest and dissipate resistance and anger, and to open up a new horizon and dynamic. We will all have examples in which surprising, inspired acts of outreach or courage have changed the course of events. 'Civil courage', practised and developed in small day-to-day ways (speaking up for someone who is being insulted or threatened, or challenging derogatory references to some person or group), is a vital ingredient in some of the essential work of conflict transformation.

Constructive programme

One of Gandhi's insights was that it was not enough to know what you wanted to get rid of: it was even more important to know what you were working towards, your understanding of what positive peace would look like. You needed not only to have this understanding, but to start living through a 'constructive programme', beginning to build, if only in small ways, the alternative society in whatever ways you could. This is how micro-transformation relates to the big vision. Small peace projects translate the idea of peace into practice, even in a largely unpeaceful present: networks and communities that transcend divisions, schools' mediation programmes, multi-ethnic village councils, community peace monitors and peace councils, experiments in cooperation, even single acts of disobedience to the rules of violence – all are present embodiments of the peace that is the goal. Such endeavours are important not only because they change things in the here and now, but also because they prefigure what can be and sow the seeds of a possible wider future. They are not simply 'peace writ small': they are the essence of peace as such.

Such initiatives may in themselves require considerable courage. They may be seen by the powers-that-be as an affront and a threat to their interests; and the energy of hate reacts in unpredictable ways to the energy of friendship. But in some circumstances such do-it-yourself peace may represent the most powerful way forward, and also the most possible.

I think here particularly of the struggle for gender justice, and resistance to the globally widespread subjugation of women and children through violence. This is never seen as 'a violent conflict' because the victims and perpetrators are inextricably mixed together, and much of the violence takes place behind closed doors. But the violence is undoubtedly structural, too – permitted and indeed encouraged by laws made on the basis of male dominance: laws, for instance, that allow women to be killed for crimes that, when committed by men, go unpunished; that prevent women from inheriting, and force them to marry relatives when their husbands have died; that prevent them from keeping their children if they are divorced, or that prevent them from participating in economic activities or in the most basic of political processes, like voting. This global 'low-intensity conflict', which for each individual is acute and makes the lives of many women a living hell, needs to be addressed for what it is, in a coordinated, high-intensity, global manner.

A large proportion of men and women consider themselves to be interdependent, and do not wish to live separately. Yet structural change is needed in the manner of coexistence. It will come not only through campaigns and changes in policy, but also through the almost imperceptible shifts that begin with small acts of courage and communication, through the education of men and women, both separately and together, through domestic experimentation and the evolution of new patterns of relationship.

Incremental change of this kind goes hand-in-hand with overcoming internalised oppression: the feeling that, because one is treated as inferior, one really is so. The liberation of spirit that this produces releases personal power that has been unimaginable until then, and which each step of courage increases.

Campaigning as bridge-building

Finding the courage to resist violence and create a space for alternative voices to be heard is the essential first step in transforming societies. In one sense it can be seen as its own constructive programme. But, if wider changes are to be made, the awakening of the few needs to be translated into the mobilisation of the many. Their courage and belief in change need to be infectious, their values need to be transferred to others, and their analysis needs to be shared and owned more widely. Small circles need to be expanded and to embrace others who have been seen as part of the problem, so that they can be brought instead into the circles of support for change. This will at the same time weaken the forces of oppression.[10]

10.   Francis, *People, Peace and Power*, p. 125.

It is useful here to think again of the mutually influential roles of attitudes, systems and actions. If positive, durable peace is to be established, a systemic shift in power will need to be accompanied by a shift in thinking. Norms often need to begin to change in order for structures to change. At the same time, a structural shift in power – brought in by legal, policy and constitutional changes, or changes to the way in which economic power is deployed – will be likely to influence the way people think. It will in time change attitudes. Behaviour is influenced by all these things, but at the same time people and their actions are the embodiment and engine of structures and cultures.

In changing attitudes, systems and actions, in influencing people, winning them over and mobilising them, effective communication is the key to success. Indeed, all the key skills of 'conflict resolution', and its insights related to needs, empathy, conflict dynamics and bridge-building, can greatly strengthen movements for nonviolent change. The world of struggle needs to incorporate the skills and the ethos of conciliation.

In my life in the peace movement, I am often frustrated by my fellow-campaigners' apparent preference for talking to themselves rather than engaging in dialogue. If we are not prepared to engage in serious discussion with those who disagree with us, we shall fail to engage the wheels of change. I believe that campaigners often overestimate their power of coercion and underestimate their power of persuasion or conversion. In human societies, minds and hearts are the main arena. I say 'minds and hearts' in the belief that we are governed by feelings as much as by thinking, and that this is true of men as well as women (though, for cultural reasons, men are generally less likely to acknowledge it).

In oppressive situations, where talking to people you do not know is a risk, outreach needs to be circumspect, and is likely to be confined either to very closed contexts, or to the deliberately very public ones of demonstrations of one kind or another. In the latter case, the wording of slogans, placards and so on (and of press statements, where they are possible) can make all the difference between provoking anger and rejection or touching hearts and minds.

And just as power struggles take place – sometimes necessarily – within organisations and networks committed to conflict resolution, movements for change have to contend with a great many internal conflicts that need to be managed, and where possible resolved. Here, too, the skills of conflict management and resolution need to be deployed. This really is one field.

Levels and connections

The notion of a pyramid of social levels has already been discussed, but I have suggested that it needs to be developed or complemented by a mapping of 'vertical' connections. It is all too easy for people to stay within their own spheres, and for the potential connections and lines of influence to be lost.

Social and political activists at the middle level are often so alienated from those at the top, or operate in such different circumstances, that dialogue and cooperation are extremely difficult – or else it is obstructed by the kind of financial dependency I have already mentioned. We have seen that the NGO world is beginning to take more seriously the need to engage with policy-makers. This must continue. The constraints on NGOs (including those of funding) are probably more manageable than those felt by policy-makers themselves, who feel all the weight of electoral expectations, political patronage and a conservative political culture.

In terms of movements for change, one can see that if the most vocal members of the lower two levels of Lederach's pyramid were to come together in putting pressure on those at the top – particularly if that pressure combined both specific requests and action to back them (or non-cooperation with the status quo) this would, if sustained and given mass backing, prove irresistible. Equally, the incremental changes in attitude and practice that are needed to build peace need to take place on all these levels. However, despite all our theory, rhetoric and aspirations about popular participation, most people are too preoccupied with the task of managing their day-to-day existence to be motivated to engage systematically in public affairs, so that the ongoing organisation and shaping of movements is carried out largely by a more restricted group of people often at the middle of the pyramid.

This depends, of course, on how a particular society is structured. Where social, geographical and political units are formed on a human scale and public affairs are managed within their compass, it is relatively easy and 'natural' for people to be involved. Alternatively, if there is a strong labour movement there may be habits of assertive participation. It may be that those who are publicly active will remain, in most societies, a relatively small minority; but their influence will be self-extending, and its aim should be to win the tacit, if not active, support of the majority, and achieve an eventual shift in collective norms and assumptions.

To achieve even this more modest ambition will require much more concerted efforts to bridge the gap between different sectors of the population. In the first place this would require new thinking and priorities, including a willingness to enter different circles, different cultures; to listen as well as to talk; to learn as well as teach. In this there is much to be learned from the Freirian approach to education, but the context in which Freire worked was very different from those in which some of us find ourselves. What are the venues in which bridge-building can take place? And are we willing to be exposed to what, to us, is the crude bigotry of some popular opinion in order to discover the real experiences and concerns that underlie it – especially when we often avoid conversation with others in our own circles who do not share our views?

As we have seen, the turbulence and suffering involved in conflict often have their roots in deprivation, and are most sharply felt at the base. The mere fact that we can represent our societies as pyramids is evidence of 'unpeace'. Any really inclusive change must eventually be grounded in change at the grassroots, even if it does not begin there. This will involve community development. Those of us who aim to work with 'key people' have a lot to learn from community-based organisations about how to identify and build transformative energy, how to nurture natural leaders and support them in finding their way into actual leadership, and how to identify and develop the values that lend purpose, dignity and motivation to work for change.

Perhaps we could make more progress by thinking and behaving as if different social and political levels did not exist as such, being simply a self-perpetuating construct, as writers such as Bourdieu, Giddens and Habermas have suggested. Maybe we should focus simply on who can do what is necessary in any given instance, and work hard to broaden our sociopolitical horizons beyond those of 'people like us'. (Clearly, some NGOs – especially local ones – already do this, but it needs to happen more.)

One colleague of mine had the idea, which alas was not implemented, of enlisting barbers, bakers and other shopkeepers to spread ideas conducive to peacebuilding. I also had colleagues working in the medical field who created dialogues in their clinics, because mental health issues were intimately related to prevailing social, political and economic conditions. Service-providers bring people of all levels together. The idea of connectors is not new, but it should lead us to fresh thinking rather than always down the same familiar routes.

Just as there are locations of interaction, there are other lines of existing connection that we could exploit more, which, in theory at least, are not in themselves hierarchical. Women's groups, for instance, may involve women from many walks of life, as may religious groups and voluntary organisations. Professional bodies often comprise people whose work status and function are very different, but who are equal members of those bodies and can unite behind a given cause and carry its message into different circles. Companies that have a social life and role as well as a commercial one can become vehicles for exchange, concerted influence and service.

When it comes to reaching people in government, it is possible to gain influence through those within 'the system' who have access to them. Where there is no system of representative government, experience has shown that popular mobilisation can have remarkable impact. In countries where parliaments are elected and governments formed on the basis of representation, the central route of influence is through the ballot box. In practice, however, the wider political processes (such as party activism, issue-based campaigns and lobbying, consumer boycotts, public debate, and media presentations), or the lack of them, have a huge effect on the character of parliamentary politics. We need to encourage others and ourselves to take politics seriously, because cynicism is corrosive and does not enable change.

Another route to influencing governments is through economic bodies, such as companies, which are important to the government's existence, and which, in turn, can be influenced by consumers and shareholders, who can choose to boycott certain outlets or products, or to vote against certain company policies or lines of production. Here we are back in the world of nonviolent campaigns and action for change, and the idea of collective power that the pyramid so elegantly illustrates.

Governments as peacebuilders at home

I realise that I tend to present governments as the problem rather than the answer. They can also play a key role in successful peacebuilding, and can guide their people into positive attitudes and action. This would seem to be the case currently in Rwanda, where the atrocities of 1994 have been so visibly and ubiquitously memorialised, and the message of 'never again' is so pervasive; where the inculcation of a common sense of identity and the organisation of common work for the common good are so strong; where the *gacaca*, or participatory village courts, have involved so many in the processing of past crimes, and in arranging for reparations to be made; and where the economic needs of the country are being so determinedly addressed, that the future seems almost unbelievably bright, given the events of the past.

One can only hope that the acquiescence and participation of the people in all this indicates genuine support rather than psychic numbness or a sense of compulsion – and that the systemic measures and behavioural changes that have been delivered by strong government nurture a culture of personal, as well as collective, responsibility and tolerance. In the last analysis, peace depends on populations. The involvement of Rwandans in the fighting in neighbouring parts of the DRC does not mean that there is nothing positive to be learned from the measures taken.

The Aceh peace process provides intriguing examples of the strengths and weaknesses of governments, in all their forms, with regard to peacebuilding. The negotiations process was a tightly controlled affair, mediated by recent Nobel laureate Martti Ahtisaari. It involved small negotiating teams from the Indonesian government and the Free Aceh Movement (GAM). It delivered a peace agreement that resulted in an immediate, drastic improvement in the security situation in Aceh, a new self-government arrangement for the province, and new rights for local political parties to contest elections. Three years on from the peace agreement, Aceh has a GAM-led local government administration – an outcome inconceivable to many at the turn of the millennium.

The process inevitably had its weaknesses. The post-agreement negotiation of self-government arrangements saw some backtracking by the Indonesian government, under pressure from constituencies in Jakarta who were not part of the process. GAM's transformation into a nonviolent political party is still an ongoing process, complicated by the demands of ex-combatants and undermined by allegations of profiteering from new commercial contracts for the province. Other significant tensions remain, including new efforts to break up the province into smaller political entities.

To a certain extent, these challenges beg the question of what constitutes a 'good enough' peace process. Could the outcomes have been better if other stakeholders had been able to participate in the negotiation process, influence the agenda, and better shape the post-agreement political landscape? Has the structure of the negotiation process left too much power in the hands of self-interested politicians, either in Jakarta or Banda Aceh? Or was the imperative to manage an efficient process that could end the war, create the conditions for change, and then allow politics to take care of the rest? There are many shades of opinion on the matter among the population of Aceh. These opinions are likely to keep shifting over time as people assess how those that they elected to govern them address the significant peacebuilding challenges that remain.[11]

The acid test of what governments do is whether they provide the framework and encourage the attitudes and behaviour that support and enable productive coexistence among their people. The role of any external government in support of peace should be to support them in these central tasks.

Third-party roles

Non-governmental

What constructive roles can be played by non-governmental third parties in increasing the power of civil action to correct structural violence, prevent violent conflict, and reduce the risk incurred by those who are directly involved in action for change?

Although there is overlap between internal and external third parties (in the case of diasporas, for example) and in the roles they can play, there are also differences. Internal third-party roles are potentially more flexible and informal. I know, for instance, of one citizens' group that is working for reconciliation and plays multiple roles: facilitating and mediating between armed factions; mobilising a peace constituency; promoting reconciliation between tribes; and interceding on behalf of people who have been kidnapped, and negotiating their release.

While they are likely to have their own interests, and connections to parties to the conflict that may complicate relationships, internal third parties have the advantage of being well-known to all concerned, and this may in practice more than compensate. If they include individuals with a range of connections, this may give them a kind of collective impartiality. Their very closeness to events and to people gives them insights and connections that are simply not available to external actors. Their connections may also confer some influence which, if used carefully, can be of use.

External third parties can, if asked to do so, assist local actors, bringing in experiences from elsewhere. They can increase the visibility of what is being done, raising public awareness of what is at issue at home and internationally (as appropriate), about what

---

11.   I am indebted to Celia McKeon for this example.

is happening and why, affirming the need for change, mobilising support at the popular level and in international forums. If asked to do so, they may call for public statements to be made or for political or economic sanctions or incentives to be applied. They may also ask for more constructive engagement from their home governments, either directly or through the UN.

Third parties, whether local or from outside (especially, perhaps, the latter) can also provide a protective presence for activists, acting as unarmed monitors who, through their contacts with the world beyond a particular context, can make those at risk and those who threaten them more visible to the wider world – which, experience suggests, makes arbitrary killings and disappearances less likely. When they do take place, international attention can minimise the risk of further crimes and increase the chances that those who are still alive will be released. Several such schemes are currently operating, for instance in the occupied Palestinian territories, in Sri Lanka, and in Colombia.[12]

While the bridge-building and mediatory activities outlined above are familiar, those related to standing against violence and protecting those who do so would constitute a major departure from the kind of 'impartial' activity currently undertaken by most international NGOs, and some national or local ones. Though I have suggested that seeking support for such work would help educate donors, such attempts might not succeed, and could have an adverse effect on other funding bids. For these reasons, those who find this work important may raise funds from individuals and independent bodies rather than from governments, in order to support their own mobilisation or solidarity work and to channel funds to help activists in whatever ways are needed.

If popular mobilisation is to be taken seriously, NGOs (whether national or international) will need to make alliances with community-based organisations and find other ways of connecting with people at the grassroots level. They will also need to educate themselves more deeply about popular movements and what helps them to succeed.

What is important is that this kind of work for change is incorporated into the way we all think about conflict transformation and do our work. It should also be incorporated into our

---

12.   For an up-to-date discussion and a broad range of cases of nonviolent solidarity, see H. Clark (ed.), *People Power: Unarmed Resistance and Global Solidarity*, London: Pluto Press, 2009.

education and training. Since there are always power struggles at any stage of conflict, addressing power relations in training has always been essential. And since dialogue and bridge-building are needed even during nonviolent struggle, both within movements and with those whom they seek to change, the related skills are essential to its efficacy.

Governmental and intergovernmental

International support can uphold the witness and the will of those within a society who are asserting the values of conflict transformation and taking action to promote justice and build bridges, at whatever level. By building and articulating moral norms, external governments can encourage their counterparts elsewhere to behave in ways that will gain the respect and cooperation of other governments and international institutions. They can offer economic support for changes that will contribute to peacebuilding and provide funding for non-governmental organisations working in support of local activists.

Whether it is better to exclude countries whose governments are deemed to be undemocratic from institutions like the European Union, or to use the prospect of joining as an incentive for change, is a matter for intelligent and honest debate. The isolation of Robert Mugabe, for instance, can be regarded as morally inevitable, but it does not appear to have done much good. And would the playing of a more supportive role by, for instance, the UK over the last couple of decades, and reparations for past injury (which would have had their own intrinsic merit) have saved Zimbabweans from dictatorship? It is impossible now to know.

If we are to have sanctions as well as incentives, I believe there should be a strong preference for the latter, with sanctions being used only when the local population is judged to support them, and when they are focused in such a way that they do not add to the suffering of those who are not responsible or able to bring about the changes required.

I also believe that the way incentives are offered makes a huge difference to the way in which they are received. An offer of support in doing something, made within the frame of human equality and respect, will have a very different impact from an offer 'from on high', in a situation where need makes refusal difficult – in which case it will feel more like a threat and humiliation than an incentive. Interventions for conflict transformation should reflect its values and insights.

If action from outside a country is to serve the cause of peacebuilding, it must be taken in the interests of those where peace is to be built, undistorted by the self-interest of those who intervene. Mediation in particular needs to be carried out with true impartiality. (Some countries, such as Norway, already do provide excellent services as mediators.) An international organisation that can command the respect and trust of all needs to be internally democratic and to rise above the interests of particular members, rather than being dominated by those that are the most militarily and economically powerful. Without having reached that stage of perfection, the UN can in some circumstances, even now, provide financial and legal services, expertise and good offices in an impartial way.

National governments can supply people as well as money to help build institutions and services, and offer training where it is needed for roles vital to peaceful administration. They may also provide monitors or police at times of transition. As I suggested earlier, I am sceptical about the added value of sending soldiers as peacekeepers, believing that, if there is a peace to be kept, that will best be done by police, and that this is important to the demilitarisation of both the immediate situation and the global system.

Although the need for effective and stable government is clear, I believe we should seriously question the assumed primacy of the nation-state, and begin to articulate new ways in which the principle of subsidiarity can be put into operation: ways that recognise the interdependence whose reality has been thrust in our faces by the recent economic meltdown and the growing impact of climate change.

There are mountains to climb if we are truly to put peacebuilding at the top of the governmental agenda. Meanwhile, in the words of the e-bulletin of Transcend, in Sweden, issued on 23 October 2008, 'While the world's countries spend some 1300 billion dollars on their military, the budget for the UN organization is 2.1 billion, or 0.2%. Development aid amounts to about 70 billion. With such priorities, is it any wonder the world looks like it does?'

However, if we believe that it is important to support nonviolent resistance and assertiveness, we should make our case for it, and discuss with civil servants and policy-makers or influencers who we can reach the things we think they could do to help, and the ways in which we could contribute that they might fund. We can, after all, point to the impact of the support given to activists in Serbia, Ukraine and Georgia, however unprincipled some of it may have been, hoping, little by little, to share our understanding of the principles and efficacy of nonviolent mobilisation for change.

The responsibility to protect

I have referred many times to this concept. Here I will add some further reflections and summarise my argument.

All that I have said about nonviolent action to address violence presupposes that there are people who have both the space and the capacity to act. If we look at the most intensely violent situations, it is hard to believe that this is so. People's lives are so shattered, 'normality' is so distant, that it is hard to see who could find the inner resources or material power to do other than be a victim (of forced conscription, brutal physical violence, homelessness and hunger, or all of these), or to choose to plough into the violence.

As I have suggested, 'peacemaking', if understood as military action in the midst of ongoing violence (even if there were the will to take such action), would in reality constitute joining battle and killing more people (including non-combatants) in a bid to gain control. The occupation that followed would be likely to bring its own violence (and counter-violence), and the entire process, which might be very long even in a best-case scenario, would leave a bitter legacy. Temporary protection may be necessary, but it needs to come in a form that does not create new victims, further victimise or disempower the current ones, or strengthen the cycle and system of violence.

Even in the darkest moments of extreme violence, some individuals do in fact manage to refuse violence themselves and protect their neighbours, showing that other responses are possible. Civilian action to uphold human life and dignity is the best possible foundation for a peaceful future, protecting those who would be victimised without violating the life and (unconditional) human rights of those who are acting violently. It is the sheer helplessness that most people experience in such situations that needs to be addressed. So the questions for us all must be what kind of preparations can be made that will give people the capacity to act and make widespread atrocities unlikely in a given context, and what kind of protective intervention could be undertaken, if they begin, that would support rather than displace potential local action to protect life and transform violence?

A major investment is needed in the development of nonviolent forms of intervention. If we can have armies standing ready for violence, we could, if necessary, have nonviolent forces of comparable size and mobility. As it is, no protective intervention is made in most situations of extreme violence. The human condition is to be vulnerable to each other, as we are to natural forces. The prevention of violence does not mean building a protective wall of some kind, or holding down a lid; it means transforming the situation from which a crisis of violence is likely to arise. Populations will be protected from arbitrary violence by having the chance to develop their own capacities to organise, to make themselves heard, and to exercise collective choice and influence. Unfortunately this is long-term work. We had better start now.

TRANSFORMATIVE POWER: BUILDING CAPACITIES FOR NONVIOLENCE

We need to build capacities for aspects of conflict transformation that require the courage, skill and moral clarity for challenging the power of violence, in whatever form. A curriculum for nonviolence training needs to include a profound consideration of its underlying values and approach. These will not differ, in essence, from those of conflict transformation more generally, or of conflict resolution specifically, but they do need to be related, precisely, to the question of risk and the exercise of power in a way that is morally partisan.

At times moral partisanship may take a political form, in which case it will require self-challenge that goes deeper than the ideological and political. It will presuppose an ongoing openness to 'the other' and to dialogue. It must have nothing to do with scorn and hatred. It must frame the other as capable of change and the self (individual and collective) as fallible, and therefore needing to accept the possibility of change. It must weigh the possible cost of both action and inaction, to the self and to others – not only those who are personally close, but people in society at large.

Nonviolence training therefore involves deep reflection, as well as developing skills of analysis, strategy, imagination, judgement and reflexivity. It also needs to enable participants to gain insight into their sources of strength and inspiration, and to learn how to minimise risk and manage fear.

Bridging the gap between training and action

Sometimes, I believe, we resort to training almost as a form of displacement activity, when we cannot see what else can be done. But training can, even in the hardest of times, lift people out of their sense of complete powerlessness, showing them the possible spaces for action, however limited they may be. Training can also prepare people for the time when something shifts and the space grows wider.

However, I believe we could do more to ensure that training does enable action of some kind, even if that action seems very small. The tiniest step can build courage for the next one, and can begin to make cracks in the solid wall of oppression. Exploring the idea of civil courage, of asserting one's own dignity and that of others in everyday ways, discovering one's own strength and identifying one's own approach to risk, is a vital element in training of this kind.

But the skills that we try to share in relation to resolving conflict – those related to creating connections between people – will also be highly relevant to training for those who want to challenge and change the status quo, enabling them to do so with the minimum of confrontation (so reducing both risk and resistance) and the maximum of outreach and persuasion.

The most important way of ensuring that our training is relevant to action is to ensure that those who participate want to act, making it known that the training is for those who wish to do so. If we have action in mind, or even if we are offering general training for those who wish to consider taking action, we will tailor the content very precisely to the situation at hand. We will help the participants identify the particular skills they most need, on the basis of their analysis and sense of what is possible, while at the same time helping them to deepen that analysis.

An excellent new resource for this work is the *Handbook for Nonviolent Campaigns* produced by War Resisters International, which is both practical and comprehensive, and is available online[13] in English, Spanish, Russian, Hebrew, South Korean and Turkish (and perhaps by now other languages).

Building groups, organisations, movements

Forming small groups of like-minded people is easier than growing into an organisation – and even that is easier than building a coherent movement. I mentioned in Chapter 1 the role CCTS members played in helping with the consolidation of groups and organisational development. The core values of inclusiveness, respect and care that inform conflict transformation, if they are translated into an organisational ethos and the understanding and implementation of good practice, really do contribute to collective effectiveness. Failure to embody the values that underlie the work at the heart

13.   WRI, 'Handbook for Nonviolent Campaigns', available at <wri-irg.org>.

of a group's purpose can cause bitterness, tension and instability, undermining that work.

Shared values and goals, shared analysis of the situation and how it can change, and a shared strategy, with specific plans to put it into practice, are essential to constructive relationships and effective work in collectives of any kind. Also essential are clear agreements about roles and processes for carrying out the work, along with regular reviews.

Opportunities to talk about the things that matter, recognition of personal as well as collective needs, and time for relaxation and celebration, will all help add the vital glue, inspiration and staying power that are needed. Building capacity must include establishing these things in any organisation, however informal they may be.

Building movements is altogether more problematic. Making single organisations work is far more difficult than those few words above would suggest, particularly when society all around works to very different norms. It is all the more difficult in movements, which by nature are ungovernable and do not lend themselves to steering. They are often too diverse to share deep values, and working towards a narrowly defined goal, while it may get over that problem, does not reduce the likelihood of clashes of ethos and ways of doing things, or of competing interests and agendas. Since change needs movements, these are important issues to include in training. They are also important to us, ourselves, if we are to mobilise ourselves to contribute to global change.

Evaluation and learning

I have indicated my scepticism about the utility of the 'logical framework' as a tool for strategic analysis and planning. Maybe this says more about me than about logframes, which may be helpful to many. In any case, we – peace professionals and peace movements alike – do need to think hard about what we are doing, holding ourselves and our work to account, and learning from our experience in order to maximise our chances of contributing to the changes we want to see.

What will be the review process that compares our analysis, goals and strategy with how things are working out? How will each step in our action be evaluated, in terms of how it was carried out and its immediate impact? How will it be related to our broader strategy? And how will our broader strategy be evaluated in the light of events?

I hope we can begin to learn more systematically about the ways in which analysis and strategising do and do not help us, and about the apparently unsystematic energies with which we can and must engage. Action research and action learning are ways for us to become more systematic in the way we learn from our practice, involving close observation of our own behaviour as well as the wider dynamics of how things happen and the different influences at work.

Within the conflict-transformation field we need to develop, in particular, the praxis of civil resistance and action to change violent systems, learning from those movements, organisations and individuals that already have knowledge and experience to share with us. We must incorporate this into the way we understand conflict transformation, in the action we take, and in the support we seek to give.

Beyond logic and control

I have noted the key role given to capacity building in the field of conflict transformation, in theory and even more in practice. I think it is time to re-examine our assumptions about the capacities that are needed to transform conflict.

At the time when the CCTS began its life, we used to discuss the utility or otherwise of what we sometimes jokingly referred to as 'touchy-feely' training. Most of us were uncomfortable with the sometimes rather formulaic and intrusively emotional nature of what was done, and what seemed like a tendency on the part of some trainers to 'psychologise everything'. We were keen to balance attention to inner processes and emotions with tough, analytical thinking about what was going on in the external world.

My impression is that, since then, the pendulum has swung too far in the direction of analysis and strategy – or perhaps, rather, that we fail to take emotional and other 'irrational' aspects of conflict into account when we analyse and strategise. The kinds of awareness exercise that were used were not always the most appropriate, but alerting participants to their own emotional and psychological needs and to some patterns in their interpersonal relationships was valuable, and bringing hidden prejudices and assumptions to light made them more self-aware and enabled them to gain fresh insights into the human psyche. Such training can increase our own alertness to factors that may be important in collective conflicts, at whatever level. In my experience, it is also important to make space for the deepest conversations about personal vision, motivation and belief, since these are the wellspring of all commitment and courage, and the necessary reference point for all judgements.

I have pointed to the apparently chaotic complexity within which we try to operate – the multiple influences and the innate unpredictability of collective, societal dynamics, which often make prediction and attribution impossible. Yet analysis is vital in ordering and making use of complex information, and we need the strategy that can come from analysis to find our direction and give us a framework for ongoing evaluation.

I believe, however, that we need to find a very different approach to strategising: one that is infinitely responsive to ongoing change. A flow-chart approach could help us to be clear but provisional in taking a longer view. We need a sense of direction that is formed and re-formed as we go, as circumstances change around us. I cannot avoid a 'satnav' analogy. The voice from the machine tells us which direction to take, but when we make a mistake or find the chosen road blocked it seamlessly gives a new, 'reconsidered' instruction, in response to the new reality. Many of us will have experienced the need to do something similar, in a process we are facilitating or dialogue we are engaged in: to move quickly to plan B or to plan C, or to invent a plan we never had. *This* is a capacity we need to develop, whether for hands-on work or for planning. It is a capacity – and an approach – that we can help others to develop. We cannot control events, but we must work with them. This is the 'aikido energy' that I discussed earlier in this chapter – a kind of powerful and benign opportunism. We must learn to convince donors of its power, encouraging them to see how we have worked and how we think, and to assess for themselves whether they can trust us to do the very best that can be done in inhospitable and unpredictable circumstances.

Recent experience of the reconciliation process that is being led by civil society leaders in one particular land (still too fragile for me to name it) has brought home to me in a very forcible way the power of those who can seize the energy of the moment and use their own gifts of courage and charisma to build its momentum and capture the hearts and minds of those who have the power to transform a conflict. I have seen magic at work – not the magic of the supernatural, but the magic of intuition in the service of love: love of people, of a vision of justice, of beliefs and ideals, uplifted by the magic of music and poetry, of symbol, ritual and shared silence.

I have seen this coupled with the parallel magic of solid, clear, analytical thinking, steady guidance and sensitive facilitation, with an effect that has for so long been no more than a dream for those concerned: the real hope of steps towards peace after many years of cruel fighting. I have seen the way that, when hearts are touched and opened, rationality becomes possible where it has seemed impossible. That has not removed the need for hard negotiation, but it has made it a serious and hopeful option.

We cannot train people – ourselves or others – to be magicians; but we can recognise and nurture the gifts of charismatic power and intuition, and begin to include them in our analysis. These, along with position, influence and connections, are factors that make 'key people' key. If we emphasise structural matters too much, and our position within them, we fail to see the human characteristics that can break out of structures and transform them.

Any analysis is made on the basis of given information and what has been perceived intuitively. We need both, to do good analysis. We certainly cannot do without analytical, logical thinking in negotiations or in planning, and, unless we hand over all power to the seers and charismatic leaders, we have to find ways of grounding transformation in the considered will and participation of the largest possible number of people. But the internal computers of the intuitive subconscious are faster and more subtle than the conscious brain, and in the last analysis most of us trust our intuition or our gut more than we do our reason.

Perhaps if we can get below the radar of our particular ways of thinking, we can also begin to dig beneath the cultural assumptions and constructs of identity that imprison and divide us, opening us up to the things that bind us and to the deepest questions we all face: to our values and ethics, our beliefs, loves and longings. If we can find a way to talk to each other about the things that matter most to us, our evaluation of what we do will be grounded in a way that can both guide and inspire us.

In my own diagram of 'stages and processes of conflict transformation',[14] and in much of the language of this book, I have suggested that power can somehow be balanced, as if it were a commodity, referring to 'shifting power relations' and talking about symmetry and asymmetry. The truth is that the ability to act and to have influence takes an infinite number of forms. Power is process and energy. It will never be symmetrical, though there are doubtless huge power disparities and abuses of power to address in given instances.

14.   See the Appendix.

Sometimes people are influenced to do something new by their own inability to achieve the things they wanted to – for instance, turning to negotiation because violence has failed them. Situations are sometimes created in which enemies find themselves becoming friends. Sometimes they change their minds because they are touched by a sudden insight into the humanity of the other, like the man who could not shoot his fleeing enemy because his trousers fell down as he ran.[15] Perhaps our common frailty, our mortality, which I believe drives our will to control, is also what most deeply binds us together.

Coercion is an overrated kind of power. Courageous confrontation is necessary at times, and can be hugely affirming. But reaching out and connecting is the greatest power of all, and it is movements that connect the small- to the large-scale, and that transform cultures, structures and events. They are the route to global transformation, as I will argue in the next chapter.

15. J. Glover, *Humanity: A Moral History of the Twentieth Century*, London: Pimlico, 2001.

7
Challenging the System

In this chapter I will begin by reflecting on the current global state of affairs and summarising my case against militarism. I will then go on to suggest how we might begin the transformation process, starting within the field of conflict transformation and exploring its capacity to contribute to a much wider movement, both through its existing work and through new thinking. I will also explore ways in which the many movements for peace around the world can become more effective, both deepening and broadening their scope.

AN OPPRESSIVE SYSTEM THAT HAS HAD ITS DAY

At the beginning of Chapter 1, I painted a gloomy picture of the world. In many places it is made ugly by chronic violence, and people live in constant fear. At times the violence reaches such proportions, or has such an impact on other nations, that it attracts their attention, and sometimes this may create the opportunity and the will for change – but too often that is not the case: the attention and the will are insufficient. At the time of this book's completion, the suffering continues in Zimbabwe, the DRC, Sudan, Sri Lanka, Palestine, and many other parts of the world. All these cases are manifestations of the culture and systems of violence. Violence has not brought them to an end, but is self-perpetuating.

Violence is fuelled by the arms trade and by hegemonic interests. Wars are launched in the name of security, costing unimaginable amounts of money, destroying countless (and uncounted) lives, and achieving nothing beyond destruction and new instability. A global financial crisis has added to the gloom, and demonstrates the fragility of the economic power that supports military dominance.

The system of militarism is oppressing us. The global 'we' – that is, most people in the world – are endangered and impoverished by it, and have our environment threatened by it, while a vast number of our fellow human beings have perished or suffered terrible loss because of it. Many of the countries that seem to have relatively low levels of violence at home are the biggest beneficiaries of the cruel global inequities that constitute structural violence, and some of them, with their weaponry and will for dominance, threaten the safety of our very planet.

At the same time, and perhaps for these reasons, I believe that a growing number of people around the world are losing their belief in war as a means of achieving anything good. They are beginning to see the wisdom of the aphorism, 'If war is the answer, it must be a very stupid question.'[1] The idea of 'just war', with its own principles and laws, seems to bear little relation to war's realities. 'Proportionality', which in essence means doing more good than harm, presupposes an ethical purpose. It also requires that any war should be won by the 'good side' (which, if there were one, could never be guaranteed – quite apart from the fact that even 'winning' a war always involves great loss). The objectives of winning a war and protecting civilians may clash, as the 2009 events in Sri Lanka demonstrated.

Moreover, in the case of Western countries, ever-increasing public sensitivity to losses on the home side, combined with the need to maximise damage to the adversary, encourages the use of high explosives launched from a distance, rather than engagement in close combat. This inevitably increases civilian casualties.[2] How can any kind of just war theory be squared with minimising risks to a country's own soldiers at the cost of causing heavy (sometimes massive) civilian casualties through aerial bombardment?

Civilians are also victimised by suicide bombings, the chosen means of resistance to the big military powers. The idea that it is glorious to *die* for a cause or for one's country is enthusiastically embraced by suicide bombers. The language of 'laying down' life and 'making the ultimate sacrifice' is still used of all soldiers when they die; but when the countries for which they have been fighting are militarily and economically powerful, their deaths are increasingly regarded as politically unacceptable. They are often met with protests from grieving relatives and others – protests framed in terms of soldiers' right to life, and accompanied by accusations of inadequate protection and substandard equipment. (No one asks about the right to life of those whom 'our' soldiers would like to kill more efficiently, with less risk to themselves.)

I would argue that the suffering of soldiers and their families matters, in fundamental human terms, as much as that of civilians,

1.   A slogan in use by peace activists during the wars in the former Yugoslavia.
2.   For a fuller discussion of just war theory see Francis, *Rethinking War and Peace*.

even if they can be seen as having had some choice in the matter that civilians have not. But, in any case, war is incompatible with the right to life. It is about killing and being killed. Those who fight, on whatever side, may do so because they have been coerced into doing so, or need a 'livelihood' (an ironic term in this context). They may also truly believe in what they are doing; and wars are characterised by acts of great courage as well as terrible cruelty. But they are by nature destructive and inhumane: part of the problem of human suffering and degradation – no way to a solution. Robots are now being developed to make the killing more efficient, taking us into new nightmare scenarios in which the 'war machine' is increasingly just that – and increasingly beyond the scope of human compassion.

Wars seek to crush the life out of conflict, rather than to resolve it; but without popular acquiescence, at the very least, there can be no peace. After years of Iraqi occupation, a British air chief marshal announced that only the Iraqis could deliver the things that Iraq needed.[3] How sad that this was not considered before the country was wrecked and hundreds of thousands had died. Then a former defence minister declared that the Taliban would have to be included in any future peace in Afghanistan.[4] So why the years of slaughter? Was there really no other way to bring about change and build peace? As I write, there is no sign that the slaughter has been justified by events, even if the death and maiming of thousands could ever be seen as justifiable.

Though it left 50 million dead, and led seamlessly into the Cold War, World War II – the second of two catastrophic 'wars to end all wars' – changed, to some degree, the attitude to war as such. This was particularly true in Europe,[5] where huge efforts have been made to ensure that, within its territory, war should not be repeated, and that cooperation and shared structures will make it impossible. Within the European Union, it seems that the appetite for war, at least within its own expanding territory, has decreased – at least for the time being. But there remains an insufficient aversion, in some member countries, to involvement in wars 'abroad'. The US, which has in the past woefully abused its power, seems to be shifting in its approach to international politics, and perhaps the world more widely is ready for change. Let us hope that this is so. The insight

3.   Sir Jock Stirrup, on BBC Radio 4's 'Today' programme, 12 September 2008.
4.   Geoff Hoon, on BBC Radio 4's 'Today' programme, 25 September 2008.
5.   J. Sheehan, *The Monopoly of Violence: Why Europeans Hate Going to War*, London: Faber & Faber, 2008.

that cooperation is better than antagonism and violence needs now to be applied globally.

If war is to be abandoned as uncivilised, it will be necessary to establish ways of dealing with conflict and addressing violence peacefully – that is, by nonviolent means[6] – so that inevitable disagreements can be processed fruitfully rather than destructively, and wrongs can be righted without the addition of further wrongs. The concept of a responsibility to protect is an important one, but when this is seen in military terms it becomes part of the old, discredited 'just war' theory. Pursuing our responsibility for each other's well-being through violence is a desperate and contradictory way of 'building peace'. We need to stop seeing war as an answer to any sensible question and resolve to overcome our addiction to it, saying 'never again', not 'just one more', and looking elsewhere for what is needed. We must turn away from the model of security-through-control, or pacification, and focus instead on common security, achieved through cooperative peacebuilding.

For this we need conflict transformation not only writ large, but global, displacing global militarism. We who work for conflict transformation presumably believe in it. How, then, can we apply our conflict-transformation praxis to the task of global transformation? What would that look like? What is the vision, and how can it be achieved? Just as disbelief can bring about collapse, as we have seen in our global financial system, belief also has positive power. It will be essential to the creation of a new reality. What we believe is possible and desirable shapes our worldview and our culture, which are what most need to change.

Such transformation will require a Herculean effort of imagination and a reconnection with our moral being and the inspiration it can provide. A world without armies may seem a million miles away from the current reality. Yet we should acknowledge that, for the more fortunate among us, daily life goes on without a gun in sight. We have first-hand experience of the possibility of coexistence without violence, even in the face of disagreements, conflicting interests, mistrust and dislike – and often, fortunately, involving comfort, kindness and laughter. Our fixation with our supposed genetic programming for selfish aggression is being countered by new books on human morality and altruism.[7] Their authors

6. J. Galtung, *Peace by Peaceful Means: Peace and Conflict, Development and Civilization*, Oslo: PRIO, 1996.
7. See S. Rose, 'In Search of the God Neuron', *Guardian Review*, 27 December 2008 (and the four books listed by him in that article).

argue that our success as a species is predicated on our capacity for cooperation and coexistence. Kindness is one of our most basic and pleasurable human qualities.[8]

GLOBAL TRANSFORMATION: AN AGENDA FOR OUR FIELD

Constructive programme: continuing the work of conflict transformation

Working for global demilitarisation does not mean giving up on local and regional conflict transformation, which is the 'constructive programme' of that wider political and cultural agenda, putting into practice in the present the principles and behaviour that constitute our goal for the future. Such current, localised work is vital to those caught up in existing violent conflicts, and gives life to the vision we have for our world. It is the means of building global 'peace capacities'. It can also help create conditions that are conducive to change and contribute to the process of demilitarisation and genuine peacebuilding.

The work that is currently being done by local communities and conflict-transformation organisations around the world continues, therefore, to be vital, and indeed needs to be extended and intensified. To be effective, however, it will need greater support from donors of every kind, and in many cases a change in the attitudes of those influential powers whose pursuit of hegemonic agendas obstructs the resolution of conflicts. Educating donors, particularly governments, not only to support conflict-transformation processes but also to change their own behaviour and contribute to them, is a key aspect of the challenge.

Conscientisation

It is one of the fundamental insights of nonviolent action that change agents need to begin with themselves – which is what we must do. In the first place, we need to wake up to the stranglehold of militarism and its impact on individual lives and international relationships. This 'conscientisation' is necessary if we are to mobilise for change that will arrest the endless recourse to violence when conflict arises and, instead, 'grow' the culture and systems of cooperation.

One key way of exposing the endlessly recycled assumptions of militarism is to switch on the light of our own awareness of the prevailing discourse on security, deconstructing its language, taking key terms – like 'conflict prevention', 'force' (as a euphemism for

8.   A. Phillips and B. Taylor, 'Kindness', *Guardian Review*, 3 January 2009.

violence), 'security forces' and 'international community' (those countries that 'call the shots', globally), exposing their true meanings and the worldview they embody. Having uncovered the militarism that is often hidden in these terms, we need also to identify the bedrock of beliefs and aspirations that underlie the things we take for granted in conflict transformation, so that we are able to reclaim the words that express them and construct a new, common language to embody our purposes: a language that is as honest as we can make it, illuminating rather than obscuring what is being done and what could be done. If we can do that, we will already have made significant progress.

One essential task in understanding the depth of our conditioning will be to uncover the ways in which male children are conditioned, from their infancy, to perform their roles as boys and men, and the role of mothers and daughters, as well as fathers and other boys, as participants in this mutual construction of gender. (In my country, sexism is in many ways stronger than ever, with military imagery, toys and clothes still pushed at little boys, and little girls left in a pink world of domesticity.[9]) To achieve the awareness we need in order to play the catalytic role that is required of us, we must make a concerted effort to think and talk with each other about our attitude and relationship to militarism and violence and to radical alternatives, so that we are able to move together in a new direction.

How far is that achievable? We can only see where the conversation goes, but if it is really serious and self-challenging, if we acknowledge the bitterness of much of our own experience in trying to swim against the tide, if we decide to turn our frustration and disappointment into motivation to think and act more radically, and if we go back to the values that first motivated us to work in the field of conflict transformation, I believe we can go a long way together.

The sticking point will be our own doubts about 'alternatives to violence'. We too have at tendency to credit violence with powers for good that it simply does not have. We too are affected by the fact that other ways of addressing it have never been tested on a scale and with a degree of commitment, belief and expertise that could give them a chance of convincing us. The cultural change that is needed to transform the chronic, structural conflict of endemic militarism needs to begin with a change in our own consciousness and focus.

9. B. Francis, *Toys, Gender and Learning: Report to the Frobel Educational Institute*, London: Roehampton University, 2009.

Part of the conscientisation process must be learning about the history and possibilities of nonviolence. We need to re-educate ourselves and others about power: its sources in all their variety, and the ways it can be exercised. The current widespread obsession with violent power hides so much from us. We need not simply to receive nonviolence as a pre-existing body of knowledge, but to inform it with our own particular expertise, born of experience, so that it becomes richer and more nuanced, building our understanding of the complementarity between the different energies of resistance, assertiveness and accommodation in processes whose goal is inclusiveness and cooperation. This is essential for our own work, and it will be a vital part of our contribution to the peace movement.

Perhaps this is as far as we can get, together, to begin with. But I believe we can at least be more unequivocal in our rejection of violence, more committed to finding ways out of it, more wholehearted in our determination to push to its furthest lengths the power of nonviolent solidarity and protection. We can also prepare to speak out more strongly and clearly against the violence-based policies and actions of our governments, and those that are based on the will to dominate rather than the wish to do right.

If we can come together on these issues, not only will we assist and encourage each other in our thinking, but our solidarity will give us protection against any potential 'punishments' of lost funding and marginalisation. Furthermore, we will be more externally persuasive. We can achieve far more together than separately. That is why we need to begin by building a common approach and platform. There are many existing networks and talking shops where this preparation can begin, as well as blogs and websites that invite the pooling and interchange of information, perspectives and ideas.

It is hard to make time for such conversations, whether face-to-face or otherwise. However, if we want to mobilise our power as trans-formative peacebuilders, both in particular instances of violent conflict and in the global system that fuels them and prevents their resolution, and if we want to build solidarity around a new, wider analysis and strategy, the process will need initiators. Which of us will take this on? Many, I hope – each at the centre of a circle that can be expanded, until we begin to overlap and coalesce.

Developing visionary thinking

Global conflict transformation will require the establishment of 'peaceful relationships',[10] presuposing a massive shift in global

10.   Curle, *Making Peace*.

power relations, economic and political. Indeed, it will require a radical shift in the very nature of international relationships, from self-interest and the desire to dominate to mutual respect and the desire to cooperate for the common good.

A radical shift in international relationships will have to go hand-in-hand with a new understanding of the function of a state, such that the currently idealised and nationalistic notion of statehood is challenged and 'relativised', and new, overlapping, networked and fluid units and relationships can emerge. Statehood would no longer be regarded as a totem of ethnic or other identity power, but as a unit of cooperation, both internal and external.

'Foreign' policy (renamed, for instance, as 'international') would no longer be seen as needing to be developed, above all else, 'in the national interest', but would aim to be truly ethical; or perhaps, rather, 'self-interest' would be viewed through the lenses of inter-dependence, becoming the basis for recognising and honouring the needs and interests of others and working for the common good. In line with conflict-resolution practice, the particular interests of others, as they identified them, would be set alongside those of one's own populace, on the basis of parity of esteem and equality of rights.

It is the idea of otherness projected onto 'foreigners' by the current notion of the state that makes such a shift seem fanciful. It is this idea that we need to deconstruct, so that richer and more creative understandings can develop. We need to develop robust, flexible and multidimensional notions of personal and collective identity and belonging, whose most fundamental aspect would be a sense of being part of humanity – consciousness of a shared existential experience that binds us all and enables us to recognise one another as 'kin', and to regard each other with the kindness that this implies.

Kindness is an important concept to reclaim. It is the natural and nurturing human disposition and behaviour that arises from our being of one kin or kind. It takes us straight to the notion of interdependence, and thence to that of security based not on antagonism and competition, but on mutuality: common security. It includes giving protection when it is needed. It can call for strength, assertiveness and courage. Why is it a word that seems so out of place in political discourse? Is that something we could change? If so, I believe that would signify a new understanding of humanity as undivided by gender, race, class, and the like.

The currently dominant model of 'democratic' politics is based on antagonism. (Domestic politics, that is. The notion of democracy has never really been translated into international form, though regional institutions are attempting the transfer, and some members of the UN might aspire to it.) Antagonistic or adversarial models do not necessarily preclude all human kindness, but they do constitute one of the many ways in which the model of human interaction based on dominance is embodied and promulgated. They are, I would argue, often inimical to the best governance, and therefore to meeting the needs of the governed.

While argument is essential to thought,[11] and debate is crucial to democracy, so are synthesis, continuity and cooperation, along with the recognition of competing goods that need to be reconciled and the accommodation of different views and interests. This is another area for radical re-examination. The ways in which antithesis and synthesis, conflict and cooperation, can work together creatively deserve further analysis and imaginative exploration.

The artificial positioning, discontinuity, and (often) disrespect of antagonistic politics, and the distance between politicians and electorates in many systems, point to a need for change in our understanding of democracy. Truly democratic systems must be established in international relations (through the UN, for instance), displacing forever the notion that organised killing can be a substitute for them. Sharing the privileges of power will spread the load of responsibility and enable cooperation for the common good. The resources released by the abandonment of militarism will be enormous, bringing within reach the now distant, unreal dream of peace and security for our planet and its peoples.

Again, it is not foolish to believe that such a change in thinking and systems is possible. Many of us have experienced ourselves and seen in others the opening of understanding and identification that can be brought about by educational processes and through experiences of meeting with 'the other', working through fear and hostility, and discovering commonality. Such opportunities must not be confined to the few. Indeed, with ever-increasing global migration, it is essential that they are greatly multiplied, as a matter of policy, so that we learn to recognise and enjoy this diverse and pluralistic oneness. And that oneness must include the fundamental oneness of male and female, liberating us all from gender constructions that are used to justify and promote violence and oppressive relationships.

11. Billig, *Arguing and Thinking*.

Strategising for global demilitarisation

We have a body of experience-based theory on local demilitarisation, which we can bring to bear on the global task.

Demilitarising culture, patterns of behaviour, and relationships

Most important will be our insights into the powerful influence of culture and the need to demilitarise minds and societies. Changing the culture of domination, and the reliance on violence to achieve it, is the biggest task of all. Hence the importance of the kind of visionary thinking discussed above.

Such a shift in thinking would pave the way for building new relationships that are not based on or affected by military power. Dissolving the conflicts and conflicts-in-preparation between the big powers would help make the world a far safer place. These are conflicts whose main purpose is to achieve or maintain dominance, whether economic, political, territorial or military. They inflict immense suffering and provoke violence in others, leaving those who engage in them at risk, and often impoverished. Cooperation would be a more productive strategy for all concerned.

Suicide bombings and other acts classified as terrorism, though by nature smaller in scale, achieve the greatest possible impact for those whose capacity for violence is limited. Although this form of violence is motivated and justified by a sense of victimhood, it is both cruel and unproductive. It could be prevented by a recognition on all sides of the right of all to respect and participation.

Cultural demilitarisation would include a radical change in relationships between men and women, ending the chronic war of gender violence and liberating men from the oppressive cultural obligation to be dominant.

Disarmament, demobilisation and reintegration

Our planet is bristling with weapons of all kinds, some of them brutally simple, others so technologically advanced and powerful that they could destroy the earth as we know it. Reversing the arms race and its systems, and collecting and destroying the weapons in circulation, would take many years to negotiate, but would be a vital aspect of demilitarisation. We can add weight to the campaigns of others by drawing on our widely accepted theory on disarmament in demilitarisation processes, translating our prescriptions for local and regional programmes into proposals for global action. We can also offer our expertise in support of the negotiation processes that will be required.

The cost of current competitive militarisation is astronomical, in terms of inflationary (because unproductive) military spending by governments and an arms trade that is lucrative for the few, but which robs the many of much-needed resources. The nuclear arms race, which has given rise to 'horizontal' proliferation, threatens the safety of our planet. Cooperative, mutually supportive relationships, accompanied by radical programmes of disarmament, would release resources for peaceful purposes and real security, while removing one massive threat to our future existence as a species.

Many industrialised economies currently rely heavily on militarism, despite its non-productive nature and its consumption and destruction of resources. Weapons industries and trade will need to be converted to constructive alternatives (which typically will create more jobs) to provide honourable and productive employment. Here again, our experience of local programmes can provide templates for wider application, whether through international, or, more likely, national schemes (of which many countries will already have had experience – for instance, following the world wars of the twentieth century).

The demobilisation of soldiers will require an economic shift, as well as a cultural one. Not only is military service, whether 'regular' or 'irregular', seen in most cultures as manly, and therefore good; it is also, in too many situations, one of the few available sources of employment and income. Global peacebuilding will require the creation of civilian jobs and strong peace economies around the world. This will be a key element in achieving demobilisation and reintegration, as well as disarmament. In 'developed' countries, one focus of advertising for military recruitment is the transferability of the skills that will be acquired during military service to civilian life; but where no transferable skills have been acquired there will need to be effective training programmes, with wages for participants.

Economic reintegration will, I believe, be made possible by the release of minds and resources from military agendas. Material and mental demilitarisation will need to go hand-in-hand, as we become increasingly aware of (and averse to) the way violence has been glorified in our cultures – sometimes to the point of addiction. New measures of heroism will need to be found, along with new sources of meaning, identity and excitement, for women and men.

Building civilian capacities to protect

The protection of fellow human beings, as far as possible, from the violence of others is a moral obligation. One major policy change that will be needed is for a massive increase in international capacities to monitor and protect human rights. (Remember the very substantial impact of CSCE monitors in Kosovo, even in very small numbers, before they were withdrawn to make way for the NATO bombing?) Having substantial numbers of well resourced, trained personnel ready for policing duties abroad would give us the chance to test new models of protective peacekeeping.

There are serious ongoing attempts (despite the currently pitiful resources being made available) to develop nonviolent civilian protection for civilians in violent situations – both governmental and nongovernmental. The European Union's training and deployment of civilian monitors showed its potential in Kosovo, for instance; and Nonviolent Peaceforce is an international humanitarian NGO which recruits, trains and deploys unarmed civilians as peacekeepers to reduce violence and protect civilians.[12] These current efforts lack the scale necessary for effective deployment in acute situations, but given the necessary resources they could do much to address the vulnerability of populations.

In the meantime, we can work with the military on how, progressively, to demilitarise their own peacekeeping work. Colleagues who have worked with armed personnel, whether official or unofficial, have found them eager to learn how to deal constructively with confrontation – as have I – and this is one way to bring about change from within the current system.

Encouragingly, a new emphasis is being brought into the ongoing discussion of R2P: that of a 'responsibility to prevent' the kind of violence that would create the need for emergency protection. A report to the US Congress stated that 'Prevention is the single most important dimension of the responsibility to protect.' The Friends (Quakers) Committee on National Legislation, citing this text, asserts that 'real policy change ... will require new investments in non-military tools to protect civilians and help prevent deadly conflict'.[13] A current UK Commission on National Security also has

12. At the time of writing it has teams in Sri Lanka and Mindanao in the Philippines, and is seeking funds for a project in South Sudan. See <www.nonviolentpeaceforce.org>.

13. B. Moix and T. Keck, 'The Responsibility to Protect: A Report to Congress from the Friends Committee on National Legislation', available at <www.fcnl.org/issues>.

a major focus on the responsibility to prevent (before going on to talk at length about military intervention).[14]

The best protection for populations will be the building of societies and systems of governance that create the security that comes with positive peace. In other words, it is peacebuilding that will best prevent violence. What peace requires, above all, is engaged and active citizens of all ages and both sexes, who, whatever their personal capacities, take on the power and responsibility of social and political cooperation, and establish nonviolence as the universal norm for all relationships, whether between parents and children, men and women, different clans and ethnicities, or different countries and continents.

Engaged 'citizens' (though this may not be the most appropriate word in all societies) are the stuff of participatory governance, in whatever system. Such is the cynicism about politics that is felt by a high proportion of citizens in many Western democracies that their engagement is minimal or nonexistent. New hope and determination need to take the place of disaffection, and systems will have to be reclaimed and remodelled. The women's movement will be vital in this. Notions of women's political success have so far been predicated on their profile in existing institutions. What is essential is that those institutions should be reconceived and transformed, or replaced.

MOBILISATION: BUILDING ALLIANCES FOR GLOBAL TRANSFORMATION

Those of us who work for peace in the midst of violence, whether as professionals or as active citizens, have a vital role to play in a movement for global transformation, and have particular insights to bring. We have the chance to influence and build alliances with different categories of people, so helping to mobilise a global movement for the demilitarisation of minds and societies. We will need to connect with overlapping circles of people.

Connecting with expert international NGOs on global demilitarisation

There are many highly expert and effective NGOs, national and international, that are already working to end the arms race, reduce military spending, formulate disarmament policy, reduce the flow

14. Institute for Public Policy Research, *Commission on National Security in the 21st Century* (interim report published September 2008), available at <www.ippr.publicationsandreports>.

and quantity of weapons of different kinds, outlaw particular kinds of weapons, prevent forced recruitment, support conscientious objection, and so on. If we are not already part of them, these NGOs should be close allies for us and for the peace movement. We should support them and draw on their expertise.

Demilitarising local conflicts has been predicated on substituting peace processes for warfare, and it will be important to draw on the learning garnered from the substantial experience of international NGOs in bringing about the negotiated resolution of conflict and addressing the factors that have given rise to it. This experience-based knowledge could contribute greatly not only to the reduction of existing armed conflict, but also to a wider capacity for addressing geopolitical conflicts constructively, and a greater willingness to transfer trust from the armed to the peaceful conduct of conflict.

Excellent work has been done recently in studying how to involve armed groups in negotiations.[15] One key focus for future thinking, research and practice will be how to do this kind of work without reinforcing the power of militarism in a given context, thereby contributing to its local and global perpetuation. This will involve increasing public participation in peace processes and making them transformative of all those who are engaged in them. The way in which the achievement of peace is understood and represented will also be crucial. It will be necessary for the peace, when it comes, to be represented as a victory for the people, rather than for the 'heroes of armed struggle'. That discourse will need to be eroded.

Working with policy-makers

We already have friends in these circles. How can we support them and increase their number? How can we use our conflict-transformation expertise to inform and inspire the mending and transforming of global relationships, and to encourage global demilitarisation and demobilisation? Can we project our work into the arena of national policy and international relations? Existing work to change the way policy-makers think needs to be supported, expanded, deepened and intensified.

There are among us organisations already working in that arena. I am greatly heartened to know, for instance, that one of the organisations with which I am associated has been asked to brief opposition politicians in the UK (as well as staff of the existing government) on conflict-transformation options in foreign policy,

---

15.   See, for example, Ricigliano (ed.), *Choosing to Engage*.

and readers around the world could no doubt cite many such examples. There is no doubt that we are seen as having expertise that can be useful. We must use such opportunities to challenge existing assumptions and offer radically different ways of seeing things.

Can our policy work be further supported and strengthened to gain a higher profile? Can it be more radically challenging and visionary? Can those of us who work in more localised and practical ways contribute with our hands-on knowledge? Can peace academics and other thinkers provide detailed policy proposals on structural changes, such as the reform of the UN; the ending and reversal of nuclear proliferation, horizontal and vertical; general arms reduction and verification; economic demilitarisation; and an ending of the arms trade? Can they help us to develop scenarios in which reliance on arms becomes an anachronism, and they are finally scrapped? Can it show how military forces can be turned into police forces, and how police forces can be demilitarised? Can we ourselves join our efforts with those within the military and the police who are already using some of the skills of nonviolence, and build those skills for defusing and containing violence without counter-violence?[16]

Is this all fantasy? I believe not. The use of conflict-transformation terminology by government bodies (for instance, the British Foreign and Commonwealth Office) shows that we already have a toehold there. Even if the use of such terms is sometimes specious (and the approaches of more enlightened wings of government are countered by more pugilistic elements), it gives us an entry point for dialogue. It is also a sign of shifting norms, and a consequent desire to be seen to be changing, becoming more enlightened.

Connecting with the peace movement

The research of academics needs to be communicated not only to politicians and policy-makers, but also to movements, so that it can inform and strengthen their advocacy work. Were the true cost of militarism – in human, environmental and economic terms – widely known and understood, the will that is needed for change would surely be there.

The experiences and ideas of those who are working for conflict transformation can also contribute a great deal to the peace

16. The 3D Security Initiative launched by the Eastern Mennonite University in the US is working to engage with both the military and the peace movement in order to influence policy. See <www.3Dsecurity.org>.

movement. So, at the same time as talking among ourselves and with policy-makers, we need to begin to build stronger connections with peace organisations that work to change public perceptions and policy through public action. Those of us whose daily work is on conflict are relatively few in number; but peace activists are many and, at present, in some Western countries at least, the connections are thin and sporadic. That is a great loss to both sides. We need each other.

In order to fill out our 'menu' of conflict-transformation strategies, we need to keep ourselves thoroughly grounded in activism, learning continually about how movements work and constantly adding to the fund of experience-based knowledge that we are able to share with colleagues and partners in other parts of the world.

Such involvement will also help bridge the gap between professionals and activists. And when we come to other countries with our organisational missions to help address conflicts nonviolently, it will increase our political and moral credibility if we are also in the business of addressing the military postures and the violence of our own governments. Furthermore, it will give us the satisfaction of knowing that we are not only working for peace in specific conflicts, but also helping to address the global culture and systems from which they arise and which block their transformation.

Just as we have much to learn from working in movements, we have our own contribution to make within them. We can bring the inspiration of our first-hand experience of what local activists are doing to address conflict in nonviolent ways, including a wealth of ideas for symbolic action and resistance. We can help create a sense of global connectedness in a way that increases the positive, hopeful side of the movements' motivation, and to counter its more cynical tendencies. We can give a human face, or many human faces, to the cause we are campaigning for, taking us beyond slogans and anger to human recognition and compassion, and to the challenge that we all have to face – of how to create a world that is not fashioned according to one rigid ideology or another, but by people and for people, in an ongoing process.

Ironically, while governments often cloak their violence in the language of peace, movements sometimes use the language of violence to describe their activities – for instance, advertising themselves as ready to 'smash' the arms trade, or whatever. This not only seems misguided and contradictory, but also reveals that the reality that the values of peace do not always permeate peace movements and inform their demeanour. Ideology is good and necessary if it is informed by kindness as well as passion and if it leaves room for change, accommodation and constant, mutual reformulation. Anger is constructive if it is an expression of grief at avoidable suffering, and of determination to do something about it. Neither ideology nor anger is good for anything when it turns us into demonisers or purveyors of hatred. Movement activists do not always understand that, while anger may feel good to the one who is expressing it, the effect it produces in others may be very negative. If changing hearts and minds is the goal of activism, such a lack of understanding is bad news.

Often, within established groups and coalitions, the lines of difference are already drawn – for instance, between the 'hard left' and the 'soft liberals'. This makes it difficult for anyone inside existing groups or networks to 'break ranks' and call for the kind of open conversation that can lead to greater clarity of purpose, fresh and shared analysis, and more productive ways of working towards agreed goals. The new perspectives and hands-on skills that could be brought in by those working in our field could revitalise struggling groups. But, to be accepted and respected and allowed to contribute in this way, we must come in not as superior external experts, but as fellow movement members with particular experiences and skills to share, as well as plenty to learn.

Many peace movement activists have had years of experience. They may themselves have become experts in public communication and private dialogue through the regular practice of sharing their ideas with people they meet – whether on vigils or through the newspapers, in public meetings or on doorsteps. They may also have participated in strategy workshops years ago, and remained informed by them ever since. They will have their own hard-won insights to share with us.

For instance, having been involved for decades in the UK's Campaign for Nuclear Disarmament, I remember a time when we spent weekends training ourselves for outreach, for instance through the use of petitions and questionnaires, which were presented to people in ways that would enable them to feel respected and listened to, drawing them into real conversations (as against word battles) in which we would be looking for the common ground that would make our message intelligible, rather than threatening.

That training was useful, and we may now be able to help fellow-campaigners who have not benefited from something similar to understand for the first time their goal of winning people over – of reaching out rather than attacking. The ethos and values of conflict resolution may deepen the source of their energy, as well as softening the aggressive edges of their assertiveness.

It is the function of movements to bring issues into public awareness, confronting or exposing what is oppressive, unjust and destructive, and calling for change. While public confrontation and opposition may be an inevitable, and indeed healthy, aspect of democracy – necessary to change and to bringing issues into the public arena – strengthening dialogue and seeking cooperation should, I believe, remain paramount. Aikido energy is simply more effective than the dynamics of confrontation, and we should be on the lookout for opportunities to harness it. Moreover, experience in many non-Western countries enables us to encourage the use of cultural and artistic forms of communication that touch people at the emotional as well as the cognitive level.

Most of the peace organisations and movements that I know tend to focus on specific wars or weapons systems, rather than addressing the underlying culture and system of militarism or war as an institution. Could we, having deepened our own analysis, help them to deepen theirs, so that every specific campaign begins to contain a more radical anti-war and pro-peace message, and every organisation starts to build this into its ethos, analysis and strategising? If this were to happen, the public impact of campaigns would be very different, producing a growing awareness that there is an alternative vision for human society, that fundamental change is needed, and that popular support is needed for change.

Maybe our skills can also be put to good use in helping broker a greater degree of unity within the peace movement at large, both within and between our own countries. A unifying focus on the need to abolish war as an institution might be the kind of catalyst that is needed for renewing and combining our energies. The task would be to generate the will and impetus for radical change; to create a peace constituency with a global agenda, calling for the dismantling of militarist policies and institutions and the development of the politics and systems needed for peace.[17]

Peace movements will doubtless continue to confront the specifics of militarism – particular wars or weapons systems, recruitment, the arms trade, and so on – and these are necessary objects of their

17.   Visit Cynthia Cockburn's website (<www.cynthiacockburn.org>) to read about her research project, 'Hearing Each Other: Towards Coherence in the Anti-war Movement'.

attention. But I am arguing, and hoping, that they can begin to set those specific issues in a wider context, and to bring before the public and before governments the need to dismantle the whole edifice of militarism. I also hope that they will do this in the most constructive ways possible, because those will be the most effective and the most consonant with the ethos of demilitarisation.

Those of us who are already engaged in movement work will be familiar with the forms its action can take. I suggest that methods of action should be selected (or developed) and carried out in such ways that they embody the good, creative energy of cooperation and kindness, even when anger and grief are felt and expressed. Confronting and laying bare what is wrong need not involve insulting and alienating people, though messages need to be clear and strong. Public demonstrations of different kinds, leaflets, petitions, questionnaires, letters to the press, acts of civil disobedience, public meetings – all have their place, if achieved in the spirit of respect and dialogue. The values we wish to uphold should be evident in the way we act and communicate, and our messages should always point to our vision, whether short- or long-term (though preferably both). This should rule out violence of all kinds.

There is a tendency within the peace movement (as I know it) to paint something of a caricature of the world. Polarisation of opinion and the desire to win arguments can be enemies of honesty. Facts are chosen selectively, distorting the picture and exaggerating asymmetries of violence and its justifications (or the lack of them). The language of hatred soon follows. Bringing to the centre of our campaigns a values-based, principled resistance to militarism will make it clear that our goals are inclusive and positive. When it is necessary to protest, we need to get to the heart of what is wrong, denouncing actions rather than demonising people, countries or governments.

Finding the right words to encapsulate our arguments (like those I quoted at the beginning of this chapter) is potentially a more powerful means of change than any gun or bomb. Cartoons, too, can be an excellent ways of exposing the absurdity of war. Humour may in some circumstances need to be trenchant, but not vicious. The point is to win hearts and minds – not to humiliate or engender hatred. We need to uncover the common ground of shared values, hopes and fears.

Transcending the political divisions between existing tendencies in the peace movement will not be easy. The vision will need to be strong, and it will need to be shared. I believe that we have skills to help achieve this, and that the inspiration of the stories we have to tell and the people we can introduce will help to dissipate dogma and liberate the spirit. We have a wealth of first-hand knowledge and experience of what violence and violent ideologies can do. We can also give life to the notion of global solidarity in such a way that it is too many-stranded and interwoven, too richly textured to be dominated by '-isms'. One way of strengthening this sense of human connectedness and common cause would be to develop the grassroots funding of international peace work. This could also help support work that is at present unattractive to most large donors.

In my local peace group, activists from many different backgrounds and perspectives have found each other to be excellent colleagues and friends, and recent campaigns have been characterised by far greater cooperation and wider coalitions than in the past. Internet communication generates the kind of global and multi-channelled networking that was scarcely possible before, so that it is hard to maintain the rigidity of old divisions – though maybe some prejudice-reduction workshops would still help! We need to open up, not only to fellow activists, but also to people and institutions we have tended to regard with too much dislike, or too little hope to communicate with them in ways that might bridge the divide.

What we all need to focus on is getting the message across to those who have not yet had the chance to hear it. We need to cultivate alliances with journalists and storytellers, find our way into schools (where the military are regular visitors and Officer Training Corps are all too often present), address societies, both secular and religious, and display our badges and stickers. We need to form peace societies within all unions and professions. In all this outreach work, those of us who have seen at first-hand what militarism does, and have witnessed resistance around the world, have a powerful story to tell.

The message must be threefold: that militarism is no answer to the violence and injustice that need to be addressed; that it is in itself at the heart of those problems; and that there are ways in which people can act together nonviolently to cope with crises and to change the system. Underlying that threefold message, and projected along with it, must be a positive vision of peace and an ethos of respect and interdependence.

Transcending levels and professional boundaries

I have suggested that we have done too little to turn theory into practice on the potential synergy between different levels of society and politics. This is the time for serious experiment. Can we make links with local governments, for instance, to formulate and adopt policies for peace and against war? This could include policy on investment and trading; on the movement of military goods on local roads and railways, and planning permission for military camps and installations; on peace education and the exclusion of military recruitment from schools; on employment and the maximising of non-military jobs; on information about the impact of wars in creating drug dependency, depression, suicide and homelessness; or on what is advertised on local authority vehicles and buildings, and so on. Could we ask local politicians to make these local policies known within their national political parties, and represent them to those who make national policy and decisions?

Our outreach work could include community groups, where such issues could be aired, along with the deeper questions underlying them, so that those groups in turn could help persuade their local elected representatives to contribute to the policies of peace. Active citizens are to be found in special interest groups and advocacy groups of all kinds, and these often organise at both local and national levels. Local activists in these groups can take their views and agendas to the central body of their organisations and ask for action.

The same can be said for religious congregations and their central bodies. Religion is seen by many as one of the chief causes and motors of violence – a sad reflection on the way in which it has often been perverted. But the yearning for meaning, the capacity for inspiration, the role of moral approval, and a sense of integrity in contributing to human happiness can transcend the divisions between religions and the secular–religious divide. They lie at the heart of our humanity. It is time that the organisations that express our beliefs and values, our longings and our commitments, whether religious or secular, became the vehicles of peace.

Within and beyond all other circles of common purpose and solidarity, the women's movement that continues to grow across the world is essential to transforming the military culture and engendering new models of coexistence and inclusiveness, new ways of valuing each other.

Positive peace means far more than the ending of war. It presupposes a worldview that sees the well-being of others as interwoven with our own. It means providing what I have called 'the space for conditions for human thriving'.[18] That includes economic justice, social inclusion, human rights, political freedom, and the chance to participate in public affairs, as well as freedom from direct violence. Our societies have activists working on all these issues, and there are highly organised and expert NGOs working on them. In the final chapter I will trace some of the connections between these different aspects of positive peace, and argue that, together, we could make the kind of breakthrough that is needed to turn our world around.

In all these fields, there are local activists and organisational employees, thinkers as well as doers, academics as well as practitioners, with an overlap between the two. Academics have their own access to governments – through their research, through think tanks, and so on. They can also influence public opinion through the media.

This is the challenge: to mobilise together effectively, drawing new people into activism, creating a common vision, and cooperating to the full – and, in so doing, beginning to challenge and transform the very system of violence. If we can do this, it will in itself be the best possible testimony to nonviolent people-power. It will provide much-needed evidence that civilian-based defence could be strong enough to deter any invasion, that uprisings can overthrow dictators, and that, given a fraction of the resources consumed by militarism, nonviolent protection could indeed work. It will inspire belief in the human spirit.

18. Francis, *Conflict Transformation*, p. 11.

8
Agenda for Humanity

My focus in this last chapter is on positive peace – what it comprises, and the power we have that can enable us to build it.

However hackneyed it is to say this, a time of crisis is also a time of opportunity, since change is underway. Thus far, the comfort and fear of the powerful has hindered change. Now no one can feel altogether comfortable. The idea of the end of history has long seemed foolish. Of late, the notion of a unipolar world on which it was predicated has been supplanted by recognition that the dominance of the West is being eroded by the growing power of the East. At the same time, fears for the future of our ecosystem and the collapse of capitalist institutions have made it clear that none of us is secure.

Will this sharpen our understanding of what insecurity means for those who have long lived (and died) with it, and hence awaken our compassion, or will it heighten our eat-or-be-eaten mentality? This is a question we must put to ourselves and determine by our actions. It is a matter for choice, not prognostication. For reasons of ethics, dignity and efficacy, I believe we must choose the model of interdependence and work together. The many must no longer cede power to the few, but must exercise their collective will for the common good. And the common good, as we are beginning to recognise, must include our planet and everything in it.

An agenda for positive peace can be conceptualised in terms of four familiar 'territories': peaceful relationships and processes, economic well-being, environmental protection, and democracy.[1] Since they are so intimately and integrally connected, separating them for discussion will be difficult, but I will address them in turn and trace at least some of the connections. What I say may seem obvious. It will not be erudite or exhaustive. However, I hope it will be sufficiently indicative to convince the reader that a new political movement is needed for a positive peace that embraces all

---

1. D. Francis, 'A Project to Transform Policy, Starting in the UK', *CCTS Review* 35 (November 2007), pp. 5–8. See also Fisher and Zimina, 'Just Wasting Our Time?'; and <www.dansmithsblog.com>.

these things, and that each needs renewed and urgent effort, both philosophical and practical.

PEACE

For the purposes of this discussion I will define peace in its narrowest sense as nonviolent relationships and processes that can embrace conflict and deal with it constructively. War is by definition its opposite, as well as being an assault on all aspects of positive peace.

Any society will include human relationships ranging from the wonderfully nurturing to the desperately destructive, with everything in between. In situations that can be regarded as tolerably peaceful, most people rub along together well enough to want to live and work with each other. Harmful behaviour is minimised, largely by social pressure and where necessary by enforcement systems. (Sometimes such systems are violent in their nature or destructive in their impact, but the best are focused on reform and restoration.)

In public affairs a great deal of cooperation is taken for granted in providing services, setting standards, implementing legislation and the like, within localities, countries and regions, as well as globally. There are also institutions that enable conflicts to be dealt with in an orderly manner without fighting or killing, and it is coming to be recognised that, through conciliation processes, it is possible to move from damage limitation to something more positive.

Even in war the values of peace struggle for expression. Enemies take pity on each other, are nursed in the same hospitals, play football at Christmas. The laws of war represent an attempt to apply humane values in inhuman conditions.

Yet alongside these relatively peaceable norms and systems for the management of conflict and protection of persons, the norms and systems of war make it possible for a political agenda to be understood as justifying acts of gross cruelty on a grand scale, which in itself is at odds with any notion of lawful behaviour, human rights and democracy. Instead of being dealt with through due process of law or by conciliation, conflict is seen as a reason for mass slaughter, even though the outcome cannot be predicted, and the cost, human and otherwise, will be immense. When war crimes that are designated as such are investigated, the collective punishment of war itself is not under judgement, and only losers are arraigned.

Full-blown war is overwhelmingly inimical to human security – causing death and misery, destroying infrastructure, homes and other fruits of human endeavour, and causing mass migrations. But the smaller, chronic wars described in terms of 'insurgency' and 'counterinsurgency' also inflict great suffering, and displace democracy with violence and coercion, making normal life impossible and displacing the rule of law and political processes.

Not only is war the antithesis of democracy, but in both its preparation and its execution it inflicts immense damage on the environment, through the plunder of minerals and burning of fuels (for the manufacture of weapons and machinery, and for powering aircraft and tanks, for instance); through the destruction of vegetation and animal life of all kinds by bombing; and through catastrophic events such as the release of immense quantities of carbon and other toxins into the atmosphere when oil fields and refineries are attacked, the bombing of chemical factories, or the poisoning of the earth with plutonium.

And although, since World War II, the use of nuclear weapons has remained a threat rather than a fact, their continuing presence, and the threat of their use in a regional conflict, or their detonation (whether intentional or accidental) remains. Proliferation, both vertical and horizontal, continues to be a matter of contention and of danger (though there are signs that at last it might be taken seriously). The impact of the use of nuclear weapons, both immediately and in the long term, would be catastrophic – both in humanitarian terms and environmentally.

Dismantling the institutions and the mindset of war will involve addressing the violence inherent in current constructions of gender and relationships between men and women. The violation of women in war is an intensified expression of the chronic gender violence that goes on in the homes, on the streets, and in the courts of the world. By the same token, the transformation of our understanding of gender and of the equal humanity of men and women will be fundamental to global demilitarisation.

For all these reasons, the abolition of war and all that goes with it is not a fantasy but a priority for positive peace and all that it requires: the physical safety, human rights and political participation, the economic well-being and healthy environment that constitute positive peace.

ECONOMIC JUSTICE AND WELL-BEING

The greatest cost of war is that it generates further wars, with all that this entails in terms of human insecurity and suffering.

But the economic impact of war is also immense, and economic human rights are too easily overlooked in the affluent world. War is the enemy of economic well-being. Militarism is an industry as well as an ideology, but a very costly one – destructive rather than productive, and dependent on war's continuation for its survival. It enriches a few: those who run companies supplying mercenary soldiers; those trading in armaments, large and small; those making careers in military research and development. But societies are impoverished by military spending (whose global level has reached $1.2 trillion per annum[2]), and this is contrary to economic justice and well-being.

War puts immense pressure on natural resources. It wastes labour and materials that could be used for the relief of poverty and the provision of health services and education, of clean water and food. It stands in the way of human flourishing. As President Dwight D. Eisenhower famously put it, 'Every gun that is made, every warship that is launched, every rocket fired signifies, in the final sense, a theft from those who hunger and are not fed, those who are cold and not clothed.'[3] If a third of the money that went into weapons manufacture and the running of the military machine went instead into resources for the support of genuine peace-making and nonviolent human protection, the other two-thirds could be spent on developing the things that are needed for economic well-being and human development. The erstwhile costs of repairing the ravages of war could be invested in research and the development of technology to help address climate change and other environmental threats, making habitats habitable and livelihoods possible.

War, at whatever level, is also the means by which those engaged in it gain illicit control over natural resources and rob communities of their wealth. This is done not only through the resource wars between the big powers, but also by those who build their own economic fiefdoms through civil war – for instance, through control of the diamond trade, by extortion, or by drug running. Abolishing war is essential to addressing economic injustice.

While war itself is both a means of plunder and a cause of poverty, economic marginalisation can be one of the causes of war. Poverty is one of the reasons why the dispossessed may be enlisted as fighters – either because they support an attempt to oust the government

2. A. Shah, 'World Military Spending' – article published on their website by Global Issues, at <www.globalissues.org/articles>.
3. From a speech of Dwight D. Eisenhower before the American Society of Newspaper Editors, 16 April 1953.

they see as responsible for their marginalisation, or because they lack any other source of income. It follows that economic justice is a prerequisite for the prevention of war, and that war, which exacerbates poverty and is a means of economic injustice, needs to be recognised for what it is, and that goals must be set for its abolition.

But economic justice and well-being are priorities first and foremost in themselves. They are a matter of moral responsibility, which in turn is essential to our dignity as human beings. Without them no peace can be worthy of the name. Economic well-being for all is not an impossible dream but an attainable goal, if it is finally seen as more important than the 'right' of the few to control an ever-increasing share of the world's wealth. The religion of unfettered capitalism has been revealed to be not only cruel and demeaning, but also an ill-founded belief in a system liable to collapse as soon as doubt creeps in and the bubble bursts.

Positive peace will require a re-examination of the relationship between democracy, justice and market mechanics. The current system has not delivered what is needed. It has proved disastrous for the majority of the world's population, and recently has even failed many of those who were its beneficiaries. It has proved fragile indeed.

International norms will need to be established, and made operational in international treaties and national legislation, on terms and conditions of employment, and on taxation for social welfare, its services and institutions, as well as on providing civil infrastructure and sustaining political life. An international body that can be trusted and respected by all, such as a reformed and truly democratic UN, will be needed to guide a process of global economic adjustment (as well as to mediate or arbitrate in disputes over natural resources), so that trade agreements and levels of production and consumption are established that are sustainable and equitable for all – which, in the long run, will contribute to global economic well-being.

Any new model will need to be based on a more sane assessment of what constitutes economic well-being, catering for our health and fullness of life, but not for the kind of 'conspicuous consumption' that has no ceiling and drives endless, unsustainable growth. Such growth has been shown to create unstable economies. It is also environmentally disastrous.

The new economic order will also need to cater for the needs and rights of both women and men, so that economic dependency does not perpetuate perceptions of inferiority and attitudes of dominance.

It must be designed for the well-being and inclusion of children, people with disabilities, and old people, as well as those who are at the peak of their capacity to work, fostering between them all a sense of true equality, respect and cooperation.

ENVIRONMENTAL PROTECTION

Environmental protection will not be achieved without profound cooperation on a global scale. Again, is this possible? Our track record to date is not encouraging. The continuation of competitive growth economics, unfettered and ungoverned, would certainly make it impossible. Current responses to the economic downturn militate against environmental protection, making for a far greater disaster than the one that is already unavoidable, and for many has already begun. Yet if we can only grasp the magnitude and intensity of the storm we are in, and the fact that we are all in one boat, this could be the moment when the paradigm shifts, and when we at last begin to order our economic life in a way that respects the needs of all people and of the planet that is our common home.

If the urgent needs of our time are to have any chance of being met, a process of principled negotiation must begin to find a way forward that meets the needs, if not the greed, of all, in such a way that our common habitat – the source of our well-being – can be secured as far as is possible at this late hour. Again, a trusted international body will be needed to facilitate, and where necessary arbitrate, on the basis of equity and the common good. But no such process will take place unless those who benefit from the current dispensation are persuaded to loosen their grip on the controls. This will require a breadth and intensity of popular mobilisation greater than any achieved before. It will mean that many must choose to have less in order that others will have more. I believe that the very size of the global crises can help to make this possible.

One matter for negotiation will be the way in which those who have caused the most damage to date, and in so doing have reaped the most economic benefit, will help the less wealthy to carry the costs of environmental protection, as well as sharing the costs of the harm already done. If the haves do not take care of the have-nots, the consequent disorder (such as food riots, mass migrations and the lawless appropriation of basic necessities) will not be controllable, even if violence is used to quell it.[4]

4. See C. Abbott, *An Uncertain Future: Law Enforcement, National Security and Climate Change,* Oxford: Oxford Research Group, 2008.

Environmental degradation and the depletion of much-needed resources, along with our multiplication as a species, have already become a source of conflict, as the oil wars of recent decades illustrate. Water is increasingly a matter of contention, even within countries that are not thought of as 'water poor', but all the more so in arid regions. The current sporadic conflicts could become endemic and take place on a much larger scale. But wars will only exacerbate the problems, consuming more resources and inflicting more environmental damage. Global democracy, economic justice, and the maintenance of peaceful relationships all require that scarce resources be shared equitably, on the basis of constructive negotiation, rather than becoming the arbitrary spoils of war.

I have already indicated the direct and immense environmental damage done by war. Our dominatory and extractive approach to nature has brought us close to catastrophe. Indeed, for some other species and for some members of our own, it is already too late. International cooperation has gone into fuelling the arms and space races; now it must be put to the urgent but necessarily patient and painstaking task of building our expertise to halt climate change (as far as it can be halted), and to cope with its ongoing impact. Thinkers across the world – philosophical, creative and scientific – will be needed to lead us into a new understanding of our place in the universe: one which encourages wonder, humility and a sense of common belonging, and in which our puny attempts at control are seen as foolish and unattractive.

Care for our planet will be promoted and encouraged by a shift from the current privileging of dominance, as a source of pride, to a preference for nurture, and the satisfaction that goes with it. The fact that our future makes care a necessity may in fact help to bring this shift about.

DEMOCRACY

By democracy, I do not mean the replication of existing models as practised in any particular country: I mean the freedom to participate in public affairs and to be the co-determinants of them, as well as the right to do so freely and without adverse consequence, and to live safely in one's society.

Human rights

Behind the apparent given-ness of human rights, there lies a wide range of related cultural norms, some of which have a profound

effect on the (non)observance of human rights. Violent discrimi-
nation – according to gender, race, caste, ethnicity, tribe, religion
and more – is still too widely prevalent, and the assumptions of
superiority and inferiority on which it is based mask the systemic
violence perpetrated by some human beings against others. The
scale of this violence around the world can be compared to that of
war. In all cases, the relationship in which the violence takes place
is one of domination, in which the equal humanity of the other is
denied and the violence used is not recognised as such, but is seen as
'normal'. However culturally sensitive these issues may be, human
rights are just that: the rights of all human beings.

Yet democracy cannot be imposed, only lived. A war for
democracy is a contradiction in terms: a tyranny perpetrated by
those who claim to oppose tyranny. The only way to promote
the observance of human rights and political participation is by
demonstrating unfailing respect for them, through the exchange
of ideas and steady, persistent, respectful persuasion. This must
be done with due humility, on the basis of human equality rather
than of assumed superiority. Those who have the skeletons of war
in their cupboards have no cause to set themselves up as models of
respect for human rights or for democratic processes. They must
win respect by putting their own houses in order: the human rights
of those who were bombed to pieces in Baghdad or Gaza were
utterly disregarded.

The right not to kill or be killed as a combatant in war is a human
right denied in many countries, despite international legislation to
support it. Children, in particular, are in urgent need of protection.
And the rights of women must at last be recognised as identical to
those of men.

It is increasingly argued by internationalists that there is an
obligation on all states to be ready to intervene to protect the human
rights of people in other states.[5] I would argue here, as I have
throughout, that war is not an effective or appropriate mechanism
for doing this, being the polar opposite of human rights, and by
nature inimical to human and planetary well-being. That means
that it is incumbent on states to develop the means and provide the
resources for nonviolent forms of protection. A state that had done
this could be seen as truly civilised.

5. See M. Walzer, *Thinking Politically: Essays in Political Theory* (ed. and
    introduced by D. Miller), Yale: Yale University Press, 2007, p. xix.

Political participation

The idea of governance by the people for the people seems a very long way from what is experienced by many of those who live in countries that are deemed to be democratic: the kind of representative democracy in which a citizen has the opportunity to vote once every few years, but between elections has little role to play. In open societies it is possible to lobby one's representative on the local council or national parliament, and some countries provide opportunities for direct participation through referendums. But many long-established democracies have lost their shine. Their people may have become apathetic, and the practice of democracy may have atrophied. 'Security' may have become a pretext for the undue curtailment of civil liberties, while preoccupation with individual rights and freedoms may have contributed to the loss of any real sense of participation in society and any meaningful commitment to the common good. At the same time, countries trying to shift from totalitarianism to democracy struggle (and not always with sufficient resolution) to consolidate a culture of engagement and the accountability of the leadership to the governed.

And what of the electoral systems in which it is possible to vote for a lifetime and never once have one's views represented as a result? What of political menus so similar that there is no effective choice, and where none on offer coincide in any way with what one wants to see? What of politicians whose only interest seems to be their own election or re-election, so that policies are endlessly tailored for short-term popularity and fail to address real needs?

I realise that, even where there is the will to create a society and systems for perfect democracy there will still be apparently 'competing goods' that need to be balanced, and that the balance that is struck, or the creative solutions that are found, will always be contested.[6] Typically, the tension lies between the demands of security and freedom. Yet I believe that, if security is rightly understood, it will be clear that the best route to it will not be through violence-based control, but through cooperation and respect for human rights.

Democracy is an idea and an aspiration. It has no single form, though its attributes may be agreed upon. I recognise that different societies will, given the will, find different ways of achieving political participation. It has been assumed in the West that the one true model of democracy is adversarial. As I have indicated earlier, I

6.   I. Berlin, *Concepts and Categories*, London: Hogarth Press, 1978.

have no doubt that contestation is a healthy part of the democratic process – the contest of ideas, and where necessary the confrontation of wrongdoing. But contestation can be understood and carried out in the spirit of common purpose, and rooted in a cooperative endeavour to find the best way forward.

Electoral reform can introduce systems that encourage a plurality of voices rather than two-party confrontation. That seems relatively simple. But we also need to look more radically at our assumptions about the way politics works, and find a new balance between conflict and cooperation. The macho style of politics, in which success is the ability to triumph over one's opponent, needs to change. It is detrimental to good governance. It is preferable to tyranny, but it is not good enough. We need to build an understanding of political life as something that is shared, in the service of the common good.

There are many politicians who are driven by the will to serve and to make their society, or the world, a better place. There are excellent, cooperative processes within political systems – for instance, cross-party committees in which politicians are allowed to work together on particular issues in a largely non-partisan way, pooling their knowledge, skills and wisdom. As with the local practice of conflict transformation, this existing good practice not only does good in its own context, but points the way forward and provides a model to build on.

But politics needs more than professional politicians. Representative democracy alone is unlikely to remain democratic. The people need to express their will in other ways, and to take action on their own account; they need to create the context in which elections are held, and their own 'constructive programmes' will not only have direct effect but also influence the way people think, which in turn will shape the political platforms on which politicians stand for election and the policies they later implement. Thinkers, political activists and voluntary workers all contribute to the creation of cultural, political and social norms. Indeed, every alert and concerned citizen, in conversation with others – whether at the bus stop, at work, or over a meal – is helping to create political reality.

'Society' and 'citizens' are Western terms, and other cultures have their own, different ways of understanding and naming the collectivities to which they belong and the ways in which people coexist. We can learn from each other. In the end all of us, individually and collectively, must take our own responsibility for our ways of being and acting in the world. But I believe that a sense of solidarity, actively expressed in day-to-day life, is both the best protection for human rights and the essence of cooperative living. It is the only rational and ethical response to the fact of our interdependence. The political participation that it can engender is vital to positive peace.

Again, it is important to bring gender into the frame. We need the equal participation of men and women at every level of public life and the creation of new models and norms that will give life to a different kind of politics, and enable us to benefit from the strengths of all, in their own right.

GROUNDS FOR HOPE

A great deal needs to change, and we are faced with vested interests and inertia. Yet the seeds of change are already active in the soil. Global disgust with war has been growing, and a strong popular movement could contribute to the election of politicians who see that war serves no one's purpose. As I write, there is a reawakening to the threat of nuclear weapons. Resistance to the 'missile defence' programme is growing. New voices are speaking out for the abolition of all nuclear weapons, and an international commission has been established on nuclear non-proliferation and disarmament. (The US president seems set to take a positive lead, though without popular support around the world he is unlikely to take things as far as the times require.) The 'war on terror' has been discredited, having been recognised as a pretext for hegemonistic wars and as counterproductive for anyone's security. Research is demonstrating the efficacy of nonviolence campaigns, as compared with violent resistance.[7] More and more people around the world are standing up for human rights, and the tyranny of war is itself being resisted ever more widely. Let us now build the movement for its abolition.

The global economic downturn has not only forced a major reassessment of the current financial system, but also heightened awareness of global poverty and injustice. There are signs of a growing current of opinion favouring equity in the face of massive inequality, sufficiency and contentment in the face of uncaring greed.

There is a danger that action to escape recession by stimulating renewed economic growth will undermine efforts to reduce global warming, and that economic preoccupations will weaken determination to address the looming environmental crisis. We must

7.   S. Elworthy, *Insider Power: Saving Lives, Saving Money. Why conflict prevention policy needs to be joined up* – speech made to the All Party Parliamentary Group on Conflict Issues, House of Commons, London, 24 February 2009.

hope that scientists and activists have done, and will continue to do, enough to convince us all that economic well-being cannot be achieved at the expense of ever-increasing environmental destruction. We have to digest the fact of our interdependence with our whole ecosystem. I believe this is beginning to happen.

Fear can stimulate action. It can also produce denial. It is essential to focus not only on what is dangerous and wrong, but also on the values and the vision that can give people the will to take action to secure a better future.

By the time this book is published, President Obama will have been in office for long enough to show to some extent how far a change at the top can produce change on the ground. He became president because enough of the electorate wanted change and voted for it. He owes his power to them. The maintenance, and indeed the growth, of popular support for radical steps will be crucial – not only in the US, but in countries around the world. We need not only to support the right kind of political lead, but to go ahead of the politicians and prepare the political ground, going ever deeper in our analysis and challenge of the system, to ensure that there is a gathering momentum of change.

GLOBAL SOLIDARITY AND THE POWER OF HUMANITY

We must build a constituency for positive peace: one so powerful that it cannot be refused and which, by its own energy, itself begins to create the transformation that is needed. A global political agenda that embraces demilitarisation and nonviolence, economic justice and well-being, the protection and nurturing of the environment and the building of global democracy, could provide the focus for effective global solidarity to transform global conflicts and build positive peace.

These are huge ambitions. They are, however, both necessary and possible. 'Yes we can' has become a cliché, but it expresses the spirit of belief that is essential to change. There is nothing in the agenda I have outlined that is by nature impossible – though it would represent a seismic shift, involving every level of society.

It is human identification and solidarity that can transcend all divisions. It is these above all else that can protect human rights and transform relationships: active solidarity expressed both 'on the spot' and through global political mobilisation.

This takes us back to the question of agency, and how change happens – of complexity, and what can and cannot be predicted.

What is needed is a growing energy for change – collective energy and the synergy of different efforts too complex to be consciously coordinated, like the astonishing, swirling dance of a flock of starlings or a shoal of fish, not planned but governed by common purpose, constant communication and intuition. I assume we have too great a capacity for conscious thought to be able to behave with the same degree of coordination as birds or fish, and must hope that our rational capacities to strategise and organise will, at least to some degree, compensate for the deficit. But, like fish and birds, we shall need to find our direction as much by responding to those around us as by trying to discern and order the big picture.

'Going with the flow' sounds careless and uncommitted, but it is important when it means putting our energy to maximum use by combining strategic thinking with opportunism, slipstreaming in behind the efforts of others, and in return having their support for the moves that we make. At the cost of some attentiveness, this will maximise our impact, so long as we hold our direction and our vision: keep our eyes on the prize. We must use our brains to the full, but we must also let go of the futile desire to control outcomes.

There are no fixed outcomes, only moments in a constant unfolding of unimaginable complexity. Within that unfolding, there are points of great significance. What we most need is the capacity to recognise those moments and to grasp the opportunities they offer; the insight to see what can be done at a given moment and in a given context; the ability to set out on a journey with a plan, but then to keep navigating and re-planning, and to do so in communication with others.

I have identified four elements of positive peace – a four-fold political agenda. I see six sources of human power: the intellect; the emotions; the will; the skills we are born with and can develop; the imagination; and the aspect of human awareness, the spirit or inspiration, whatever its source, that takes us beyond our own individual capacities and lifts us up, uniting us with others in ways we cannot express but which give us a collective power that is far more than the sum of its parts. This is the deepest level of our humanity that makes us long for meaning, and that manifests itself in 'the promptings of love and truth'.[8] I believe it is the most

8. The words of Isaac Pennington in 1667, at the Yearly Meeting of the Religious Society of Friends (Quakers) in Britain, *Quaker Faith and Practice*, London: The Society of Friends, 1995, para. 10.01.

powerful source of our capacity for good, and can be the motor for the change we need.

These are the powers that can enable us to flourish, and our planet to remain hospitable. Whatever our strengths, we must contribute them. Men and women, young and old, whoever and wherever we are, we need each other and we need peace. Conflict transformation is an idea and a practice that gives form to this worldview. Let us begin to apply it globally.

Appendix: Stages and Processes in Conflict Transformation

In any consideration of conflict and how to engage in or respond to it, it is necessary to take into account its causes. Violence, not conflict, is the problem. Conflict in itself may be necessary to address structural violence. The prevention or premature 'resolution' of conflict may therefore mean in practice the suppression of just aspirations: 'pacification' rather than 'peacemaking'. At the same time, those wishing to enter into conflict in the name of a cause they consider to be just need to do so with some understanding of the likely cost to all concerned, and of their current and future opportunities, in the light of the distribution of power.

The diagram opposite aims to show the stages and processes that will typically need to be passed through if a situation of oppression, with an extreme imbalance of power, is to be transformed into one of genuine peace. (The words contained in the oval shapes describe conflict stages, while those contained in rectangles describe the actions or processes by which new stages are reached.)

Such diagrams do not present reality, but ideas about it, and should be seen simply as tools for thinking and discussion. In practice, the 'stages' represented here are not in themselves static – they have their own dynamics and in reality may merge with one another. Neither are they likely to follow each other in a clear and orderly sequence. It will often be a case of 'two steps forward and one step back', or even vice versa; and frequently processes need to be repeated, built on, or reinforced by other processes in order to bring about substantial progress. And the ideal of conflict transformation is often no more than that, at the stage of confrontation. This reality is reflected in the diagram's later stages, which are largely about recovery from violence.

In addition, large-scale conflicts are not simple or single affairs, but usually involve multiplicities of issues, parties and sub-parties. They will, in all likelihood, also involve conflicts and power struggles within as well as between parties, and the stages of these internal conflicts will not coincide with the stage the overall conflict has reached.

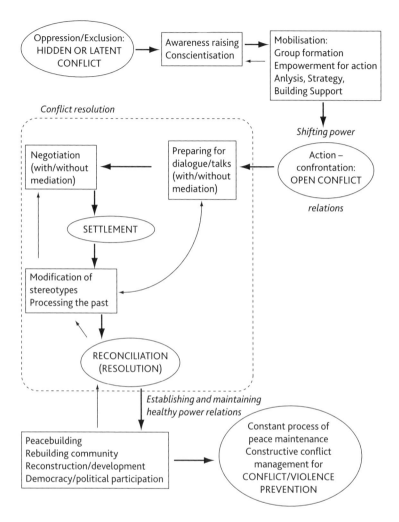

The diagram begins with a situation in which the oppression (or exclusion) is so complete that the conflict is hidden or latent, the oppressed group remaining passive in the face of extreme injustice or structural violence (often maintained by physical violence, or the threat of it). They may remain passive because of tradition, or lack of awareness, or because the power imbalance is such that they have no chance of being taken seriously in any demands or requests they might make. In order for this to change, some individual or group must begin to reflect upon, understand and articulate what is happening, and encourage others to do the same: a process described in the liberation language of Latin America as 'conscientisation'.

This process will, if it generates sufficient determination, lead to the formation of groups committed to change. Their first task will be to continue the process of reflection and analysis, formulating a common purpose and strategy, then developing organisation-ally as they begin to take action to build support and so increase their relative power.

Some oppressed groups choose to use violence in their struggle. For others violence is not something to consider, or is not seen as a practical option. For yet others it is a matter of clear strategic choice or principle to act nonviolently. The term 'conflict trans-formation' implies the nonviolent option.

As their power and visibility increase, as their voice begins to be heard, these groups will increasingly be seen as a threat by those in power, and a stage of open confrontation becomes inevitable – a stage which might well involve repressive measures, including physical violence, on the part of the oppressive power-holders, even if the oppressed group has opted to act nonviolently. (At this point, nonviolent resistance will sometimes turn to violence.) During this stage of open conflict, the power relationship between the opposing parties will change as a result of their ongoing confrontation, and other developments may occur within the parties or in the wider environment.

Even if the confrontation takes the form of armed conflict, eventually a road back to dialogue has to be found. Once the oppressed group has increased its relative power or leverage sufficiently, it can expect to be taken seriously as a partner in dialogue. At this stage it is possible to begin the processes grouped together and described as 'conflict resolution', in which communication is somehow restored and settlements reached.

This will not be a smooth process: talks may break down, agreements may be broken, and conflict may flare up again. Non-partisan intervention can help, for instance in the form of mediation, both in preparing the parties for negotiation and in the negotiations themselves. And through the work of preparing the ground, and through face-to-face dialogue, some of the heat may be taken out of the situation, some more hope and trust generated, and some of the prejudice dissipated, which in turn will facilitate the reaching of (and adherence to) agreements. Once these are in place, it may be possible to begin to deal with some of the remaining psychological damage that the conflict and its causes have occasioned, and to develop more positive relationships between the previously conflicting groups.

These more positive relationships will be consolidated through a long-term process of peacebuilding, and will find expression in social, political and economic institutions. But societies never remain static, and the final phase of 'peace' will, in fact, need to be a process (made up of a thousand processes) of maintaining awareness, of education, of management of differences, and of adjustment and engagement at all levels, so that some new situation of oppression – or other major source of conflict – does not develop, and just and peaceful relationships are maintained.

Bibliography

Aba, E., and M. Hammer, *Yes We Can? Options and Barriers to Broadening the Scope of the Responsibility to Protect to Include Cases of Economic, Social and Cultural Rights Abuse*, One World Trust Briefing Papers 116 (March 2009).

Abbott, C., *An Uncertain Future: Law Enforcement, National Security and Climate Change*, Oxford: Oxford Research Group, 2008.

Ackerman, P., and J. Duvall, *A Force More Powerful: A Century of Nonviolent Conflict*, New York: St Martin's Press, 2000.

Anderson, M. B., *Do No Harm: Supporting Local Capacities for Peace through Aid*, Cambridge, MA: Local Capacities for Peace Project, 1996.

Ball, N., and L. van de Goor, *Promoting Conflict Prevention through Security Sector Reform*, London: Price Waterhouse Coopers, May 2008.

Banfield, J., C. Gunduz, and N. Killick (eds), *Local Business, Local Peace: the Peacebuilding of the Domestic Private Sector*, London: International Alert, 2006.

Barnes, C. (ed.), 'Owning the Process: Public Participation in Peacemaking' (*Accord* 13), London: Conciliation Resources, 2002.

Berdal, M., and D. Malone (eds), *Greed and Grievance: Economic Agendas in Civil Wars*, Colorado and London: Lynne Rienner, 2000.

Berlin, I., *Concepts and Categories*, London: Hogarth Press, 1978.

——'My Intellectual Path', *New York Review of Books*, 14 May 1998, pp. 53–60.

Billig, M., *Arguing and Thinking*, Cambridge: Cambridge University Press, 1987.

Boulding, E., *Cultures of Peace: The Hidden Side of History*, New York: Syracuse University Press, 2000.

Boutros Gali, B., *An Agenda for Peace*, New York: United Nations, 1992.

Burton, J. (ed.), *Conflict: Human Needs Theory*, London: Macmillan, 1990.

CDA, *Reflecting on Peace Practice*. Cambridge, MA: CDA Collaborative Learning Project, 2004.

Clark, H., 'Demilitarising Minds, Demilitarising Societies' (*CCTS Newsletter* 11, Winter 2001), <www. c-r.org/ccts>.

——*The Evolution of the Committee for Conflict Transformation Support, 1992–2006*, 2006, <www.c-r.org/ccts>.

——(ed.), *People Power: Unarmed Resistance and Global Solidarity*, London: Pluto Press, 2009.

Cockburn, C., *From Where We Stand: War, Women's Activism and Feminist Analysis*, London: Zed Books, 2007.

Conciliation Resources, 'Choosing to Engage: Armed Groups and Peace Processes (*Accord* 16), London: Conciliation Resources, 2005.

——*Accord Policy Brief: Incentives, Sanctions and Conditionality in Peacemaking*, London: Conciliation Resources, 2008.

Curle, A., *Making Peace*, London: Tavistock Publications, 1971.

——*True Justice: Quaker Peace Makers and Peace Making*, London: Quaker Home Service, 1981.

Dudouet, V., 'Nonviolent Resistance and Conflict Transformation in Power Asymmetries', in M. Fischer et al. (eds), *The Berghof Handbook for Conflict Transformation*.

——'Cross-border Nonviolent Advocacy during the Second Palestinian Intifada: The International Solidarity Movement', in H. Clark (ed.), *People Power*.

Eisler, R., *The Chalice and the Blade: Our History, Our Future*, London: Unwin Paperbacks, 1990.

Elworthy, S., *Insider Power: Saving Lives, Saving Money. Why conflict prevention policy needs to be joined up*, speech to the All Party Parliamentary Group on Conflict Issues, House of Commons, London, 24 February 2009.

Fischer, M., H. J. Giessmann and B. Schmelzle (eds), *The Berghof Handbook for Conflict Transformation*, Berlin: Berghof Research Center for Constructive Conflict Management, 2008.

Fisher, S., and L. Zimina, 'Just Wasting Our Time? Provocative Thoughts for Peacebuilders', in B. Schmezle and M. Fischer (eds), *Peacebuilding at a Crossroads? Dilemmas and Paths for Another Generation* (Berghof Handbook Dialogue No. 7), Berlin: Berghof Research Center for Constructive Conflict Management, 2009.

Francis, B., *Toys, Gender and Learning: Report to the Frobel Educational Institute*, London: Roehampton University, 2009.

Francis, D., 'Conflict Transformation: From Violence to Politics' (*CCTS Review* 9, Summer 2002), <www.c-r.org/ccts>.

——*People, Peace and Power: Conflict Transformation in Action*, London: Pluto Press, 2002.

——*Rethinking War and Peace*, London: Pluto Press, 2004.

——'A Project to Transform Policy, Starting in the UK' (*CCTS Review* 35, November 2007), <www.c-r.org/ccts>.

——'Pacification or Peacebuilding?' (*CCTS Review* 30, March 2006), <www.c-r. org/ccts>.

——'Pacifism and the responsibility to protect' (*CCTS Review* 31, June 2006), <www.c-r.org/ccts>.

Francis, D., and N. Ropers, *Peace Work by Civil Actors in Post-Communist Societies* (Berghof Occasional Paper No. 10), Berlin: Berghof Research Center for Constructive Conflict Management, 1997.

Freire, P., *Pedagogy of the Oppressed*, London: Penguin, 1972.

Galtung, J., 'Cultural Violence', *Journal of Peace Research* 27: 3 (1990), pp. 291–305.

——*Peace by Peaceful Means: Peace and Conflict, Development and Civilization*, Oslo: PRIO, 1996.

Glasl, F., *Konfliktmanagement: Ein Handbuch fur Fuhrungskrafte, Beraterinnen und Berater*, Bern: Reies Geistleben, 1997.

Glover, J., *Humanity: A Moral History of the Twentieth Century*, London: Pimlico, 2001.

Goss-Mayr, J., and H. Goss-Mayr, *The Gospel and the Struggle for Peace*, Alkmaar, The Netherlands: International Fellowship of Reconciliation, 1990.

Institute for Public Policy Research, *Commission on National Security in the 21st Century* (interim report published September 2008), <www.ippr. publicationsandreports>.

Keegan, J., *A History of Warfare*, London: Pimlico, 1994.

Kelly, R., *Warless Societies and the Origin of War*, Michigan: University of Michigan Press, 2000.

Kurlansky, M., *Nonviolence: The History of a Dangerous Idea*, London: Vintage Books, 2006.

Lederach, J. P., *Building Peace: Sustainable Reconciliation in Divided Societies*, Tokyo: United Nations University Press, 1994.

Liebmann, M., *Restorative Justice: How It Works*, London: Jessica Kingsley Publishers, 2007.

Mathews, D., *War Prevention Works: 50 Stories of People Resolving Conflict*, Oxford: Oxford Research Group, 2001.

Max-Neef, M., 'Reflections on a Paradigm Shift in Economics', in M. Inglis and S. Kramer, (eds), *The New Economic Agenda*, Inverness: Findhorn Press, 1985.

Miall, H., O. Ramsbotham, and T. Woodhouse, *Contemporary Conflict Resolution*, Cambridge: Polity Press, 1999.

Minic, D., 'Gender and Peace Work', in H. Rill, T. Smidling, and A. Bitoljanu, *20 Pieces of Encouragement for Awakening and Change*, Belgrade–Sarajevo: Centre for Nonviolent Action, 2007.

Mitchell, C. R. *The Structure of International Conflict*, London: Macmillan, 1981.

Moix, B., and T. Keck, *The Responsibility to Protect: A Report to Congress from the Friends Committee on National Legislation*, <www.fcnl.org/issues>.

Pennington, I., at the Yearly Meeting of the Religious Society of Friends (Quakers) in Britain, *Quaker Faith and Practice*, London: Society of Friends, 1995, para. 10.01.

Phillips, A., and B. Taylor, 'Kindness', *Guardian Review*, 3 January 2009.

Pleydell, A., 'Giving meaning to "Never Again": The International Responsibility to Protect' (*CCTS Review* 31, June 2006), <www.c-r.org/ccts>.

Prager, J., 'The Funder's Perspective', in 'Funding Conflict Transformation: Money, Power and Accountability' (*CCTS Review* 25, November 2006), <www.c-r.org>.

Ricigliano, R. (ed.), 'Choosing to Engage: Armed Groups and Peace Processes' (*Accord* 16), London: Conciliation Resources, 2005.

Ropers, N., *Peaceful Intervention: Structures, Processes and Strategies for the Constructive Regulation of Ethnopolitical Conflicts*, Berlin: Berghof Research Center for Constructive Conflict Management, 1995.

Rose, S., 'In Search of the God Neuron', *Guardian Review*, 27 December 2008.

Rouhana, N. N. 'Unofficial Third-Party Intervention in International Conflict: Between Legitimacy and Disarray', *Negotiation Journal*, July 1995.

Shah, A., 'World Military Spending' – article published on their website by Global Issues, <www.globalissues.org/articles>.

Sharp, G., with B. Jenkins, *Civilian-Based Defence: A Post-Military Weapons System*, Princeton: Princeton University Press, 1990.

Sheehan, J., *The Monopoly of Violence: Why Europeans Hate Going to War*, London: Faber & Faber, 2008.

Stubbs, P., 'Civil Society or Ubheha', in H. Rill, T. Smidling, and A. Bitoljanu (eds), *20 Pieces of Encouragement for Awakening and Change: Peacebuilding in the Region of Former Yugoslavia*, Belgrade–Sarajevo: Centre for Nonviolent Action, 2007.

van Tongeren, P., M. Brenk, M. Hellema, and J. Verhoeven (eds), *People Building Peace II: Successful Stories of Civil Society*, Boulder and London: Lynne Rienner, 2005.

Ugresic, D., *The Culture of Lies*, London: Phoenix, 1998.

Verkoren, W., *The Owl and the Dove: Knowledge Strategies to Improve the Peacebuilding Practice of Local Non-governmental Organisations*, Amsterdam: Amsterdam University Press, 2008.

Vuskovic, L., and Z. Trifunovic (eds), *Women's Side of War*, Belgrade: Women in Black, 2008.

Walker, B., 'A Grant-Seeker's Perspective', in 'Funding Conflict Transformation: Money, Power and Accountability' (*CCTS Review* 25, November 2006), <www.c-r.org>.

Walzer, M., *Thinking Politically: Essays in Political Theory* (ed. and introduced by D. Miller), Yale: Yale University Press, 2007.

Index

Compiled by Peter Ellis

academics, peace, 35, 36, 160, 167
accompaniers, volunteer, 28
active listening, 5, 14
advocacy, 26–9, 40, 62, 93, 117, 160, 166
Afghanistan, 81, 97, 100, 115, 148
Africa, 36, 82
African Union, 82
Ahtisaari, Martti, 133
aikido energy, 126, 143–4, 163
Albania, 80
altruism, 78, 94, 123–4, 149
analytical grids *see* logframes
armed groups, working with, 30–1, 97
arms,
  economy, 72, 146, 171
  race, 70–1, 84, 88, 92, 155–6, 163, 174
  reduction, 158–9, 160, 171
  see also demilitarisation; disarmament; police
art, and peacework, 23

Baath Party, 52
Baghdad, 175
Banda Aceh, 133–4
Bangladesh, 124
Billig, Michael, 77
Bosnia, 81
Bourdieu, P, 131
Boutros-Ghali, Boutros, 8
boycotts, 132
Brecht, Bertolt, 93
bridge building, 23–6, 120, 121, 128–30, 131, 135, 136
Burma (Myanmar), 67, 101, 124
Burton, John, 4

Campaign for Nuclear Disarmament, 162
Canada, 92

capacity building,
  global, 83, 150
  for nonviolence, 102–4, 139–40, 142–5, 157–8
  of organisations, 19–21, 54, 55, 141
  training, 15–19
Caucasus, 89
Chechnya, 68, 97
children,
  and education, 21
  needs of, 28, 173, 175
  as soldiers, 24, 33, 49–50
  and violence, 117, 128
China, 67, 68, 100, 101
civil resistance, 115, 120–1, 125, 142, 158, 167
  see also non-violence; women
Colombia, 27, 135
colonialism, 39, 52
Commission on National Security (UK), 157–8
Committee for Conflict Transformation Support (CCTS)
  aims, 1, 25, 34, 38, 99, 140, 142
  origins, 3, 8, 9, 41
communications,
  and shaping opinion, 23, 93
  skills, 3, 5, 14–15
conditioning, gender, 151, 154
conflict,
  asymmetric, 6
  frozen, 90
  prevention, 8, 45, 58, 61, 88, 115
  resolution: aims, 2–6, 11, 184; in domestic politics, 88, 153, 163; and nonviolence, 129, 139; and power, 45, 59, 60, 129
  transformation: difficulties of, 38, 45, 56, 57–62, 66–70; global, 84, 89, 92, 93, 109, 150, 181; and militarism, 71–3, 75, 77, 78, 79, 81–2, 149, 151; and nonviolence,

104, 113–16, 120, 121, 139–40, 184; and peace movements, 161; and politics, 27, 96, 98, 99, 101, 102, 104; practice of, 4–9, 12, 13, 105, 107, 135, 136, 144, 159, 177; stages of, 182–5
conscientisation, 15, 56, 150–2, 183, 184
constructive programmes, 127–8, 150, 177
consultants, use of, 20
Cook, Robin, 87
Coordinating Committee for Conflict Resolution Training in Europe (CCCRTE), 3
CSCE, 157
culture,
    of constructive conflict, 76
    and male domination, 23, 66
    and needs theory, 46
    and power, 122, 177
    and violence, 4, 69–70, 91–5, 105–7, 113, 155, 161
Curle, Adam, 7, 76

dealing with the past (DWP), 33–4, 44, 50, 52, 102
demilitarisation,
    economic, 160
    and funding, 109–10
    global, 72, 116, 150, 155, 158–9, 164
    practicalities, 49–53, 82, 84–6
demobilisation, 155–6, 159
democracy,
    and economics, 172
    global, 179
    and participation, 114–15, 176–8
    practice of, 86, 154, 163
    and war, 169, 170, 174–5, 183
Democratic Republic of Congo (DRC), 65, 82, 100, 133, 146
demonstrations, 27, 129
Department for International Development (DFID), 86
dialogue, 3, 4, 48, 79, 94, 110, 130, 139, 183, 184
disarmament, 84–6, 155–6
displaced people, 50, 51
donors see funding

East Germany, 52, 63
East Timor, 80
Eastern Europe, 2
education, 3, 21–2, 34–5, 62, 69, 83, 128, 131, 136
Eisenhower, Dwight D, 171
electoral reform, 177
environmental crisis, 91, 108, 137, 168, 170, 171, 173–4, 178–9
ethics, 77–86, 87–8, 97, 99, 105–7, 153, 168
ethnicity, 6, 153, 175
European Union, 136, 148, 157
evaluation, 19, 20, 42–5, 111, 112, 141, 145

family and clan, 63
Fatah, 59
films, and peacework, 22
Foreign and Commonwealth Office (FCO), 86–7
foreign policy, 87, 153
Freire, Paolo, 15, 107, 131
Friends Committee on National Legislation (US), 157
funding,
    dilemmas of, 39, 40–2, 44, 109–12, 130, 135–6
    external, 9–10, 103
    of non-professional bodies, 64, 165
    and politics, 53, 59, 62, 152
    and training, 16, 17, 20
    widening scope of, 150

gacaca, 132–3
Galtung, J, 118
GAM (Free Aceh Movement), 133–4
Gandhi, 100, 125, 127
Gaza, 70, 110, 175
gender see male dominance; masculinity; women
Georgia, 48, 60, 67, 89, 96, 98, 137
Giddens, A, 131
global poverty, 91, 108
'good offices', and peace work, 29, 30, 97
governments,
    and arms expenditure, 71, 88, 155–6

and conflict transformation, 27, 92, 110–12, 132–4, 135–7
and consent, 61, 84
local, 166
and militarism, 53, 57, 58, 59, 72, 102, 150, 152
and nonviolence, 113, 121
see also democracy

Habermas, J, 131
Hamas, 59
human rights,
 advocacy, 26
 and conflict resolution, 48, 108, 113, 123, 167, 174–5, 178
 economic, 171
 education, 3
 violations, 10, 28, 33, 57, 99, 102, 169
humane disabling, 85–6
humanitarian intervention, 79–80

India, 65, 67
Indonesia, 133
international relations, 86–8, 153
intervention, external, 8, 80–1, 89–90, 99–100
intifada, 59
Iraq, 52, 65, 75, 81, 97, 100, 148
Islam, 64
Israel, 59, 67, 70

journalists, 22, 165
'just wars', 147, 149
justice,
 and advocacy, 26
 economic, 170–3
 and needs theory, 48
 restorative, 33, 51
 see also human rights

Kendall, Bridget, 80
Kenya, 70, 117, 120
Kosovo, 39, 80, 82, 89, 100, 157

labour movements, 130
latent conflict, 26, 45
Latin America, 123
Lederach's pyramid, 5, 130
Liberia, 80

logframes (logical frameworks), 20, 141
LTTE (Tamil Tigers), 67–8
Luttwak, Edward, 81

machismo *see* masculinity
male dominance, 66, 69, 76, 108, 128, 155
Manila, 126
Manipur, 120
masculinity, 65–6, 76, 126, 151, 177
 see also male dominance
Max-Neef, M, 46
media, 22–3
mediation,
 practice of, 5, 7, 97, 106, 135, 137, 172
 in schools, 21, 127
 victim–offender, 51
Meijer, Guus, 7
militarism,
 conflict transformation and, 70, 71–3, 80, 90, 146–50
 costs of, 154, 156, 171
 culture of, 114, 121, 150–1, 161
Milošević, Slobodan, 6, 60
Ministry of Defence (MOD), 86
Moldova, 89
monitoring, 20, 28, 135, 137, 157
Mugabe, Robert, 102, 136

Naga, 120
nation states, 66–8, 89–90, 137, 153, 175
NATO, 38, 67, 80, 157
needs
 basic human, 4, 96, 113, 153, 172
 theory, 45–9
negotiation,
 facilitating, 58–9, 102, 184
 practice of, 3, 119, 156, 173, 183
 and war, 97, 145, 159, 173
neo-colonialism *see* colonialism
Nepal, 100, 124
NGOs,
 and nonviolence, 99–100, 158–9, 167
 and partnerships, 13, 14, 26, 39–40, 101, 136
 and politics, 60, 82, 89, 97, 105, 110, 112, 113, 130

NGOs *continued*
  practice of, 9, 16, 22, 30, 31, 36,
    41, 54–5, 65, 135
  professionalisation of, 12, 40, 55,
    62, 63
  scope of, 24, 27–28, 36, 102
non-cooperation, 120, 125
nonviolence,
  and advocacy, 26, 27
  character of, 2–3, 6, 7–8, 10, 107
  and civil resistance, 84, 121–7, 160,
    161, 178
  *Handbook for Nonviolent
    Campaigns*, 140
  importance of, 74, 75, 79, 94, 138,
    152
  practice of, 48, 60–1, 113–16,
    119–121, 129, 138–9
  and relation to violence, 99–104,
    138–9, 158
  training, 21, 103, 125, 138–40
Nonviolent Peaceforce (NGO), 157
Northern Ireland, 29, 42, 117
Norway, 137
nuclear arms, 68, 86, 88, 92, 156, 159,
    160, 170, 178

Obama, Barack, 67, 177, 178
Orissa, 70, 117, 120
Oslo Accord, 59
Otpor movement, 60

Pakistan, 68
Palestine, 59, 65, 67, 110, 135, 146
parity of esteem, 11
partnership, 2, 8–9, 38–40, 104, 110
peace,
  activists, 161, 162
  character of, 8, 43, 152–5, 169–70
  and conflict studies, 35
  constituencies, 28, 30, 114, 121,
    163, 179
  movements, 27, 160–5
  positive: attributes of, 75, 76, 127;
    building, 168–81; and coercion,
    79; and organisations, 12, 158;
    and popular participation, 61, 68,
    101; and transformation, 83,
    129, 166–7
  zones, 27

peacekeeping, 8, 77, 85, 137, 157
people power, 2, 6, 57–62, 83, 100–1,
    113–16, 167
Philippines, 2, 68, 124
police,
  and firearms, 85, 160
  and peacekeeping, 137, 157
power,
  asymmetric, 6–7, 39, 55, 59, 61,
    106, 145
  and conflict, 38, 45–53, 56, 72, 109,
    136, 184
  and decision-making, 30, 38–9
  and money, 40–2
  and needs, 90
  and nonviolence, 83–4, 94, 113, 139
  structural, 2, 31, 58, 74, 79, 129, 152
  see also people power; violence;
    women
Prime Minister's Office, 86
psychological recovery, 32–3, 34

radio, and peacework, 22
rape, 65, 80, 81
  see also violence; women
Real IRA, 42
reconciliation, 34, 50, 143, 183
religious organisations, 63, 166
'responsibility to prevent', 157–8
Roma, 80
Ropers, N, 96
Russia, 67, 68, 89, 96, 97
Rwanda, 100, 132

Saakashvili, 98
sanctions, 136
security, 72–3, 74, 77, 79, 80, 81, 85,
    90–1, 109
self-interest, enlightened, 88, 91, 94,
    153
Serbia, 39, 60, 80, 100, 137
Sharpeville, 124
Sierra Leone, 80
soldiers,
  attitudes of, 147–8
  help for former, 21, 32–3, 49–50,
    156
  refusing to fight, 119
South Africa, 2, 50
South Ossetia, 96

sovereignty, 89–90
Soviet Union, 2, 3, 100, 124
Sri Lanka, 67, 68, 135, 146, 147
Stubbs, Paul, 13
Sudan, 65, 82, 146
suicide bombing, 147, 155
Sweden, 92

Taliban, 148
television, and peacework, 22
terrorism, 58, 81, 155
third parties,
    governmental, 136–8
    non-governmental, 134–6
Tiananmen Square, 101
Tibet, 57
tracks (levels of actors), 5, 13, 56
training,
    conflict transformation, 3–6, 107,
        136, 137, 142–3, 156
    fundraising, 20
    nonviolence, 21, 103, 125, 139–41
    outreach, 162–3
    workshops, 15–19, 23, 26, 29
Transcend, 137
Truth and Reconciliation Commission,
    50

UK,
    and conflict transformation, 88
    foreign policy, 75, 80, 87
    government structure, 86–7
    knife crime, 70
    military spending, 68, 115
    pressure groups in, 36, 159
    and Zimbabwe, 136, 159
Ukraine, 60, 137
UN,
    and conflict transformation, 137,
        154, 160, 172
    in DRC, 65
    Resolution 1325, 28, 65
    and third parties, 135
    US attitude to, 75, 86
US,
    and conflict transformation, 36,
        157, 179

foreign policy, 59, 67, 68, 72, 75,
    86, 88, 90, 97, 148
gun crime, 70
and nonviolence, 61

values, of peacebuilding, 10–11, 74,
    104, 107, 122, 140, 143–5, 149,
    152–5, 163
Vietnam, 97
violence,
    addressing, 6, 21, 77–86
    and nonviolence, 99–100, 119,
        122–7, 151, 152
    recovery from, 31–5, 49–53
    rewarding, 31, 32
    structural, 4, 69–70, 76, 89, 91, 92,
        103, 116–18, 146, 151, 155, 175
    against women, 32–3, 51, 64, 69,
        70, 81, 117, 128, 170
volunteers, 28, 32

war,
    cost of, 115, 171
    failures of, 97, 178
    reality of, 31, 49, 52, 81, 82, 103,
        107–8, 146–7, 169–70
    on terror, 68, 122, 178
    see also just war; violence
War Resisters International, 126, 140
women,
    and civil resistance, 120–1, 123,
        158
    and conflict transformation, 20–1,
        23–4, 28–9, 31, 49, 166
    and gender inequality, 65, 66, 69,
        76, 108, 151, 155, 175
    and power, 64–6, 76, 81, 126, 178
    soldiers, 49
    and violence, 32–3, 51, 64, 69, 70,
        81, 117, 170
Women in Black, 6
workshops see training
World War II, 148

Yugoslavia, former, 6, 13, 25, 33

Zimbabwe, 102, 136, 146